"Aaron was a true competitor, [...] teammate off the ice. If you want to learn about the power of the human mind, you need to read this book!"
Daniel Sedin

"Aaron's life experiences exemplify the delicate psychological balance associated with adversity and resilience. His story of triumph, powered by his visualization practice, offers great insight into how we can all move our personal fulcrums to find pathways towards growth and resilience in the wake of adversity and trauma."
Dr. Jacinta M. Jiménez – PsyD, BCC, Psychologist specializing in motivation and peak performance, Author of The Burnout Fix

"After playing against Aaron in the NHL, I had an inclination that he had an amazing story to tell. I was right. His story will serve as an inspiration to so many people as it is a true depiction of mind over matter."
Jordin Tootoo – NHL Alumnus and Author of:
All the Way: My Life on Ice
Mind Over Matter: Hard-Won Battles on the Road to Hope

"As a rookie coming into the NHL, I didn't have to look far to see the perfect example of extreme work ethic, perseverance and leadership. These attributes that Patti possessed came as no surprise after I learned about his story. I was lucky to be able to battle next to him as his linemate. He was fearless, always had my back, and was the ultimate professional day in and day out."
Tom Wilson – Washington Capitals

"Aaron's book will leave a lasting impact on your soul. He's candid about his struggles and brings you into his journey, which leaves you rooting for him the entire way. Hockey is simply a conduit, but this story is about human perseverance under great odds. A marvelous read."
Sami Jo Small – 3x Olympian (2 Golds, 1 Silver)

"Aaron's inspiring story epitomizes the use of visualization to overcome the unthinkable."
Emerance Maschmeyer – 2022 Olympic Gold Medalist

||

Published by Defiant Publishing House, October 2022

ISBN: 9781738700608

Written and Edited by: Aaron Volpatti
Proofreader: Dana Micheli
Typeset: Greg Salisbury
Book Cover Design: Michel Vrana
Portrait Photographer: Heather Pollock

NOTE TO THE READER: This book explores themes around general trauma, mental health, and life as a hockey player. There are raw and graphic descriptions of injuries (specifically burn injuries), disease, pregnancies, and miscarriages.

FIGHTER

Defying
The NHL Odds

AARON VOLPATTI

"Aaron was a great teammate and his road to the NHL
is like no other." —ALEX OVECHKIN

To Dad:
Here's to livin'

Contents

Part II

Author's Note

I had no business making the NHL. While I was an above-average hockey player, I was the smallest kid in Revelstoke and had barely snuck into Junior hockey. But I had something that separated me from all the other kids with big dreams. I was gifted with a powerful sense of courage and a spiritual awakening through my discovery of the powers of Visualization – a superpower that got me through the deepest lows in my life and brought me out to the other side as a survivor.

By all rights, I shouldn't even be alive to share my story with you, and sometimes I'm not sure how I actually overcame all the adversity I have faced, both personally and professionally."

Yet I did, because I am a fighter. And I'm hoping that by reading my story you will get to know the real me, both the hockey player who nearly died, and the Coach that I am now who wants to help you unleash your true potential.

I hope my journey inspires you to do something, start something, create something, or change something. That my words will help you tap into your inner powers of Visualization and be enough to push you to take those first steps toward a new mindset.

By sharing my story of grief, terror, personal tragedy, uncertainty, and happiness, I hope you will be inspired to dig deep within yourself to find your own strength to walk into your darkest moments and come out of them with a determination and mindset to achieve your wildest dreams. Think of this book as a guide to find the fighter inside of you. A guide that will push you to fight for what you want and what you love in this life.

Believe me, if I can play in the NHL, you can achieve anything you want.

And I want to be right here cheering you on.

Part I

"You never really get the smell of burning flesh out of your nose entirely, no matter how long you live."

J.D Salinger

Chapter 1

Inferno

—

A loud rushing noise filled my ears. My whole body was engulfed in an intense, warming sensation. Oddly, it wasn't painful, but it felt completely wrong, and my body reacted by telling me to run. As I bolted into the woods in a panic, I thought, *Holy shit, why isn't this hurting?* But I had no answer. I had no control over what was going on. Adrenaline was coursing through my veins, and I raced blindly for what seemed like an eternity. My body then screamed at me to drop to the ground and roll around to get the flames out. I frantically slapped the palms of my hands against my body, willing it to disappear. But the flames didn't subside. I vaguely heard people calling my name, telling me to stop moving, but I ignored them. Panic pushed me up off the ground and I continued to run, and in hindsight, I still don't know why that action seemed sane. The thought of dying flooded my mind. But still, no pain.

I thought I heard screaming and didn't realize until later that the guttural howling had been coming from my lungs. Finally, I felt a sudden push from behind me and I was thrown to the ground. My body landed sharply in the dirt, with the sensation of rocks pushing into my raw skin as my friends tackled me and started beating me with their jackets. Finally, someone smothered the gas induced flames. My skin was still smoldering as they peeled off what little remained of my clothing.

My breathing slowed and when I looked up, all I could see was a crowd of horrified faces. Some of my friends had their hands covering their mouths and noses, some turned away in shock, and some were crying and shaking. I couldn't make sense of what had happened but as I followed their gaze down to my naked body, I saw piles of gnarled, white skin lumped around certain areas as if a giant candle had been melted and deliberately poured all over me.

I grabbed the dangling skin around my right hand and pulled it. The skin kept coming and coming, continuing down my entire arm. It released near my elbow, and I chucked the pile of skin onto the ground. I did the same thing to the pile of skin on my chest. It kept coming off as I essentially skinned myself. Months later, one of the guys on my team told me, "I thought you were taking off your shirt. When I got closer, I realized you were peeling your skin off. That's when I knew you were fucked up pretty bad."

My stomach and the inside of my legs looked like a grotesque cooked fish with its skin still on. Charred on the outside and a mixture of deathly white and bright red on the inside. Rocks were embedded in the skin, poking out like small mountains through a crispy landscape. My thoughts finally collected themselves in a jumble. *What just happened? What have I done to myself? This is serious. Fuck.*

My friends were able to sit me up on a cooler and I still felt like I was having an out-of-body experience, trying to recap what had just happened. A cooler that had once been overflowing with beer was now filled with peoples' hands as they tried to soothe their burnt skin after wrestling me to the ground.

I could hear conversations between my friends, but I don't

think I was really comprehending everything that was happening. The tell-tale signs of shock were setting in.

"We need to get you to a hospital, Patti."

"We have no service out here to call 911!"

"How the fuck are we gonna get him out of here?"

"Can anyone drive?"

That last question brought forth another serious problem. My friends and I were out in the bush, camping up at Bluenose Mountain and drinking hard because we had just lost in the league finals in the BCHL (British Columbia Hockey League). Most of us were on the Vernon Vipers team, and in the early hours of April 20, 2005 we had been drinking straight for two days. My seared flesh, however, had sobered most of them up instantly.

Luckily, my teammate Ryan was there with his girlfriend, who hadn't been drinking. Someone gingerly put me onto the front seat of Ryan's car with her behind the wheel. Unknown hands passed me a cooler full of ice. The first hint of pain was pushing through into my consciousness, and I plunged my burning arms and hands into the cooler, which, unbeknownst to me, would save my right arm and hand from a lifetime of disuse.

Ryan's girlfriend started the car, and the wheels skidded as we slid out of the woods and sped along the winding dirt road. That's when the smell hit me. Imagine the smell of burning hair, but infinitely worse. A nauseating and torched odor mixed with a sour stench of copper and liver or pork. It's a smell that permeates your nostrils and stays etched in your memory forever. It penetrated the air and saturated every particle in that car. Every time I smell something burning today, I get flashbacks to this terrible thirty-minute car ride.

The shock was wearing off, and the pain became more intense. My right hand and arm felt like someone was slowly carving into the flesh with a dull saw. Ryan was in the backseat trying to keep me calm as my anguish was evident on my face and small moans were escaping from my lips. "You're going to be okay Patti; we'll be at the hospital soon."

"Ahhh fuck, this is getting bad, drive faster! Drive faster!"

"I know, I'm trying!" his girlfriend barked, her voice full of panic.

"We'll be there soon, Patti," Ryan replied.

I looked at my naked, mutilated body.

"This is bad, isn't it? How bad is this?" Just as the pain heightened, I felt my spirit returning from the out-of-body experience. The shock was really wearing off now, increasing the feeling of dull saws carving my raw skin.

Until this point, I thought I had experienced pain. Playing hockey, I had broken several bones, been punched in the face hundreds of times, and received many stitches to repair the cuts from pucks and fists. But this was something different. This was something new and awful — it dwarfed all my previous experiences. *Was I going to die?*

I started humming and rocking back and forth. Nothing was helping. From deep in my chest I let out a maniacal scream. I couldn't help myself and could do nothing to stop it as the feeling of scorched flesh took hold of my mind. I vaguely heard Ryan try to reassure me again.

"You're gonna to be okay man," he said, hesitantly this time.

My response was a scream.

"Ahhhh help! Fuck, I'm not going to make it. Please help, drive faster!"

The last ten minutes of the ride were pure torture. My screams became louder and more distressed. I had no idea pain could be this bad. For a few precious seconds, the pain subsided, and everything went dark as spots swirled in front of my eyes. I was passing out.

"Patti! Come on, man, stay with me," Ryan said, as he shook

me and slapped my face. I knew he meant well, but I would have preferred to stay passed out. I'm sure he was thinking the worst and was trying to keep me alive and conscious. I would have done the same thing.

As the pain came rushing back, so did my screams. I think I tried to cry but couldn't. The dull saws were now cutting my whole body, moving deeper into my flesh with every passing second.

"Oh my God, please get me to the hospital," I croaked out of a parched throat.

We blew through every red light and sped through town.

The lights of the emergency entrance came closer and as we turned into the hospital, I felt my body shake as I anticipated my torturous exit from the car. As the car slowed, for some incomprehensible reason, I opened the door and dove out skidding, my skin sloughing off onto the pavement as I hit. I rolled to a stop, and then found the energy somewhere to jump up and sprint into the emergency room, screaming "Help!" like I'd never screamed before. I wonder what all the people thought at the sight of my naked, bleeding, filthy, charred body careening into their space. I'll never forget the horrified look on the first nurse's face, as she registered the state of my situation and turned back and ran into the doors for help. Then everything went black.

Chapter 2

Blue Genes

—

I was a tiny blonde-haired kid with big blue eyes. A cautious overachiever, I always over-planned before taking action. This would eventually change in my teen years.

My dad, Tony, was tall and athletic, standing six feet two inches tall and probably one hundred and eighty-five pounds. Although I was the smallest kid in town, he always told me I would grow up to be big like him. He too had been small, just like me. He had long brown hair, vintage tinted glasses, and a booming personality. Someone could have easily cast him for the classic movie Dazed And Confused.

Dad worked for the Canadian Pacific Railway as a machinist and my mom, Lana, was a server at a local restaurant, who later went into nursing. Mom was, and still is to this day, a very striking woman. She has defied aging and continues to pass as my sister in the eyes of strangers. Her laugh is contagious, and she has the thickest brown hair you've ever seen.

My younger sister Brianne and I grew up in Revelstoke B.C. The town was founded by the Canadian Pacific Railway in the 1880s, so a large segment of the city housed the company's blue collar workers, and that included us. Some people may have referred to us as trailer trash, but we were proud of it. That is, of course, until I was old enough to understand how the trailer park was perceived by the more well-off families, as sad as it was.

Our trailer was a sun-faded cream colour with a dark brown front door, and the interior was riddled with deep orange shag carpeting, flower linoleum, and wood-paneled walls. The trailer alone would have certainly pushed us to the epitome of the era.

An iconic picture from a family ski day hung on the wall of our living room. Brianne, Mom, and I were dressed in quintessential fluorescent eighties ski wear, but Dad took home the best dressed award. He was wearing blue jeans, an old Toronto Blue Jays jacket with the white faded to more of a yellow colour, and he was sporting his welding glasses instead of ski goggles.

We had a 1974 Volkswagen Westfalia van with a propane cook stove that we used as a source of heat. Not the wisest choice, but it worked. We didn't have all the material possessions, but that never stopped us from having fun. My parents put all their time, money, and energy into fostering our close-knit family.

A love of sports was cultivated early in my family. In 1985, the year I was born, my dad was the Canadian Motocross Enduro Champion. Growing up, I loved watching him race motorcycles. I couldn't wait to get to the track to observe everyone wrenching on their bikes before the big race. I fondly recall the sound of those bikes when the gate dropped – a two -stroke symphony that propelled dirt backwards into the sky.

Dad would tell me stories when I got older of his battle through pain and exhaustion to win races. These enduro races could last days. He said his hands would go numb and he could barely see, but he kept grabbing another gear. He kept grinding. The way his whole face and being would ignite when he expressed his love for the sport has stuck with me all my life. When we got older, my dad saved up for a used Honda 50cc bike for my sister and me to share. We raced around the track, but I was always apprehensive about grabbing another gear. Brianne was fearless, and I know she would have beaten me if we had been in a race. Something about the power when I torqued the throttle made me nervous.

When I wasn't at the racetrack, I was usually at the boxing club with my dad. As kids, my dad and his brother boxed and then helped to run the club in Revelstoke. These early boxing sessions certainly showed up later in my hockey career. I loved sparring and watching Dad climb into the ring with the other boxers.

In Revelstoke, the winters could get pretty crisp. Not to mention the amount of snow. Revelstoke holds the record for most snow in a single Canadian winter with eighty feet.

My dad was constantly shoveling the snow off the roof of our trailer. The roof could possibly cave in if he didn't. This meant Brianne and I could literally walk over the trailer, since the snow piles were so high. So tall, in fact, that my dad had to shovel around our windows to keep them clear in case of an emergency. We played for hours in the snow until our toes and fingers became numb.

I loved playing hockey – the Revelstoke winters were great for that. Every Canadian kid usually spends some time on skates with a hockey stick. I still remember my first pair of skates. They looked like mini ski boots made of rickety black plastic. They had enormous tongues that flapped in the air. I sported a different colour lace in each boot – one white and one orange.

There was nothing like getting outside in the cold air to hear the sound of the sharp edge of a skate blade cutting through the ice. When I was about four, my dad constructed a tiny backyard skating rink right over our garden. I don't know how thrilled my mom was to see roughly hewn tin boards patched together around an icy patch. We would push around a hard orange ball with hockey sticks, but I was always shooting it over the tin boards, so Dad would make me wait until he shoveled all the snow off the rink before handing the ball over to me.

Once the ice was clear, we would skate around, pretending we were in the Stanley Cup Finals. I was always the Vancouver Canucks. A few years later, when Pavel Bure entered the NHL, I wore his retro number ten jersey religiously.

My parents' marriage was the epitome of a true, loving partnership. Of course, they had their difficulties like anyone, but all I remember was being surrounded by love and having tons of fun.

Dad was the prank master. He was always tricking me and all of my family members. From convincing us we were lost in the woods and would have to survive off the land until someone found us, to leaving me at the airport to go on a secret mission to stop poachers in Africa at the tender age of three – nothing was off limits.

Determined not to miss a prank or a joke, Dad had glued to his side a giant eighties video camera (the big news-reporter-type camera that rested on your shoulder), so he could add to the already massive collection of family videos. Dad would often follow my mom around with the camera, which she hated. She would be getting ready for her night shift at work, or cleaning, and he would be on camera telling her how beautiful she was before going in for a kiss. It drove her nuts. The next day, we would watch the footage and laugh hysterically. We all shared a truly special bond. Underneath my parents' love and compassion was a real drive to help keep me and Brianne grounded on the right path.

Chapter 3

The Mummy

—

I don't know a single parent whose heart doesn't pound loudly in their chest when they receive a phone call at 1:00 a.m. It often means that someone is injured, missing, or dead. That's what my parents thought when Mom answered the phone in the early hours of April 20, 2005. "Mrs. Volpatti," said the voice on the other end of the line, "your son has been in an accident. He's been severely burnt and is getting airlifted to Vancouver General Hospital in a couple of hours."

They told me later that my mom fell to her knees in shock. "Is he okay?" Mom asked with trepidation.

"He is stable at the moment. I'm sorry I don't have many more details other than he will be going to Vancouver shortly."

"Vancouver?! Oh my God. We're coming. Can we see him?" She could barely get the words out as fear overcame her.

"From Revelstoke? You should make it to Vernon in time to see him off but try not to speed. Don't put yourself in danger, drive safe." My mom nearly dropped the phone as she asked my dad, "Is he going to be okay?" Tears trickled down her face. They were frantic. Mom grabbed a pair of clothes out of her drawer and was ready to leave when my dad stopped her.

"Lan."

"What?"

"We're going to need more clothes. He's going to Vancouver.

We're going to be there for a while I think," said Dad as he ran out of the room to grab every suitcase in the house. He returned quickly and dumped each drawer out into the suitcases. They loaded their truck within minutes. Before they headed out, they woke Brianne and told her they were going to see me in the Vernon hospital and they'd call her in the morning.

They later told me the drive to Vernon was grim and silent. Asking those tough questions would likely have broken them down. What had happened? How burnt was I? Would I live? They tried to stay positive, but as any parent will tell you, that's no easy feat when your child has been in a terrible accident.

My parents made it to the hospital just as I was getting wheeled out on a stretcher to the ambulance to take me to the helicopter. All my parents saw was a quick glimpse of me wrapped up like a mummy. I think the reality of how severe my accident was really hit them hard. The only part of me they could see were my eyes, which were closed thankfully because of the powerful pain medications. The extent of my injuries wouldn't be known to them until I was in Vancouver. I can't imagine how terrified they were.

Somehow, my friends and teammates were also there to see me off. How they got there I don't want to know. They were all drunk, but given the situation, it's likely they didn't care. I'm thankful no one else was hurt that night. Apparently, it was a very grim scene. Everyone was deathly quiet and in tears.

My parents then had to drive another five hours to Vancouver, a large portion of that drive on the Coquihalla Highway, which can be treacherous even in the spring. There are usually slick patches of snow and ice at those elevations, and I'm grateful they made it to Vancouver safely.

I recall my eyes squinting at the ceiling light in the hospital room as I tried to look around to see where I was, but it was difficult. My face was tight with bandages, and I was confused.

I only had a small slit to see through. I recall saying, "I'm in a hospital?" Then I saw my parents. Their eyes were filled with tears. The memories came flooding back, and I mumbled, "I fucked up."

Chapter 4

Morphine

—

Y ou're going to be okay, Hub (my nickname)," Dad said reluctantly, as I'm sure he didn't know if that was actually the case. It was all they could do to not break down completely. The white gauze and bandages were letting fluid seep through in some places, and there was a pungent smell as they leaned over me, their faces slicked with tears, trying to find some hope to get us through the trauma. I mumbled, "I'm sorry," as the morphine coursed through my veins. My mom bit her lip and resisted the urge to pat me on the arm in a reassuring manner.

I weakly looked down the bed at my wrapped arms. Menacing thoughts raced through my mind. *What do I look like under all these bandages? Will I ever be normal again? Will I play hockey again?* I thought about my new girlfriend, Claire. She had been at the party. Or had she? I couldn't remember. I moved my cracked lips.

"Does Claire know? Is she here? Is she okay?" I asked. My mom nodded. "Yeah, bud, she saw you last night. She's not here right now, but we said we would update her on how you are doing. She's still in Vernon and will come down when we know more." I tried to lower my eyebrows in confusion. "Vernon? We aren't in Vernon? Where am I?"

My dad sighed. "You got airlifted here to Vancouver last

night, Hub. Don't worry, we're staying here with you."

I felt another presence in the room as a nurse leaned over me. "How are you feeling?" I felt my eyes well with tears, only to be soaked up by the bandages. I was beyond scared. "I… am I going to be okay?" I asked.

"You're stable right now, but we won't know more until the bandages come off. We just need you to rest as much as possible. Are you in any pain?"

I tried shaking my head, but it was too tough. "Not too much then." She nodded and gave me a small smile. Looking past her, I saw a little red wheel in the machine of my IV tower turn and release something, presumably morphine. I sighed and everything went dim as I fell into a dreamless sleep.

Chapter 5

Debridement

—

For the first twenty-four hours I drifted in and out of sleep, vaguely seeing the shadows of Mom and Dad come into a fuzzy focus for a few seconds at a time. They were always right there. Sometimes I would hear them speaking to each other, but it seemed far off.

"Hun, Aaron is strong. He's going to battle through this."

I really hoped they were right.

On the second day, the little red wheel continued to spin, and I was conscious of the feeling from the morphine – high, but also dreamlike. I could tilt my head and take the odd mouthful of water. I was sore, groggy, and uncertain of what was supposed to happen next. The nurse reassured my parents that while things looked a little bleak, I wasn't going to die. There was still the risk of infection and shock complications – we still didn't know what I looked like under everything – but I was going to survive this. Although it didn't feel like it, I think my parents were reassured by this.

The nurse leaned over and asked me if I wanted to take the bandages off of my face, and I nodded. I could feel a slight pull as the gauze lifted. With each layer, I could feel the air shift and my hot skin felt cooler. It didn't hurt as much as I had expected.

"Can I see?" I asked nervously.

"Yep." She held the mirror up to my face.

I was surprised. It just looked like a nasty sunburn. There were odd little blisters, and my face still seemed to have dirt embedded in the skin. To make things even more interesting, I was sporting large black eyes and a large cut due to a broken nose I suffered just days prior, and my head was completely bald. Also, for some reason, the reflection in the mirror looking back at me seemed to have gained thirty pounds. To say I was a sight for sore eyes wouldn't do this image justice. I was confused. Handing the mirror back to her, I joked, "Why am I so fat?"

The nurse smiled.

"Your body has gone through a major trauma. These first few days, you will gain a lot of water weight. Because of the burns, your body gets dehydrated quickly, so we have IVs filled with fluid to help you heal. There will be swelling but try not to worry too much." A little later, the doctor came in to tell me all about debridement. It's a word that still sends chills up my spine. A word that means to remove damaged tissue but should really be defined as torture.

"Mr. Volpatti, it looks like you were in quite an accident the other night. So right now, our biggest concern is infection. We need to keep the burns clean while we wait for your grafting surgery. We will chat more about that later, it most likely won't happen for another couple weeks. But today, and every third day after, we are going to take you into the debridement room. We will put you under a general anesthetic and the nurses will scrub and hose your body to keep everything clean. You will be quite sore after, so we will continue to provide you with pain medication to help you manage. While they perform that procedure, I'll be able to get a good look at what's under your bandages and we can talk about what lies ahead for you."

It's difficult to describe just how vulnerable and scared I

was when I was placed onto a morgue-like metal bed as we began our trip to the debridement (shower) room. Since I could barely move, it had taken four nurses to lift my heavy, waterlogged ass onto the cold metal table. They pushed the IV tower behind me as we made our way down the bright hallway. That's when I heard the screams as we moved past different rooms (I would soon learn that the burn unit is one of the most amazing places but also one of the most terrifying. I believe at the time there were only around ten beds in the burn unit. They were the ten worst burns in British Columbia so you can imagine how severe some of these injuries were). My anxiety increased as I feared what was in store. We pushed through a set of dark, hollow-sounding doors and entered a small room that had large windows where you could see a kind of human car wash structure with shower heads hanging from the ceiling. As they pushed me into the sterile setting, I could see a bunch of surgical tools sitting on top of a metal platform. It looked like a torture chamber out of a movie. My heart started thumping against my ribcage as I pictured them slicing me open to relieve all the pressure from my massive blisters and wounds.

I recall that there were a handful of nurses and an anesthesiologist. They placed the mask on my face, and I drifted off to sleep seconds later.

The nurses wheeled me back into my room where my parents waited with anticipation. I woke up a few hours later, and I was in extreme pain. It felt like someone had skinned me alive. The doctor came into my room, and he relayed what the next steps were for my stay in the burn unit. I tried to focus on what he was saying, but it was difficult as my whole body was writhing in pain.

"I hope you were able to get some rest. I know that is an uncomfortable procedure."

Bit of an understatement, Doc, I thought to myself.

"You are one lucky young man. Your burns are serious, about fourty percent are second - and deep third-degree burns. You will make a full recovery, but it's going to be a long summer of recovery here. Someone was looking out for you. It doesn't look like we will need to graft over your joints, which is good news. But there is extensive damage to your right flank, thighs, and right arm and hand. We will hopefully get your grafting surgery done within the next couple of weeks. Right now, our biggest concern is monitoring for infection and making sure there are no complications with smoke inhalation. We will continue with the debridement procedure every third day to keep the future graft sites clean. Our focus for you will be rest and pain management."

At least we had a plan. But the debridement room was my double-edged sword. I got to escape the pain and my grim reality when I was put under general anesthetic, but when I woke up hours later, the pain was debilitating. It felt like hundreds of razor blades were being sunk into my raw skin. The morphine couldn't touch this pain. It was horrific.

Debridement, as I learned, is vital to the overall good outcome for burn patients. There is a specific inflammatory response after a serious burn injury where large blisters form and need to be cut open to remove pressure and swelling. Leaving the dead tissue and large blisters can increase susceptibility to infection and slow healing time. Without debridement and grafting, my recovery would have taken much longer, with the skin becoming more leatherlike and less mobile each day. So, it was a necessary evil.

The procedure is really just buying time for the eventual grafting surgery, where new, harvested skin is placed on top of fresh tissue – once they've found it buried beneath layers of gnarled, dead skin. They use a mix of hydrosurgical (like a high-powered pressure washer) debridement and excisions using sharp scalpels to cut open the blistered areas and relieve pressure. They slough away the layers of necrotic tissue until the fresh, bleeding tissue is exposed, halting the formation of scar tissue. There is potential for a lot of blood loss. During the three days afterward, new scar tissue would form, then they would have to repeat the procedure over and over again until the grafting surgery.

After coming out of the anesthetic, I would lie in silence, my jaw clenching and eyes shut as I tried to deal with this new level of pain. I would have cried if I had been able to. On the non-debridement days, the pain was slightly more manageable. It felt like I was constantly being tattooed over my whole body. The morphine was helping, but it was tough to get quality rest.

My parents were right by my side the whole time, advocating my need for more morphine as the pain increased to an intolerable level. The nurse would usually oblige and add more of the drug into my IV line. As soon as it trickled down the line, it would feel as if my bones were numb. It was a great, welcomed high. I would continue to lie in silence for hours, trying not to think about anything other than how much it fucking hurt.

I would get incremental chunks of sleep, then try to get some cold lunch into my stomach. I remember thinking how terrible the food was as my parents attempted to feed me in bed. The milk I drank had some serious repercussions later on as well.

At one point, during a visit from the doctor, I got up the courage to ask the question that had been a constant at the back of my mind. "Will I be able to play hockey again? Our season starts in a few months."

The doctor somberly looked at me and I could see it in his eyes. A look that said, *This poor kid has no idea what he's in for, let alone thinking about playing hockey again.* That's when I knew it. My career was over.

"I'm sorry," he said. "You won't be playing hockey in a few

months. This kind of recovery can take years. Maybe when it is complete years from now, we can look at getting you in a pair of skates in a non-competitive environment. Let's focus on your recovery for now."

Close the book, I told myself. *Your career is over. It was a nice run; made it to Junior A, and that's pretty damn respectable.*

Chapter 6

The Volpatti Way

—

I excelled in hockey soon after I put on my first pair of skates. I used to have a great time as a toddler, tripping and getting up time and time again. By the age of five, I was motoring around the skating rink pretending I was a superstar. Dad coached many of my minor hockey teams. I remember him showing up to practice in his dirty welding clothes from a long day at work, smelling like torched steel.

After my games, Dad would take me to get hockey cards and the biggest Slurpee they offered from the local 7-Eleven. I was good, but I wasn't *that* good. I would eventually get cut from several select teams and even play "house hockey" – the lowest level of minor hockey – at one point. Our Revelstoke minor hockey team got to play the short game in between periods of a Vancouver Canucks game, two different times! I don't know how we managed to do this twice, but it was amazing. My dad took me down to the Canucks' dressing room and I froze as I stared at my idols. Guys like Pavel Bure, Trevor Linden, and Kirk McLean. I took it all in and was overwhelmed with the power the game had over me. I dreamed of stepping onto that ice and becoming them. They were absolutely inspiring.

It's difficult when you look back at your childhood and

realize that the joy you had living with your family could be so easily tainted by others. I did not know that the home I had in a great trailer wasn't viewed as being normal or acceptable by some other kids. Why would I? I had a great time there with my family. But every kid has a day that changes all of their innocent views, and that day for me came around grade five when I became the target of bullies.

I knew I was built much smaller than the other boys in my classes at school. I mean, all I had to do was look at the class picture. Anyone could point me out as the shortest and skinniest one there. And bullies can prey on smaller kids and get jealous if they are more adept at certain things. Bobby was that guy. I was a better hockey player than he was, so he bullied me. Every day after school let out, he would follow me home, pushing me around and taunting me.

"Hey trailer trash, go back to your dumpster house," was one of his favourite lines. He would point out how poor I apparently was while throwing me around, and until that point in my life, I had no idea that it wasn't cool to live in a trailer park. I didn't give a fuck about where I lived because I thought I had the best life ever. And this spoiled, silver-spoon fed idiot ruined that for me. I kept hearing his taunts in my head and I did everything I could to not let it affect me, but he eventually wore me down and I had to tell my dad.

He was pissed. He spoke to Bobby's parents, but nothing changed. Then we went to the teacher and my principal. Nothing changed still. My dad's third suggestion was to punch him in the face as hard as I could, aiming directly for his nose. I listened in stunned silence for a few minutes when he told me this. I'm sure the look on my face expressed absolute confusion.

"Wait, Dad, you want me to hit him?"

"Hub, you've done everything you can to get him to stop.

Sometimes there comes a time in life when you have to stand up for yourself. Time to fight back. If you don't, he will keep coming after you. So yeah, turn around and smoke him so he knows you're not putting up with this shit anymore."

I thought about it for a minute.

"Okay, but what if he fights back?"

"He won't, but if he does, don't back down."

I was confused. How did he know Bobby wouldn't fight back? Was it because he knew that deep down, he was more of a coward than a bully?

Looking back, I shouldn't really have been surprised by this advice. I mean, he did come from a long line of fighters. His dad, Jerry, who died in a snowmobiling accident before I was born, was a gigantic man with a quick temper, and from what I understood, if anyone crossed him he would drag them out of wherever they were and beat them senseless. He was a great family man but could also be a mean son of a bitch. My dad's brother, Shane, also had a short fuse. He would whack anyone who disagreed with him before they knew what was going on. Dad had been a damn good boxer, but he was more of a lover than a fighter. I would later learn that I had some of Papa Jerry in me. I was generally a patient and compassionate person, but my fuse would blow if pushed too far.

So, while I'm sure this advice was – and still is – controversial, I fought back. I headed home from class and the bullying began with Bobby skulking behind me, taunting me, getting closer so he could yell in my ear. Without hesitation, I turned around and clocked him right in the nose. He grabbed his face, cowered, and ran home crying. He never bothered me again. Dad's suggestion worked, and that's when I learned to stick up for myself.

From that day on, I gained a ton of confidence. Dad made it very clear I was to never instigate a fight and never bully anyone. I felt good knowing I was supported in standing up for myself. Navigating school is difficult, let alone adding bullies to the equation. This is when Dawson entered the picture. I don't really even remember why he had it in for me, but he was merciless. He was two years older than me and twice my size. He not only verbally abused me, but he would pin me down, hit me, and leave me bruised on some occasions. My dad and I both knew if I swung at Dawson, he would beat the shit out of me. Nothing was working and one day I came home crying. Dad had finally had enough. Mom couldn't understand how anyone could treat her boy so badly.

When Dad walked through the door after work, he knew right away.

"Dawson?"

My mom nodded.

Dad looked at me. "Let's go." I had never seen such determination in his face before. He meant business, and it was scary.

"Where?" I whimpered back hesitantly, almost knowing what he had planned.

"I know where he lives, we won't be long," Dad said, looking at Mom as we headed out.

We drove to the other side of town to a rundown condo building. We walked through the main entrance and down the hall to his unit. I had no idea Dad knew where he lived and didn't care to ask how he knew. He knocked on the door and Dawson answered with an *oh shit* look written all over his face. "Where's your mom?" my dad demanded. Dawson pointed into the living room behind him.

"Who is it, Dawson?!" we heard a woman yell in an annoyed shriek.

"Let's go talk," Dad said as he pushed past Dawson and headed toward his mother.

I followed nervously but felt safe with Dad in front of me. His mother was sitting on her La-Z-Boy chair, and seemed to be enjoying long, satisfying drags of her smoke. As soon as she saw us, she was confused and looked right at Dawson. "What did you do now, you little shit?!"

My dad turned to her and said, "Dawson has been bullying Aaron for a long time. We have asked him many times to please stop. He's not listening. Either he stops today, or we are going to have to take some sort of action." And that was it. It didn't seem too threatening, but I think both of them knew Dad wasn't fucking around.

"I'm sorry, young fella," she said to me. "Dawson can't get his shit together. It won't happen again, will it, Dawson?" She scowled hard at him. "No," he said with his head down, eyes scanning the floor for some sort of distraction.

She nodded in affirmation. "Good, now walk these two to the door and apologize."

Dawson walked us out and said sorry. I knew he didn't mean it, but it was better than nothing. Just as we got to the door, Dad grabbed Dawson's shirt by his neck and firmly pushed him against the wall, peering quickly down the hall to make sure his mother wasn't watching.

He quietly said, "Listen here, you little shit, I can't teach you a lesson, but I know who can. You know the Johnston brothers, right?" (The Johnstons were three brothers that frequented the boxing club and had a tough reputation. No one fucked with them. Dad coached them and I had watched them spar many times. They were a few years older than me). Dawson gulped with wide, frightened eyes.

"Mm-hmm," he mumbled.

"You so much as lay a finger on Aaron again, and the Johnston boys will be coming to pay you a visit, understand?"

"Yes," he nodded aggressively.

I remember thinking differently about my dad that day. I had always looked up to him, but I felt a deep admiration and worship from that day on.

That was it. Not only did Dawson never touch me again, he never even looked at me. And, as I should have expected, the Johnston boys started checking in with me.

"You good? He's not bothering you?" they would ask, and I would feel a great sense of relief knowing that those boxers had an eye on me. So, while I learned to fight as a kid, I also learned about intimidation.

Dad always put the rest of the family's needs first. No matter what the situation was, he protected us. He was a very caring, fun-loving man and father, but he also didn't fuck around. He would do anything to keep his family safe.

The fighter inside me was lit. I had learned to fight back and stand up for myself. But most importantly, and I didn't realize this at the time, I had learned to protect my dreams and stand up for what I believed in.

This fighter mentality would become a pivotal asset in both hockey and in the burn unit.

Chapter 7

Reality Check

—

I had been chasing an NCAA scholarship before the fire. That was my ultimate goal, my NHL. I had completed two seasons with the Vernon Vipers, with not only no offers from an NCAA school, but not even one conversation with a scout. I had one more crack at it with my last season of eligibility, and that was now gone.

The NCAA was where all the best North American Junior A players, and some U.S. prep school players, graduated to and was a great path to secure an education. You could either go this route or play Major Junior which was more of a fast track to pro hockey. This was a big step up from Junior A and on a similar playing level to the NCAA, but it was never even an option for me since I wasn't good enough to catch the attention of Major Junior scouts. For every year you played Major Junior, they would pay for a year of school at a Canadian University. The caveat with Major Junior was, as soon as you played one game, you were ineligible to go to the NCAA. Most players had to choose their desired path around sixteen or seventeen years old.

I made it to Junior A on sheer grit and hard work, not talent. I had skated with a lot of NCAA players; they were much more skilled than I was. Being a late bloomer, I figured I could add this skill element to my game if given the chance. But after the doctor laid down his gavel, I sat in silence, processing this incomprehensible future. I had to come to terms that I wouldn't find out if I could secure a scholarship to the U.S.

How would I fight through this? I had to accept it. It was difficult, but I accepted the consequences of my actions, and I was just grateful that I was expected to make a full recovery and lead what I thought would be a pretty normal life, whatever that was supposed to look like.

I had been a daredevil ever since I was a young teenager. I thought I was invincible. When someone said jump, I would ask how high. I did a lot of immature and stupid things for both attention and adrenaline. But my accident forced me to realize how fragile life was.

My thoughts were racing, trying to come to terms with the possibility of a new normal, an after-fire normal. *Okay, hockey is done, but this could have been much worse—my face could be deformed or worse, I could have died. I can still go to university, get a good job, maybe travel the world, and start a family someday.*

The thought of family quickly directed my attention to somewhere I hadn't thought about yet. The burns down there. *Could I have sex again? Could I have kids? Was it even there?*

"What about my... package?" I asked the doctor.

"That will be fine, don't worry. There is some trauma, and your testicles will be quite enlarged for a few more days. But I don't see any issues there from a recovery standpoint. With that said, we are going to need to monitor your right arm and hand for the next few days to see if they're going to need grafting. You may have some level of impaired functioning down the road, but to be honest, I'm surprised they're not worse."

I tried to recall what I had done after I had raced through the barren woods on fire. I must have put my hand in front of my groin as a natural reaction to protect it. *Good work, brain!*

An image came to me – my arm in the cooler on the drive to the hospital. Relief poured through me.

"I had my arm and hand in a cooler of ice on the drive to the hospital."

He nodded. "That may have saved your hand."

Again, more relief poured through me as I thought about my guitars. My dad and I had always shared a love for guitar. He was the one who taught me when I was twelve. I had become obsessed with playing ever since I plucked my first string, playing for hours every day after school. It didn't hurt that I seemed to be a natural at it. We would jam to all our favourite Steve Earle and John Cougar Mellencamp songs.

Picking up my guitar allowed me to get lost in the music – to totally unwind and de-stress. It also didn't hurt with the ladies, which proved to be an added benefit.

"Look, I know this is a lot to digest," the doctor continued. "You're going to be okay, but let's not try to take on too much too soon. Try and get some rest. I'll check on you in a couple of days to see how you're doing."

As he walked out of the room, my parents and I shared some hope. One, I was going to make a full recovery and two, my face wasn't going to be permanently scarred.

I'm not sure if they cared about my package as much as I did, but let's just say when you are a young man you have big plans for using that thing! I'll never forget my first look down there later in the week when the nurses changed some of my dressings. My balls were the size of softballs, and my member was discoloured and even raw in some places. I was slightly embarrassed knowing that all these nurses had been tending to my deformed package. I still have a little discoloured scar on my balls as a reminder of the fire – albeit tiny compared to the other large, grafted areas – but thankfully everything works just fine now.

My mind started racing as I sat with my new reality. No scholarship, no hockey. *What was I going to do with my life now? Go work at the local mill? Get some sort of trade?* I had been so determined to get that scholarship I hadn't thought about anything else. I was still in immense pain during most of the day, so it was hard to focus on anything else. Since I couldn't move, my mind was all I had. A fact that would change the path of my life weeks later.

Chapter 8

Groundhog Day

—

As I settled into the world of recovery during that first week, my days became very repetitive. Every couple of hours, I would wake up in pain and focus on the dread of the looming debridement. After this procedure the whole day was a write-off. I thought I was going to pass out from the pain half the time. I mostly spent the day sleeping, asking for more painkillers, and trying to eat something when meals were brought in. I began to reach for some meditative place in my mind to cope with the pain, and if I wasn't sleeping, I just lay in silence, trying to manage. The feeling of being skinned from nipples to knees is debilitating.

Breakfast was at 8:30 a.m. and Mom or Dad would try to get some food in me, but I was never that hungry, at least for the first week or so.

I quickly developed bed sores since I could barely move, and non-shower days meant I still had to get most of my dressings changed in the morning, except for the large third-degree areas on my legs and stomach. My right arm and hand hurt so much that when the nurse changed those bandages, the air pierced the raw flesh. Even though she pulled slowly, the bandages would always rip off the fresh skin covering the newly formed scabs.

The first time I saw my right arm and hand, I finally understood what the doctor meant. It looked fucking terrible, like this weird flesh-eating disease had crept up my limb, encasing it in some alien covering. The nurse would gently clean the burns as fast as he or she could because the air was so painful, apply some colloidal silver (for infection), and wrap me back up.

My mom was usually tasked with wiping my ass and cleaning my package. Under normal circumstances, I would have been embarrassed about this, but I was grateful for her help. All modesty was out the window. She spent countless hours by my side every night, making sure I was okay.

Going to the bathroom was an extremely painful endeavor (when it finally happened) because someone would have to roll me over to slide the bedpan under me. It was a less-than- ideal situation for all involved. There's a reason we sit to shit. And once I overcame my constipation, I'd usually go through a couple of the tiny bed pans. To this day, I don't know why they were so small.

On top of the treatments, I had my vitals taken and I was given injections of a blood thinner every day, twice a day. This was standard practice and prevented blood clots from forming since I was immobilized in bed. My arms eventually became so bruised I looked like an addict. "Where do you want it?" they would eventually ask. There wasn't much real estate left on my burnt body, so my arm or shoulder was usually the best bet. I remember waking up one night and my arm was spasming like crazy. It was like a bad leg cramp that jolted through my body, and it would only go away if I could relax. The petty annoyances of all the blood thinner injections, IV changes, the cramps, the bedsores, the laying-down shits, the dressing changes, and the emotional rollercoaster started to compound in an unimaginable way.

One particular day it was especially hard, and I felt so defeated with all the pain I wasn't sure I was going to be able to face the months to come. The tears I shed that night were the first of many. This was almost unendurable and unforgiving. I had never experienced anything like this in my entire life. I couldn't see past it. It seemed like it was getting worse, not subsiding.

I helplessly watched my dad hold the pressure on my arm to try and get me to calm down. Eventually, I would drift back to sleep, but I did not feel rested. I was so grateful for my parents. They supported me so much and kept helping me when I was down. Without them, I'm sure I wouldn't have made it. That first week was absolute hell.

Chapter 9

The Burn Unit

—

As I rolled into my second week in the burn unit, I started feeling a little better. My appetite was slowly coming back. The portions were so small I eventually had to double or triple up. Don't ask me why but I somehow grew to love cream of wheat. Sounds terrible, I know, but throw a little brown sugar in there and, man! It's hard to say whether it was really amazing, or my taste buds just craved something sweet, but I took all the little wins. At least my appetite was coming back. I did enjoy the hospital meatloaf. I think it's the only thing they made well because the other stuff tasted like garbage. But give me a giant glass of milk and I was slowly climbing out of the funk I was in.

I killed time by watching TV, thinking about life, watching the red morphine wheel, talking to my girlfriend Claire on the phone, trying to deal with my depressed state, and playing cards with my family. I eventually had my fingertips exposed on my left hand, so I could at least hold some cards. I always beat my mom and Nannie (my dad's mom) at crib, rummy, thirty - one – you name it – I won. And I was always a little cocky with card games. I'm sure they might have let me win the first few times, but I doubt that sympathy continued, since I could tell I was genuinely pissing them off. Plus, at that point, there wasn't a lot of joy or happiness with being in the hospital, so it was a good way to keep the mood light and have a bit of fun. Claire was also able to come down and visit for a couple of days, which lifted my spirits. I was getting a piece of my old self back.

Dad and I started shooting the shit and joking around a little bit more too. Once I was through that first week and everyone knew I was going to make a full recovery, it changed the mood drastically. My dad and I not only had a strong father and son bond, but we were also a lot like brothers. One of my most cherished memories was traveling to hockey games, tournaments, and tryouts with my dad. We would blast rock and roll music, singing at the top of our lungs. If he was driving, he would make sure we had a bag of potatoes to fire at road signs along the way. I would have the bag of potatoes at my feet, and Dad would speed up and drive on the shoulder of the road so I could get close to the sign. If I hit it, the potato would explode, and we would cheer in celebration. If I was driving – that's right, I was driving by age twelve – Dad would either just talk life with me or catch a quick nap.

This might seem negligent or irresponsible on his part, but he was all about instilling confidence and independence in me. As crazy as it sounds, I actually was a skilled driver at a young age. I remember one time I was driving to Vancouver and Dad said to wake him up before we crossed the Port Mann bridge. I let him sleep as I found myself in bumper-to-bumper traffic on the bridge, getting all kinds of reactions from other drivers.

As I continued to recover, I was moved into a room with two beds, which meant getting a roommate. Week two brings patients closer to getting graft procedures done, so it was kind of a positive step forward. My first roommate was a young girl who'd had a pot of boiling water spill on her. Her face was badly burned which was heartbreaking, but she and her family were troopers. They discharged her a couple of days after I moved into her room.

My next roommate was a police officer from Vancouver. He had been on his bike when a semi-truck blew a stop sign, hitting him and pinning him under the truck, dragging him for God knows how far. I'm not sure who stopped the truck driver, or how. We didn't get into that, but most of his damage was to his arm and hand. The friction burn actually burnt him so badly he was left with only a couple of fingers and half the flesh on his forearm. He had completed his surgery a few days prior to moving in with me. We had some good chats; it was great to speak with someone who could relate to what I was going through, and it took our minds off of the craziness of it all. After he had been discharged from the hospital, he came back to visit me and presented me with a box of Krispy Kreme donuts. Now that was something I could manage to eat.

Getting woken up by a cacophony of screams from people in excruciating pain is something that will echo in my mind for as long as I live. The sounds would ricochet off the walls, and it was hard to block them out. One patient was in so much pain, I thought she was being tortured. She had been at a get-together with friends and the parking brake on a truck accidentally released, rolled down a hillside, and pinned her on the campfire.

Most of her body had suffered severe third-degree burns. She needed skin donors as there wasn't enough healthy skin on her own body to harvest from. Once she came out of her coma, the endless torture began. Her struggle for survival reminded me how lucky I really was.

Since I was feeling better, I was visited by pastors and psychologists to help with the trauma and recovery process. I guess part of the psychologists' due diligence was to make sure there was no foul play involved in my accident. I hadn't even thought about the perception of a suicide attempt. Their questions ranged from, "Do you love yourself? Do you experience any kind of depression? Could anyone you know possibly have done anything to hurt you?" The questions started to irritate me to the point where I snapped back at them. "Leave me alone! I'm not suicidal. My friends didn't try to kill me! I just fucked up, that's it!" It wasn't their fault. I just wasn't quite ready to come to terms with what had happened and really dig into my own shit.

By the end of week two, the pain was becoming slightly more manageable, except for the debridement days. I was chatting with my new roommate one day when the phone rang. It was a phone call that would change my life forever.

Chapter 10

Finding Strength

—

Hello?" It was my coach, Mike Vandekamp (Vandy). He had come to see me shortly after I had arrived at the burn unit, although I didn't know since I'd been asleep in my morphine coma.

"Hey Vandy, I'm doing okay. Better than last week. Hanging in there, but I'm going to be in here for a while."

"Well, it's good to hear you're making progress. It was terrifying seeing you wrapped up like a mummy. I know this might be too soon to be talking hockey, but I was speaking with one of the coaches, Danny Brooks, at Brown University this morning and they said they're looking for a player that can crash and bang, kill penalties, and bring some energy to the bottom six every night. Actually, his exact words were: we need someone to put the fear of God into the defencemen of the Ivy League. Obviously, I told him I have the perfect guy for you, but he's burnt himself to a crisp and is in the hospital in Vancouver."

I laughed out loud; it was nice to find some sort of humor in my predicament.

"Wow, that's great, but unfortunately, it doesn't sound like I'm going to be playing hockey any time soon," I replied, my voice wavering as my new reality hit home.

"They're aware of the situation, but I think you should give Danny Brooks a call. They want to chat with you if you are up for it. I know you have the time."

We laughed some more, then I took down Danny Brooks' number. Well, I had to relay it to my parents to write it down.

"Okay, sounds good, thanks Vandy. Do you think I'd be able to stay in Vernon for next season and just be around the team?"

"You just focus on getting better big guy. But yes, we will be happy to have you around, whatever that looks like."

"Okay, thanks. Talk soon."

"Take care bud."

I leaned back in my bed and smiled. Hearing from him brought back a connection that I hadn't been feeling since being stuck in the hospital. Vandy and I had a special bond as coach and player. We respected the hell out of each other and while he demanded a lot from me, he really saw the value I brought to the team.

I was quickly brought back to reality as I looked back at my decrepit body. All the negative thoughts tried to take hold of my mind again. As I snapped out of it, I took a chance and called Danny Brooks. My parents held the phone up to my ear and I tilted my head, tucking the phone between my head and shoulder.

"Hello, Brooksay heeaw." I'd never heard a Rhode Island accent before, let alone this strong of one. And as I would soon learn, this guy was an absolute riot, always going a million miles a minute.

"Yeah, hi Danny, this is Aaron Volpatti. I just got off the phone with Mike Vandekamp and he passed along your number."

"Aaron! How are ya, brotha? Mike tells me you're in the hospital?"

"Yeah, I burnt myself pretty good."

We mostly bullshitted for a few minutes, keeping the mood light.

"Well, brotha, I know the future is uncertain for ya. Mike mentioned your playing days may be over. Just focus on getting better. We would love to hear how your recovery progresses."

"Ok, thanks a lot Danny, will do."

"Take care, pal."

I hung up the phone, and a tear ran down my face as I talked with my parents. I had worked my ass off to get noticed by even just one NCAA team, and it had finally happened. But now I couldn't seize the opportunity because of what I had done to myself. As I lay in my bed, I just couldn't fathom that competitive hockey had come to an end. The thing I loved most in life. I started asking questions. *How could my career really be over? Why can't I play next season? Just because the doctors say? Because the pain will be too much? I'm not like everyone else. These doctors and nurses don't know me. I'm a fucking Volpatti.*

There was an extensive list of reasons why I wouldn't be able to play in a few months. For one, I was going to be in the hospital for a while, well into the summer. There was a major risk of infection, the fresh skin grafts would need a long period of maturation, as they would be very limiting and painful. I wouldn't be able to sweat from these large third-degree burn areas which could cause serious complications if my heart rate increased. Lastly, I was going to be in a full-body suit for two years (to help minimize scarring), and my full recovery was going to take years, not months.

I thought about the pain I would face in the months and years ahead. I was okay with the idea of this future pain. *It can't be worse than what I've experienced so far.* I had been stuck in a spiral of feeling sorry for myself, trying to accept my fate without my first love: hockey.

No. I wasn't going to let this happen. Up until this point,

I had just taken what everyone had told me as the way it had to be. I was letting other people dictate my future and what it was going to look like. Sure, they had good reasons for it, but I decided these reasons weren't strong enough to warrant me giving up on my dream. All they saw was a burnt husk who had made a mistake playing around with gas and fire. Why should I accept their prognosis?

Like the flip of a switch, I realized I'd always had a choice. I would not accept this fate. This opportunity was everything I had been working for. I couldn't let it slip away. Plenty of people had faced worse adversity than this and had come out the other side, not only surviving but thriving. I decided I was willing to die before giving up on my dream of achieving a scholarship to the NCAA.

For the record, the Ivy League doesn't technically offer scholarships like the other NCAA schools. Basically, this "scholarship" would allow me to pass through admissions. I excelled at school and was top of my class, but would I get into Brown without a free pass? Probably not. I would still have to write the SAT and go through the admissions process, and as long as I proved I wasn't an idiot, I should get in. This is assuming, of course, that they would eventually offer me a spot on the team. Then I would go on financial aid like every other student that attended an Ivy League Institution.

Luckily, the financial aid was based on household income and since we were a working-class, blue-collar family, Mom and Dad would only have to pay a small fraction of the two hundred fifty thousand-dollar education. Having good grades and a good SAT score also made it appealing to recruit me because every sports team in the Ivy League had to keep a certain team grade average and keep in "good standing" with regulatory bodies that governed the NCAA.

It was at this time that the gates opened to the extreme

powers of Visualization. People always ask me, "How did you discover Visualization?" This is how. By surviving extreme adversity. I was still bedridden and could barely move, so my mind was all I had. All day long, all I could do was think. And those thoughts had been flooded with negativity, pain, and helplessness. No more. I didn't realize it that day, but I had unlocked a superpower and tapped into uncharted territory in my mind. An uncharted place that's accessible to all of us. A place where the fighter inside us is sitting dormant, waiting to be unleashed.

So, as I lay there in my bed, I knew my real fight was just beginning.

Chapter 11

Vipers

—

My three years as a Vernon Viper were instrumental in many ways. Not only in my hockey career, but in life. We had one of the best teams in Canada, if not the best. It was an amazing organization and I turned into a fan favourite. Our team had an absolute blast off the ice, and I met Claire during my second season. I had experienced innocent high school love, but Claire was the first girlfriend that really stole my heart.

After I graduated high school in Revelstoke and had freshly signed with the Vipers, my dad came home from work one day and said, "I think we should throw the boxing gloves back on, what do you say? You're gonna have to start throwing down with the big boys this year because of the way you hit." I had fought a little bit leading up to that point – a handful of fights with the local Grizzlies Junior B team (one league below the Vipers) and a couple street fights (which I'm assuming Dad didn't know about).

"Let's do it," I replied with a smirk.

We wrapped our hands, put on the gloves and were ready to spar in the backyard shortly after. Mom wasn't home, obviously.

"I'll keep it to body shots," he said. "But I want you to come at me with all you got."

"Bring it on, old man."

He hit me with a couple good body shots before I popped him hard in the face, dropping him to one knee. It was on now.

"Alright, no more playing nice, protect yourself," he said.

We both smirked again and started going full tilt. By this time Mom had come home from work and was banging on the window wondering what the hell we were doing. We waved her off as she rolled her eyes.

I was protecting myself, but Dad's punches were definitely harder now. I overextended myself on a missed right and he hammered me in the stomach. Down I went. Another minute or so went by. I ended up connecting with a big right after I popped him with a jab, and he went down smelling nitrogen and freshly cut grass (in his words).

To this day I swear Dad let up on me, but he claims he didn't.

"I think you're ready," he smiled.

I loaded up my 1983 Toyota Cressida and headed to Vernon with the essentials: my hockey gear, another hockey bag full of clothes, and my guitar. I was excited to move out of the house and start a new chapter in my life.

As soon as training camp started, I knew I needed to get fighting right away. Everyone was so much better than I thought they'd be, and I knew exactly why they had signed me. There was always a ton of competition during camp, and I needed to get noticed quickly and show them I could provide that toughness element. I essentially fought my way onto the team.

The Vancouver Canucks were even having their training camp in Vernon this year. I remember being in complete awe of these huge professional hockey players. I didn't play a lot of minutes my first year and had a very defined role: skate, hit anything that moved, and fight. I quickly earned the nickname Patti-Train because I was throwing multiple huge hits every game. I even scored, wait for it, one goal my entire first year, in game fifty-five of sixty. I had one goal and about twenty fights. I had a long way to go before colleges would start showing interest, but I was just trying to stay in the league my rookie year. I had doubts every day about whether or not I was good enough to obtain a scholarship to the NCAA.

Coach Vandy and I quickly developed a deep respect for each other. I think it was because we were both a little crazy. I played fearless, and he loved that. And I liked how much he demanded of us, as crazy as some of his antics might have been. One thing was for sure, we hated to lose more than anything. Partly because of the pride Vandy instilled in us but mostly because we would pay the price the next day if we lost. Plus, as long as we were winning, we had the green light to party as much as we wanted, and party we did.

My best memory of Vandy's antics happened about halfway through this rookie season. My parents had come to Vernon early (for pre-game skate – which happened around 10:00 am for a 7:00 pm game) and brought me a brand new CCM Vector stick hoping to bring me my first Junior A goal. Back then, a lot of guys were still using wood sticks or the composite shaft and wood blade combo. But this is when the one-piece composite stick first came out.

Every hockey player remembers the first Easton Synergy and CCM Vector sticks. These sticks changed the game completely because of how hard and quick players could shoot the puck, especially compared to the wood sticks. Only the first-line players got the new one-piece sticks on the Vipers. Us fourth liners used the traditional wood sticks. Vandy saw my parents give me the stick and I could tell he was thinking something along the lines of, *You little fucker, you better not be thinking you're a goal scorer now.* I had an important role to fill at the time. Scoring goals wasn't in the job description.

It was my first shift in the game that night. I skated down my side of the ice and went to rip a shot from the top of the circles. But I whiffed it right into the corner. When I came off the ice Vandy came storming over to me with a rush of purple filling his face.

"What the fuck was that?" he said, looking at my stick as if he didn't know.

"My parents bro-"

"Give me that," he barked back. "T-Bone, give him that big Koho (the quintessential heavy wood stick)." T-Bone was our trainer and equipment guy. As he was trying to hold back his laughter, he tossed me the Koho.

The next thing I knew I was holding this huge, solid wood stick on our bench. Vandy looked me right in the eyes and said, "Your next shift, you don't come off the ice until you break that over someone."

I looked at the guys next to me; they had huge grins on their faces, but I was slightly terrified.

"Is he serious?" I asked.

They all laughed and said I had better do it. Out I went for my next shift. I was lined up next to the opposing player, and my mind was racing. *How am I going to go about breaking this two-by-four?* I brought my left hand up to meet my right at the top of my stick, and I tomahawked this poor kid right across the back of his legs. Of course, that fucking Koho didn't break. Did they ever? Naturally, this caused a line brawl, and I spent the first period in the penalty box. We ended up winning the game and Vandy made his rounds to each guy for a fist bump. He got to me and had the hugest smirk on his face. *This guy is nuts!* I remember thinking. But I loved it.

The biggest beating I ever received happened in my first year with the Vipers. We were playing the Trail Smoke Eaters in our last game before the Christmas break. We were losing badly with about five minutes to go in the game, so I decided to run their goalie when he came outside his crease to play the puck. Part of our job as fourth-line players was to "send a message" to the other team so they would remember the next time we played each other, especially if the game wasn't going our way. And Vandy made it very clear that in a situation like this, we might get beat on the scoreboard, but we would never get beat up physically.

The melee that ensued after I ran the goalie was broken up by the referees quickly, so the Trail team didn't get much retribution. Once I was out of the penalty box and back on our bench, there was about one minute left in the game. Trail put all their tough guys on the ice, and they had one of the toughest teams in the league. Vandy, of course, gave our line the tap from the bench, and I knew I had to answer the bell. I had been winning pretty much every fight up to this point, so I was feeling pretty confident.

I lined up next to this huge twenty-one-year-old from Saskatchewan. We dropped our gloves and started trading blows. He hit me so hard I dropped to the ice – not knocked out cold but very dazed. I would have stayed down, but he picked my limp body up, with what seemed like one hand, and hit me with another enormous right. Everything went foggy, and I could feel the immense pressure building in my head and mangled face – it was fucked. My nose was broken badly, and I got some stitches to repair the cuts on my cheekbone and above my eye.

I iced my face for the entire five-hour bus ride back to Vernon. My head was pounding and I'd definitely suffered another of what would be many undiagnosed concussions. Once we arrived in Vernon, we unloaded the bus, unpacked our gear, and said brief goodbyes to the rest of the team before our week-long break. I popped some more painkillers, drove to my billets, and drifted off to sleep.

My billets, Brenda, Brian, and their son, Brad, were like

a second family to me. As a young adolescent, moving into another family's home can be uncomfortable, but I felt settled with them right away.

The next morning, I woke up to blackness. I was confused. I tried to open my eyes, but everything remained black. My head throbbed, and I gently put both hands on my face. My eyes had swollen completely shut! I felt my way up the stairs when I heard Brenda say, "Oh my god, are you okay!?"

I got her to dial my parents' number and pass me the phone so I could let them know I wouldn't be able to drive home that day. They offered to come pick me up, but I figured I would just rest and ice and see what the next day brought. I'd never spent so much time with a bag of frozen peas on my face.

I made it home to Revelstoke the next day, with a couple of days to spare until Christmas. My mom cried when I walked through the door. I looked like I had been beaten with a baseball bat. Two cuts that looked like bloody, crusty caterpillars and a swollen, black-eyed racoon face.

I hugged my dad. "Damn, bud, you don't look too good. Sorry to see you like this. Maybe pick your spots better next time and don't go shot for shot with the big boys?"

I learned my lesson and never took a beating that badly ever again.

Chapter 12

The Fire

—

My second year in Vernon was much of the same. I had gone back to Revelstoke the summer after my rookie year to work at the local mill piling lumber so I could have some beer and gas money for the year. I played a much larger role on the team my second year with the Vipers. I established myself as a decent third-line player and was one of the most feared hitters in the league, if not the most feared. I increased my point total to eighteen, played some time on the penalty kill, and was still fighting often. I was only about one hundred and eighty pounds but I could run over anyone. Defencemen were terrified to retrieve the puck when I was barreling down on them. As much as my role grew that year, I still wasn't skilled enough to warrant any attention from college scouts.

With all the fighting, attention from girls, and partying we did, my ego started to grow. I became more reckless and felt more invincible than ever. The problem with being one of the fighters on the team was that local guys from Revelstoke and Vernon knew who I was and figured I was a good test of their toughness. I never went looking for fights off the ice, but if someone came at me, I wouldn't hesitate for a second to drop them. The Papa Jerry in me started showing itself. Plus, I figured it was just keeping me sharp for the on-ice fights.

We lost in the league finals to the Surrey Eagles my second year in Vernon. It was hands down the nastiest hockey I have ever been a part of. Just like the classic hockey movie Slapshot. I actually received a two-game suspension in this series for taking out their goalie. You had to commit a pretty serious offence to get that kind of punishment in the league finals of the BCHL in 2005.

There was a bounty on my head when I returned to the lineup for game five in Surrey. As I was skating at centre ice without the puck, one of the Surrey players blindsided me with a vicious elbow to the face. I never saw it coming and I wasn't sure how long I was knocked out. The blood poured out of my face as T-Bone lifted me off the ice. The tip of my nose was touching my left cheekbone (the second of my four broken noses) and I suffered another major concussion. It didn't help the situation that I had blocked a shot with my face earlier in the game, requiring a bunch of stitches. That cut was once again bleeding profusely.

The trainers were trying to get me to the dressing room for repairs, but Vandy had insisted on holding my head over the boards so the refs could see the blood pool onto the ice. I dangled lifelessly, like a puppet. He was livid, and the pooling blood added support to his claims of wanting a penalty. He stood there holding me and yelling, "Look at this poor kid, you blind motherfuckers. How the fuck can you not call a penalty? We are going to fucking kill everyone on that team if you don't call a penalty." This was not an empty threat.

When I played Junior hockey, the players made the call whether they could continue playing, not the doctors. Right or wrong, that's just how it was. We didn't want to be perceived as weak, so we took a bunch of Tylenol and sucked it up. This time was no different. I got a bunch of stitches in the dressing room, got my nose reset, knocked back a bunch of painkillers and came back out for the rest of the game in a very dazed state.

After we lost this series in Surrey, it was time for our week-long bender (our party to kick off summer and bid farewell to another season). The next day, after returning to Vernon, we spent all day and night frequenting the local bars. The second night, we spent the night camping thirty minutes out of town at Bluenose Mountain, just as we had done the previous year. This meant it was time for my annual pyro show. My display of recklessness and invincibility would be on full display.

The year before, I'd introduced my beer bombs. I would chug a beer, fill the bottle with gas, put the lid back on the beer, and set it ever so gently in a rock nest in the fire. I would yell at everyone to take cover since glass would go flying. After about thirty seconds, flames would billow out around the fire and then - BOOM! - the flamethrower would blast straight up into the air about thirty or forty feet. Everyone would cheer. I would wait ten minutes or so, and then I would repeat over and over all night long.

For our second annual trip to Bluenose, I thought, *How can I make my pyro show bigger and better than last year? Use bigger bottles of course!* I warmed up with a few "normal-sized" bombs to get the crowd going. For my finale, I decided to use a Colt 45 bottle and an empty wine bottle. I chugged the whole Colt 45, filled it with gas and put the lid back on. Then I grabbed a wine bottle, filled it up with gas and put the lid on it as well. I put both bottles in my sweater's front pocket and went around getting the crowd revved up before I placed them in the fire.

As I was stumbling around in my drunken state, my face still mangled from the devastating elbow in our last series, I suddenly felt soaking wet. *What the hell? Maybe I pissed myself. Was I that hammered?*

I went to feel my sweater pocket. *Shit!* The bottoms of the bottles hit each other and broke, spilling a litre and a half of gas all over my torso and legs.

As the minutes passed, I failed to recognize the dangers of gasoline vapors. The vapors are more dense than air, so I had a flammable cloud settling around me wherever I went.

I reeked of gas. I peeled my sweater off as broken glass fell out of the pocket and, for some reason, decided to throw the sweater in the fire. To this day, I don't know why I did this. Maybe I was being a good Samaritan by not leaving it in the woods. Or maybe I figured I might as well just watch the sweater light up in flames. Either way, I kept what I thought was a safe distance as I tossed the sweater towards the fire, giving it an extra kick as it flew through the air.

As clear as a detonating cord runs towards sticks of dynamite, a raging inferno shot out of the fire and instantly engulfed me as the extreme heat forced me to bolt into the woods.

Chapter 13

Pushing the Human Spirit

—

Week three in the burn unit. I was now slightly more mobile. I grabbed the bar running parallel with my body that hung above my bed. My left hand was now free of bandages, but still raw in some areas. The range of pigmentation on the skin as it healed was really incredible. It was almost as though I had a severe case of vitiligo. My right hand was still bandaged. I grabbed that bar as hard as I could, my hands in immense pain, and tried to do a pull-up. I had lost so much muscle that I couldn't pull myself up. The negative thoughts started rolling through my head like a freight train. *You're too weak. The doctors are right. Just wait until your hands heal, until you're out of the hospital.* I acknowledged the voice but didn't listen. I tried again. Failed. And again. Failed. *Okay, baby steps. That's fine. I'll try again later, and tomorrow, and the next day.* Although I couldn't do a pull up for the first few days, I refused to give up. After making the choice to chase my dream, I was trying to do anything I could.

Thanks to the support of my family, friends, and my new mindset, my routine had changed. When I woke up, I was no longer depressed and hopeless. I was determined and hellbent.

I started framing the pain differently, changing my internal dialogue around the adversity. The pain was always there to some degree, and much worse on my debridement days. I would imagine the pain was fuel for my cells, and this was just the process of healing. Before, I was always focusing on the pain and how bad it was. It fucking hurt and I would just focus on the feeling of the pain, feeding it. My cells now "ate" the pain and used it as fuel. The more I overrode this natural response, the more manageable the pain became. It was remarkable. It didn't disappear by any means, but framing it differently really changed everything for me. I was digging even deeper into this untapped place in my mind.

I would then close my eyes and visualize four things. The first was healing and walking out of the burn unit. But not healing like you might think. I visualized the healing process at a cellular level. I envisioned the skin cells around my burns (and eventually the grafts) nourishing the open areas and closing them. I imagined the cells changing from damaged to healthy – slowly healing my body back to its original state. My cells were powerful and full of nutrients. They were fast- tracking my healing.

Then I would imagine myself walking out the front doors of the hospital and feeling the fresh air against my face. I felt liberated and determined from manifesting this vision and creating such a deep sense of belief in myself.

The third thing I visualized was playing on opening night with the Vipers for the upcoming season. I broke it down into little details: seeing the guys at camp, the game day routine, driving to the rink in the Cressida, putting my gear on, looking at my burns, knowing they were just a part of me and my new story, and feeling the wind against my face as I skated in the game, hitting guys and scoring goals, I could hear the crowd chant my name.

I started to realize how powerful it was to create an actual experience in my mind, not just paint a picture. My imagined experience brought me such an indescribable amount of joy. It transported me into a different reality, not the one I was currently living in. I was effectively distorting my reality.

The fourth, and last thing I visualized was signing my commitment letter to Brown. I would watch it in my head over and over – feeling the pen in my hands and pressing it into the paper, watching the blue ink flow with my signature. I could see the handshake with Danny Brooks and hear his voice over the phone as he offered me a spot on the team. I imagined my parents' reaction after I told them the news that I was going to attend an Ivy League school.

My prognosis would not define me. I believed Visualization was my only hope to prove the doctors, and my old mind, wrong.

One day, I actually got busted by the nurses for doing my pull-ups. I'm sure they'd never seen anyone do pull-ups in the burn unit before. They thought I was crazy. Maybe they were right. "You need to let your hands heal and rest!" I would just smile and tell them I was going to walk out of that place before they knew it.

"That's not going to help you heal or walk!" they would say.

I would simply smile again, "Yes, it will."

Chapter 14

Long Shot

—

I was scheduled to have my graft surgery done in week three, but the procedure kept getting delayed because patients in more serious condition kept bumping me down the list. Rightfully so, but it just prolonged my recovery.

The nurse came into my room to change my dressings one day. There was some fresh blood on the side of my right hand from the pull-ups.

I was up to three of them, but that would soon change. My muscles were slowly coming back. I had been a hundred and eighty pounds when I went into the hospital, went up to almost two hundred pounds from all the water weight I gained the first week, and then plummeted to a hundred and fifty-five pounds by the end of week three. I was still chugging milk because it provided easy calories and seemed the most appealing, but I was very dehydrated. I remember looking at my catheter tube, shocked at what colour my piss was. It was a dark brown rust colour, despite all the fluids being pumped into me. That catheter sucked. It felt like I had chlamydia for three weeks straight. I'll never forget the feeling when they pulled that thing out. They warned me about how far it actually went inside my body. The nurse started pulling, and it kept coming, and coming, and coming, for what seemed like a foot of tube (it's actually close to ten inches). I couldn't tell if it felt good or terrible.

I was in a much better spot mentally. I truly believed I would walk out of that hospital and play hockey again, especially because my surgery was supposed to happen any day. That was my ticket to recovery because the rehab program would begin shortly after, which meant I was one step closer to getting out of that place. I firmly believed there was another element at play when it came to my body healing faster and using the pain as fuel. That negative voice that was always trying to creep back in eventually said, *Holy fuck, he's really going to do this.* All the pain signals my brain sent were being overridden by my new voice. My body had no choice but to listen to my mind. *Well, he's not going to stop this madness. We might as well get on the same page and speed this healing up because it looks like there's a new plan.* I truly felt this in my soul.

"What do you say we try and sit up today?" the nurse asked. "And if that goes well, we can get you standing, for a moment."

"Yeah!" I said with enthusiasm. I was tired of lying in one spot, getting my parents and nurses to adjust my body all the time because of the bedsores.

"Okay, we're going to take it slow because you're going to feel quite dizzy. If you feel nauseous or sick, please tell us."

"Okay," I said, rolling my eyes. I could handle a little nausea. How bad could it be? After they changed my dressings, I got ready to sit up for the first time. I couldn't believe the amount of energy it took to get myself upright, even with the nurses' help. I got to the edge of the bed and realized they were right. The room started spinning like crazy. My mouth filled with saliva as I tried to fight the feeling of throwing up.

"How are you doing?" the nurses asked as they held me upright.

"Pretty good," I said, lying of course.

The spinning subsided slightly, and they asked if I wanted to try standing. I wouldn't be able to walk, but just to stand would be a feat.

The nurses each grabbed an arm and heaved me upwards. The weakness I felt was unforgettable. My legs shook as they struggled to support the weight of my body. The thud in my chest increased in power and frequency. The room started spinning again as I felt faint. It was like I was in the last leg of a marathon after not eating for days.

In my head, I figured I would be totally fine. I wouldn't just let myself simply fall over, I'm stronger than that. Well, I was wrong, of course. I had nurses surrounding me in case I started a heavy lean. Right when they let me go, I quickly fell over, with all of them catching me. "Okay, maybe not quite ready for that. Let's get back to just sitting for now." The negative thoughts came rushing back. *The doctors are right. Look at you. You can't even stand up. Override. Try again tomorrow. Giving up is not an option.*

Sure enough, after the next couple days of attempting this, I became more comfortable and less dizzy. I couldn't stand for long periods of time, but I took my first steps that week. Mind you, I probably looked like I was a hundred years old.

My parents were finally able to take me outside in a wheelchair, and it was the best feeling in the world. The fresh air pumped new life into me. The hospital windows couldn't be opened, so I hadn't been able to suck in fresh air for three weeks. I was beaten down and decrepit looking. I remember getting emotional while I sat outside with my parents. My dad looked at me and said, "What a crazy few weeks, eh dude? We're so proud of you, you're going to be okay."

I looked at him and said, "Thanks Dad, but I'm going to be better than okay. I'm going to walk out of this hospital and be playing hockey in a few months. Then I'm going to go to

Brown. I might look a little fucked up, but I'll have some cool scars to tell my story."

They loved my enthusiasm, but I am sure they had doubts about this statement. I was supposed to be in the hospital for a lot longer still, and the doctors had already thrown my hockey career out the window. I don't think my parents cared if I went back to working at McDonalds for the rest of my life. They were just relieved that their son was going to live a normal life again. But my parents had always supported me in anything I chose to do, so my dad looked at me and said, "Well then, go get it, Hub. And don't stop until you call us from your dorm at Brown."

Chapter 15

Grafts

—

By week four, I had made significant progress and felt stronger each day. I was finally off of the morphine drip and was only taking pills for pain, except for the debridement days of course. I was really starting to notice the effects of morphine dependency by this point. The pills weren't enough, and I really craved that old feeling of sinking into my bed as my bones became numb. No wonder that shit is so addictive.

Claire had also visited again. It was nice that she could wheel me around outside. We would just chat, and I'd sneak in a few make-out sessions when I could.

I got wheeled into the shower dungeon for more debriding that week. The anesthesiologist and doctor relayed some new concerns to me.

"Aaron, we'd really prefer to not give you more general anesthetic if we don't have to. It's not ideal to be put under two to three times a week for this long. Are you up for seeing if you can get by with some morphine? It will be more painful, but if you can bear it, I'd like to see you try."

I thought about it and uttered, "Umm, ok I'll try."

I only had an open IV line now, not a bunch of lines pumping fluid into my veins. I had been stabbed with so many needles that I'd lost count. At one point, I was so dehydrated that the nurse had to put the IV in my foot. My hands were also not ideal, as the line would get caught in the bedding all the time. This made my pull-up attempts hurt even more.

There I was, lying on the metal bed for the umpteenth time, except awake. The nurse hooked into my IV with a fresh dose of morphine. They slowly peeled my bandages off. I still had yet to see my third-degree burns since I had always been put under for all the previous debridements. I was very curious, yet frightened, to see what I looked like. The number of bandages covering my body slowly became less and less as my healing progressed, but these deep third-degree areas needed to stay covered because of infection risk. I was beyond horrified when I saw them. Pain rushed through my body. They had warned me the air would be very excruciating.

This was an understatement. My heart rate rose as I anticipated what was coming next. If the air felt that bad, what was the high-pressure water jet going to feel like? I felt physically sick when I looked down at my body. I knew I had been injured badly, but I didn't realize it was this catastrophic. I had been completely naive in my thinking; specifically what I imagined deep third-degree burns would look like.

My thighs looked like rotten cauliflower – swollen, yellow, and bloody. The huge open areas were oozing with blood and awful-smelling pus. I finally witnessed firsthand the massive gashes left after they sliced me open every debridement day to relieve the pressure.

The pain left. I was in shock from the disgusting visual of my body. That negative voice started shouting at me this time. *I didn't think it was this bad! How am I going to play hockey in a few months? How is this not infected? It looks like my legs will have to be amputated!* It was difficult not to give this voice power. I was silent for what felt like hours.

It was time. I was about to be snapped out of my trance in a big fucking way.

"Okay Aaron, we're going to give you a little shot of the water. I'm not going to lie; it's going to hurt. See if you can manage. If you're in too much pain, tell us and we will give you more morphine."

I just nodded as I sat there naked, with nothing but a little towel over my parts. Then it came. I thought I had experienced the pinnacle of pain until this point. This was something I could have never imagined, and I doubt I will ever experience again. As soon as that jet stream of water hit my raw flesh, my vision blurred as a demonic scream left my body. It felt as if an old, rusty, serrated knife was being sunk into my leg and moved back and forth as it explored the depths of my flesh. My subconscious brought back flashbacks to the car ride to the hospital weeks prior, somehow comparing the pain without my conscious control. I didn't have to say anything.

"Give him more morphine. Let's try once more."

I grabbed the sides of the bed as hard as I could in anticipation. The water pounded my other leg. Another demonic scream. I would have cried if I could.

"I can't! Please stop! Please knock me out. Ahh please, please!"

How did they think anyone would be able to endure this kind of pain? I'm sure I would have just passed out, eventually. My flesh was still on fire from those two quick shots of water. The darkness came quickly after the anesthesiologist arrived. The darkness allowed me to finally escape this torture.

After an hour or two, I slowly opened my eyes. I was defeated. I broke down and wept like a baby. All the emotion I'd felt during my stay in that hospital came pouring out of me. I had had enough of the pain, and after seeing my deformed body, I really thought back to what the doctors said. *Maybe they were right. How was I going to play hockey like this? My body was mangled. Maybe it WOULD take a couple of years to get back to normal.* The mindset I was trying to cultivate was constantly being challenged with this fucking relentless pain.

I sat with my feelings for a couple of hours. All I had to do was stay in the fight. That's what I reminded myself of. I repeated it. Over and over. *Stay in the fight. Don't give up. Don't let the doctors tell you what you are capable of. Remember, the pain is your body healing. Visualize, visualize, visualize. Live in that other reality. The pain will come again. Embrace it. It can't break you.*

Over the next few days, I got back in a good space mentally. I was wheeling myself around the hospital, one-handed in my wheelchair. After a conversation with my parents, I mentioned that I was fine if they wanted to head home to Revelstoke. I knew they had gone into serious debt during my stay.

But they were adamant about staying with me. They had spent a full month sleeping on the floor by my bed up until this point.

Finally, the day came. I was getting my surgery. Four weeks after I arrived at the hospital. The road to recovery was truly about to start. I was ready to get out of this place and fervently signed the waiver for my surgery. I wasn't fully aware of what it entailed, nor did I really care, especially after what I had seen in the shower a couple of days prior. It was crystal fucking clear that I desperately needed skin grafts. They began to lecture me on exactly what the procedure would look like. There was a high risk of blood loss and a good chance I would need a blood transfusion while they performed the surgery.

Thankfully, I wouldn't need skin donors. They were going to harvest the skin from my calves, the outside of my legs, and the sides of my ass. I needed three large grafts, two covering my entire inner thighs and one spanning my entire right flank, as well as three smaller ones down my right hip and glute. There was a point early in my stay where the doctors thought I may have needed a bone graft on my right hand, but it had shown remarkable healing, again, thanks to that cooler of ice on the ride to the hospital.

They harvested the skin with a dermatome, which was nothing more than a glorified cheese slicer, just much sharper I assumed. The blade would be placed on the desired areas and they would essentially skin me alive (well, alive but sleeping). That skin is then meshed, which means stretching it out. This is important in split-thickness grafts because of the lack of donor skin available. It allowed for less donor skin to cover a larger area than it normally would if unmeshed. The meshing leaves little holes throughout which increases the chances of a successful take of the skin grafts. It was as if the skin was aerated; the same concept as aerating your lawn. Aerating your lawn allows vital nutrients to reach the root system. You can still see the meshing on my grafts to this day, and it's pretty cool.

The wound bed is then cleaned, and this harvested skin is laid over top and secured with staples into the healthy skin surrounding it. Then it's wrapped in dressings for several days.

The bad news? The donor sites were the equivalent of second-degree burns since the first two layers of skin are removed. So instead of being forty percent burnt, that number would climb to about sixty percent. This meant more pain, and I would be bedridden again for almost an entire week. It felt like I was going to be right back where I started.

The surgery lasted several hours. I needed a blood transfusion from the bleeding that occurred, but it was a successful procedure. They hooked me up to a bunch of IVs again, and the steady morphine drip was back in my life.

Each leg was in a sling hanging from the bar above my bed. I looked at my shins. They were covered in yellow bandages, but not wrapped, and I could see that blood had clotted into a dark brownish red colour. The morphine was helping slightly, but these donor sites fucking hurt. And this was going to get worse before it got better. The nurse came into my room the next day and said we needed to take these yellow bandages, or wax strips as I thought of them, off to allow my legs to drain and heal.

She put two troughs under each leg that were slung up from the bed. This was making more sense now. Not only were my legs in a sling to prevent my donor sites from sticking to the bedding, but they were elevated so the troughs could catch the blood that would drain from the donor sites over the next few days. *How much blood were we talking?* She started peeling it off and I couldn't bear it. I grabbed the sides of the bed and screamed, "Just rip it off!" I winced and the blood slowly started dripping into the trough. The nurses would come in a couple times a day and empty the blood and pus-filled troughs. I started forming bed sores again – much worse this time. Not only could I not move, but having my legs elevated added much more pressure on my glutes.

After a few days of recovery, I finally got a look at the grafts. They were a very dark purple colour where the skin was starting to take. The edges were even darker, almost black, where the skin was dying from lack of blood flow. Apparently, these were all normal signs, and my grafts were taking well with no rejection.

The major concern for the next couple of weeks was infection. The grafts had to be monitored closely. I still had open second-degree areas on my right arm and hand, as well as several other areas on the rest of my stomach and legs.

By the end of the week, I could get out of bed. Same

idea as the first time – sit up really slowly and stand if I felt comfortable enough. I knew what to expect with the dizziness, which helped me this time around. I got to my feet slowly, and was able to take a few steps, albeit hunched over since the grafts would pull tight if I attempted to stand up straight. This would be a major part of my rehab – stretching and working these grafts so they didn't become stiff and immobile. But man, it felt amazing to walk, even if I was back looking like an old man again.

The nurses sat me back down. I wasn't allowed to stand for too long because the blood would rush to my legs and the grafts on my thighs would bleed out. Short walks several times a day were the key. All the staples, around fifty, had been removed from my body. Or so I thought.

What started as an annoyance on the bottom of my right thigh, began to progressively get worse, and it turned out to be a missed staple. The skin had grown completely over it. They had to cut it out with a little scalpel, and I broke down again. Not because the pain was too much, but because it was relentless. Fucking never-ending pain.

Just as I would turn a corner, something small, like a little staple that had to literally be dug out of me, would set me off. Constant pain for so long can wear on a person and I was almost at my breaking point. "I can't do this anymore," I cried to my parents. They had tears in their eyes, too. My mom held my hand in silence, there was nothing to say. I had to reassure myself that I was on the fast track to healing, and therefore one step closer to walking out of the hospital. Stay in the fight.

Chapter 16

Rehab

—

My healing progressed rapidly, and I was thrust into my rehab program a week after surgery. Week five. I could now do ten pull-ups on the bar above my bed. I was feeling stronger, but I still looked terrible. My appetite was finally improving. My new routine was as follows: wake up, do my Visualization, bang out some pull-ups, eat breakfast, dressings change, coat my whole body in nonstick mesh padding, tensor bandage my legs to prevent bleeding, get myself out of bed and into my wheelchair, wheel myself over to the rehab centre, rehab for an hour or so, come back to eat lunch, take tensor bandages off, rip scabs off due to the mesh sticking, nap, play cards with Mom, watch TV, eat dinner, call Claire, put nonstick pads and tensors back on, go for a short walk and cruise in the wheelchair, take tensors off, peel more scabs off, visualize again, pull-ups, sleep. Repeat.

And I was able to have a bath! What a feeling. Air and water didn't hurt anymore, except for the few open second-degree areas. I still had to keep them covered in bandages to prevent infection. Colloidal silver and flamazine cream were going to be my new best friends. No matter what measures I took to prevent these sores from sticking to the bandages, the scabs always got ripped off when they were changed.

The nurse warned me that when I got out of the bath, there might be some dead skin floating around. Weird, another understatement. It was as if a dozen snakes joined me in my bath for their seasonal molt – I was bathing in skin rather than water. But thankfully, I was done with the debridement showers. Sayonara. I had finally made it to the other side of the relentless pain. Now I could really just focus on my recovery.

Rehab was centred around two major goals: to gain mobility back and keep the grafts stretched and supple. I was still hunched over like an old man, so I would try to stand up a little more each day. I pushed this too far most of the time and the graft on my right side would start bleeding. I had to listen to the physiotherapist and not push it too far too soon so I could continue to heal. I had to learn which pain to push through. Ripping the graft and disturbing the successful "take" of it wasn't going to help me.

The rest of the rehab time was dedicated to gaining some strength back. The pain of rehab was welcomed because I knew I was on the fast track to healing. I made huge strides the first couple of weeks at the rehab centre, and since I was off all meds, I thought, *Why do I need to be here? Can't I just do rehab at home?*

The short answer was no, for a couple of reasons. For one, I still had a significant number of open sores, and the risk of infection was still too high. And two, I was supposed to complete the first phase of rehab in the hospital. This was part of the reason my stay in the hospital was going to drag into the summer. The risk of impaired mobility was very high if my grafts weren't properly tended to.

Every day, I wheeled through the hospital and heard more screaming. As much as I liked all the nursing staff, I needed to get the fuck out of that place. I had cultivated such a deep sense of belief in myself through Visualization – I knew in my heart I needed to go home. If anyone was going to ensure they followed the rehab protocols, it was me. I pleaded my case to the staff and half-jokingly said I would just leave if they didn't grant my request. But since I was doing so well, they agreed.

I met with the physiotherapist the next morning to get my rehab program, gathered all my medical supplies (gauze, bandages, tensors, gelatin, colloidal silver, flamazine cream, iodine), and was ready to go. Six weeks had passed since that night up at Bluenose Mountain. What a ride. As my dad wheeled me towards the entrance of the hospital, I felt a great sense of pride, freedom, and hope.

Then something clicked in my mind. "Stop!" I cried out. He stopped before the doors. I slowly got up out of the wheelchair and hobbled through the doors in a hunched-over position. Although it wasn't how I visualized walking out of the hospital, I still did it. It wasn't perfect, but such is life. I still fucking did it – way before anyone said I would.

Chapter 17

Setback

—

We headed East, back to Vernon. I was going to stay with Claire for a couple of nights before heading back to Revelstoke. I kept myself covered on the drive with a blanket because I was supposed to limit sun exposure for two years. I would also have to get fitted for my compression bodysuits in the coming weeks, which I'd have to wear for two years as well, twenty-four hours a day, every day. Fitting from my nipples to my knees, these suits would prevent the scars from becoming thick and leatherlike, which could have inhibited mobility even more.

We arrived in Vernon. I gave my parents a big hug, and they briefly met Claire's dad, Rick. They were going to come get me in a few days.

Claire and I didn't do much, just went for a small walk in the driveway and watched a movie. She wheeled me around in an office chair so I could move about the house.

I woke up in the middle of the night a few times with pain in my back. My first night out of the hospital and something was already wrong. It wasn't muscle pain or burn-related pain. It was something new. I spent some time trying to go to the bathroom, but that didn't help. I was able to drift off to sleep again, but when I woke in the morning the pain was much worse. I didn't really let on how much pain I was actually in. I figured it was some weird cramp or something. Plus, my new pain threshold was extremely high.

"You okay?" Claire asked as she got ready for her shift at work before our weekend together.

"Yeah, I just have this pain in my back. Maybe I'll have a bath and see if that helps."

I was in the tub trying to breathe through the pain when Claire came in to say goodbye. I tried to hide my discomfort.

"I'll see you later. Help yourself to the kitchen and the TV is all set up. Call me if your pain doesn't get better."

"Sounds good. I'm sure it's nothing."

The pain continued to get worse as I sat in the tub for another hour. I got out and sat on the floor of the bedroom. I tried to lie in every position possible to get some sort of relief, but the pain became unbearable. I had to call Claire's dad.

"Rick? Riiiiiick!" I heard his footsteps and then a knock at the door.

"You okay in there?"

"I think I need to go to the hospital. Can you pass me a phone?" I could barely speak now.

He opened the door and found me in the fetal position, ass naked in his spare bedroom. Just picture this for a moment. This young hockey player, who's sleeping with your daughter (well, not currently but would like to again soon), whom you've only met a couple times, is lying naked in your daughter's bedroom with only a towel on him. His whole body is strewn with gnarly scars, and he is wincing in pain.

"Shit, do you want me to take you to the hospital?"

I thought for a second. *This guy barely knows me. Maybe I should just call my billet family. I'm in excruciating pain, but what's another few minutes waiting for them to come pick me up?*

In hindsight, I should have just asked Rick to drive me, but I decided against it.

"I will..." I gasped, struggling more to get the words out, "...call my billets to come grab me."

They picked me up from Rick's house shortly after and I was off to the hospital again, the same hospital I came rushing into six weeks prior. I hadn't seen Brenda, Brian, or Brad since the day of the accident. We hadn't talked much except for a few times in the hospital, so this was a bittersweet reunion. We arrived at the hospital, they put me in a wheelchair, and wheeled me into the emergency room.

One day out of the burn unit and I was back in the hospital. One of the ER nurses recognized me right as I came in.

"Oh my God, I remember you from that night. Are you okay?" she asked as she looked at my bandaged body.

"Something is wrong," I replied, hunched over in my wheelchair. It didn't take long before I was admitted and given more morphine. I had some tests done and was diagnosed with kidney stones. The doctor explained that dehydration, partnered with the copious amount of milk I had been drinking, led to the formation of these calcium stones.

I thought back to what my piss looked like passing through the catheter – a dark brownish orange. Thankfully, after the CT scan, it was determined that the stones were small enough to pass and I didn't need shockwave lithotripsy surgery this time (a non-invasive procedure where shockwaves break larger stones into smaller pieces). This would not be the last time I would get kidney stones.

Anyone who's had kidney stones knows they fucking hurt. And pissing them out didn't feel much better. One minute I would feel fine, the next I was in pain as they passed through sphincters in the ureter, which passes waste from the kidney to the bladder. If a stone has trouble passing through the sphincter, it causes spasms and potential urine backup.

The pain was manageable compared to what I had just

endured for six weeks, but why did this have to happen right after I was released? I stayed overnight in the hospital, getting pumped full of liquids and morphine. At least I got to call my parents this time. Once the pain had subsided, and I was nice and high, the nurse brought me the phone.

"Hey Mom, you're never gonna guess where I am." That was an interesting conversation, to say the least. I was monitored overnight, and my parents showed up in the morning, speechless. The stones would take a week or two to pass, and if I had the same type of pain again, which was likely, I should head to the hospital in Revelstoke.

I hit the road with a handful of filters to piss through for the next two weeks. Claire had come to say goodbye in the hospital – so much for our weekend together. At least she was going to come visit me in Revelstoke the following weekend.

Chapter 18

Last Test In Hell

—

Once back in Revelstoke, I ended up in the hospital two separate times over the next week. I was pissing blood through these stupid filters and hadn't seen a stone yet. When these spasms became too intense, IV fluids and morphine were a quick cure and I returned to my normal state, relatively speaking. I didn't care about the pain anymore. I had become numb to it.

I was mostly just frustrated because the stones were interfering with my rehab. I was exhausted enough trying to heal from a major surgery. I wanted to be pushing the limits, going for numerous short walks and working these burns as much as I could. I still managed to get out for some walks, but when my kidneys were spasming, it was less than ideal.

My thigh grafts would still bleed within a minute of standing. I really had to watch this or they wouldn't heal properly. For the most part, I spent the next month getting around like an ape, using my arms to propel me from room to room so my legs could stay somewhat elevated.

Within a couple of weeks, I'd pissed out all the stones. Now I could continue on with my plan, the next step of which was to play in the home opener for the Vipers. I continued to visualize this every day.

I was still out to prove people wrong. To show everyone that I could play hockey again. To honor what I had been through and fight for my dream of an NCAA scholarship. But time wasn't on my side as I headed into my last eligible season of Junior hockey.

Besides the countless hours of prepping my burns with gelatin, silver, cream, gauzes, and tensors, the next month was mainly focused on my rehab, pushups, short walks throughout the day, and Visualization.

I needed to get back in the gym to get my legs back. I looked like I was riding a chicken. But I was really capped at how long I could be upright. The tensors helped the bleeding, but five minutes upright was about the max for the next few weeks, and I gradually increased that as time went on. My upper body was totally back. My triceps were jacked due to my new mode of ape-like transportation around the house. By the time July rolled around, I was back in the gym for my rehab. Except now I added bodyweight leg workouts along with some upper body exercises. Man, did this feel terrible. Anytime my legs were pushed to their max range, the grafts would stretch well beyond my comfort zone. But I pushed through it; I knew I had to get stronger if I wanted to play hockey in a month's time.

I was also getting accustomed to my new bodysuits. My scars needed the pressure, more so than I realized. I was fitted for three suits – a black, a blue, and a nude coloured one. By the end of summer, I got a couple more because you can imagine how much they needed washing after wearing them for twenty-four hours every day. My scars looked very gnarly by this point; my whole body was riddled with dark purple scarring. The donor sites matched this purple colour as well.

It's amazing how much these bodysuits helped with scarring. Just the ten minutes they were off to shower would cause my burns to raise about half an inch and become rock hard. At least the hair had finally fallen out of my grafts. That's right, I had new patches of hair growing out of my stomach. The skin from my calves had hair follicles intact, meaning the hair would grow on these new grafted areas for a couple of months before finally falling out. I had no chest hair, so this was quite the look. A temporary one, thankfully.

Claire and I started falling apart halfway through the summer. There was definitely something there. I really liked her. But I was also consumed with this comeback, not just having fun like everyone else my age. She was likely second-guessing the whole thing. It was still early days, and she probably wanted to enjoy her summer too. We would end up on and off for the next year – a theme that would continue for most of our young adult lives. I figured, *Oh well, chicks dig scars, right? Let's hope so.*

August came quickly. I was now walking a few blocks to the gym, but I had to get a ride back to my parents' house because I was absolutely drained afterward. This time of year also meant the ice went back in at the local arena. I had a chat with the rink attendant about getting on the ice by myself. Camp was less than a month away. I was excited, nervous, and scared to step on the ice for the first time since my injury.

I prepped the stubborn areas that still hadn't fully healed – my right arm and the areas on my stomach and legs. It was crazy how long these areas were taking to fully heal. I couldn't seem to win with them, especially overnight. If I kept them bandaged, the bandages would just rip the scab off every time I changed them. If I didn't cover them when I slept, they would stick to the bedding and rip off in the morning. My bed was disgusting; it looked like a murder scene.

I knew I needed to cover these open wounds as best as I could under my gross hockey gear to mitigate the risk of infection. I had my black bodysuit on, with gauzes on the open areas, and sleeves to protect the donor sites on my calves and the areas on my right arm. If people only knew what I looked like under all my gear, they would have, without question, wondered what the hell I was doing playing hockey.

What a feeling it was to put on my equipment. But I was quickly humbled once I stepped onto the ice. It felt so foreign to me. I thought it would come back quickly like it did every summer after taking a couple months off the ice. But it didn't. Skating really emphasized how immobile I was due to the thick scars restricting me. After I was able to ramp up my conditioning, I was instructed to monitor my heart rate closely since I was unable to sweat from the large grafted areas.

But I said fuck it and tried to push through. Thankfully, I never noticed an issue with keeping cool from the lack of sweat. But I couldn't give more than fifty percent effort because of how stiff and sore I was. I got off the ice and went into the dressing room. I just sat there with my mind racing. The negative thoughts came rushing back again. *How the hell am I going to be ready to play a game in a month? Maybe the doctors are right. They've seen thousands of these injuries. Maybe I won't be able to play this season. Maybe I should just call the coaches and tell them I can be the video guy for the year.*

There are times in your life when it's really empowering to simply say "Fuck that" and make a choice. We always have a choice, no matter the circumstances. Sometimes it takes that defiant attitude to make the hard choice. That's what I had done after my phone call with Danny Brooks and look how far it had gotten me. I acknowledged these negative thoughts and saw them float on by. I went back to my new mindset. *It's only your first time on the ice. Give yourself a break. Come back tomorrow and take it day by day. Just stay in the fight, that's all you can do. Show up and put in the work. Start small, that's ok. Giving up is not an option. Put one foot forward and just take another step.*

Think of that guiding star, the scholarship to Brown.

I constantly closed my eyes and visualized playing in the home opener and committing to Brown. It was incredible how my visualizations manifested such a deep sense of belief and trust in my journey. They gave me the superpower to push through anything – something I would need for the months ahead.

I wouldn't sign with Brown if I couldn't play hockey, so that was that. Decision made. I would have to find a way to play with the pain and limitations. Visualize the process every day.

My skating eventually progressed, albeit very slowly. The healing process for these grafts was just slow by nature, just as the doctors had told me. I was skating a couple times a week and really pushing my limits.

I had gone back to Vernon after the first week of August. I could skate whenever I wanted, or more like whenever I could, and I could be around a few of the guys. It was an emotional goodbye with my family, as they were apprehensive about me trying to play hockey, but they ultimately understood. The worst was behind us.

I stayed with my billets and went to the rink to skate with the guys. I remained at my own end of the rink since I couldn't keep up with the pace. They kept it light with comments like, "How you feeling, charred wood? What's it like to burn your dick off? No pucks today. Let's use Patti's stones." That might sound ruthless, but it made me and everyone else laugh, something I hadn't had a lot of that summer. Sometimes, humor really is the best remedy.

More guys started rolling into Vernon, and every one of them embraced me with an enormous hug. Seeing them was the best therapy I could ask for. It helped give me that last little push I needed. I wanted to be on the ice with my brothers.

But every day that camp crept closer, I had more and more

doubts that I'd be ready. I was nowhere near where I needed to be in order to play. That doubt was cemented after my next setback. The year from hell continued.

I woke up one night with a similar pain to the kidney stones – a deep internal pain. Except this time, it was in my lower abdominal area. I sat on the toilet in hopes it was just a stomachache. I drifted in and out of sleep. When I woke up a couple of hours later, the pain was much worse. I sat on the couch for a while, waiting for the pain to pass. It got even worse, and I had a fever. Something wasn't right. *What this time?* I drove to a walk-in clinic so a doctor could check me out. I told her about my symptoms.

"Alright, let's look at your abdomen."

I took my shirt off and peeled the ultra-tight pressure suit down as far as I could, revealing my fresh purple graft and all the other smaller second-degree areas that were also still purple.

"Wow, you've done quite a number to yourself. When did you get these grafts done?"

"In May," I said.

She pressed on my stomach and then on my lower right abdomen. The grafts hurt like hell to be pushed on, and to this day they still hurt if pushed hard enough. It's odd, I can't feel light touch because there are no nerves innervating these areas but pressing hard hurts.

After a quick exam, some blood tests, and an ultrasound, the diagnosis was appendicitis. I needed emergency surgery. *What else could go wrong!?* To make matters worse, the appendix is located in the lower right abdominal area. Of course, I had a fresh graft covering my entire right flank, so they would have to cut through my graft to remove it and then stitch me back up. *Would my graft be fucked up?* The hope of playing in the season opener vanished rapidly. The doctors didn't have an explanation for the appendicitis but I must have been pushing my body too far. It was begging me to stop so it could heal and recover.

Just a casual appendectomy to add to the summer from hell. Maybe I should have prayed in the burn unit with the pastor. I felt like I couldn't catch a break. I really didn't know what else could have gone wrong.

Chapter 19

Home Opener

—

I spent a couple of days in the Vernon hospital. I figured I should have received a member rewards card for that place. Camp was starting soon, and the season opener was in less than two weeks. And now I couldn't lift or do anything strenuous. I was down again. I needed to be on the ice to even have a sniff at being ready for the start of the season. Even at that, I had doubts. I knew I could barely play as it was, let alone this last surgery derailing me. All the progress I had made that summer was slowly being destroyed.

I met with our team doctor after being released from the hospital. He looked at my incision and asked me a few questions. He had been in the dressing room with me during all my previous injuries with the Vipers, so he knew I could play through a lot of pain. "Can I get on the ice just by myself? I need to play in the home opener. This is my last year to get a scholarship."

The doctor relayed this: "In terms of your burns, I'm not saying you can't play. It really depends on what you're able to do with this limitation. As for your appendectomy, we really need to keep your exertion level quite moderate, at least for the rest of the week."

Prognosis? I could skate lightly on my own for the rest of

the week, ride the stationary bike, and continue my rehab for the burns. Since camp had started, it looked like I wouldn't have the luxury of easing into body contact. *Contact – shit!* I hadn't even thought about what that was going to feel like. I still hadn't even skated at full capacity. Hitting was the largest part of my game. It's what got me that call from Danny Brooks in the first place. The surgeon obviously advised against contact during these first two weeks after the appendectomy, but as far as I was concerned I couldn't afford to take this much time off. I put my dreams before my health. It was an easy decision because I really was willing to die before giving up. I knew I wouldn't actually die, but if they had to take something else out of me or shoot me up with painkillers so I could play, so be it. If I got an infection, my body would fight it. I couldn't make my burns worse; they were just stiff and painful. Every day the pain and adversity tried to suck the life out of me but I wasn't stopping now.

It was almost the beginning of September. I got the go ahead to amp up my skating. I put myself through some good bag skates (on-ice conditioning). My cardio was terrible and my burns were stiff, but I was managing. I missed fitness testing and the first half of camp, which meant the home opener was just over a week away. I needed to test myself and test my body. I met with our coach and told him I was ready to practice with contact. He was skeptical based on how I looked on the ice, but he said we could give it a go. I prepped my burns and stepped on the ice with my teammates. The first couple strides were the toughest because they were the most explosive, and to be explosive, you needed full range of motion, something I didn't have yet. When I had been skating on my own, I wasn't really working on quick stops and starts. I was just trying to get my skating legs back and improve my cardio.

Then the drills started. The battles. A chaotic mess of bodies colliding every couple of seconds. I was definitely rusty compared to the other guys, but I wasn't about to take it easy on anyone. And I made it clear to everyone not to treat me any differently. The first bump I took to my right flank almost paralyzed me. The graft was still too fresh to handle contact without pain. I winced and got back in line, knowing I would have to try to avoid leading with my strong side. My thighs were usually fine with contact, but since there was no padding protecting my inner thighs, I was exposed to errant sticks and pucks.

I got off the ice feeling torn. I was so happy to be back practicing, but I knew when the games started I would be in a lot of pain. We had to rig my pants up with extra padding to protect the grafts. There was no perfect scenario. The extra padding helped if I got hit there, but it only exacerbated my limited range of motion, something I couldn't afford if I wanted to skate properly.

Vandy had taken a job in the WHL, so our assistant from the year before was now the new head coach – Bernie Pimm (Pimmer). Vandy and I kept in touch, and it didn't surprise him that I was back at camp. I called him after my latest surgery. "You are the toughest kid I've ever met. I'm proud of you, young man. I know the guys are rallying around you. Go get that scholarship." I would miss Vandy but was happy that he was progressing in his career as a head coach.

I met with Pimmer after the practice and lied about how I felt. He thought I looked pretty good. I was a little surprised by this, but maybe he just said that because he knew how much I wanted to play. Truth was, I was beyond sore.

Then it was time for our Blue versus White scrimmage game, which was usually played towards the end of camp. There were still enough players trying out to form two teams. After the game, the coaches would make the last big round of cuts.

Me being "healthy" enough to play proposed a unique situation, and a potential problem for someone. We had too many twenty-year-olds on the team now. Someone in their last year of eligibility would have to get moved since there was a max number of twenty-year-old players allowed per team (I believe it was six at the time). So, there was a battle for spots on the team. I knew I was an important piece, but after my injury, I figured I was more dispensable. After all, Junior hockey was still a business and winning was a priority. Yes, the coaches liked my game and what I brought to the team, but if I couldn't show up with my toolbox, why would they keep me around? The reality was, however, I was most likely safe after all I had been through. And the team could really rally around my comeback. They wouldn't trade the burnt guy, would they? I wasn't willing to take any chances.

The first period of the scrimmage was over, and the hockey wasn't great. We were coming off an upset in the league finals a few months prior, so we wanted redemption this season. The coaches stormed into the dressing room and tore us a new one.

"What the fuck was that? If you guys don't want to show up, we'll go find other players that do. You know you're competing for jobs out there, right? Stop being pussies! Someone hit someone, or better yet, drop your gloves! Fuck me."

Message received. Troy (aka Chewy) and I locked eyes in the room. The teams were sharing dressing rooms since we only moved into our main dressing room after camp was done and the team was set. We had traded for Chewy and him and I became friends right away – we still are. We had a tough team. Out of the seven twenty-year-olds, four – including me and Chewy – were pure scrappers. He was probably thinking the same thing as me – *I might be disposable here.* We gave each other a nod, and that was it. Time to send a message to the group.

We lined up at centre ice and dropped the gloves. We traded a few good punches, but when I switched to my left, I popped him pretty good, and we fell to the ice. To this day, he will tell you the fight ended with him on top. However, there were a lot of witnesses, so everyone there knows what really happened. Sorry, Chewy. I respect the shit out of him because a lot of guys probably thought they should have taken it easy on me. But Chewy and I were cut from the same cloth. He wanted to treat me the same, no matter what. I'm sure everyone thought I was crazy for fighting with all my injuries. Maybe I was.

Most people don't understand how hockey players can get into fights with their friends. Or how two guys can beat the absolute shit out of each other and have a beer at the bar afterward, comparing cuts and bruises from the tilt. The friend card goes out the window on the ice, but the respect card is always there. Adrenaline courses through your body, so you don't feel the fist hitting your face. This was the same adrenaline effect that had numbed the pain from my burns immediately following the accident.

The game ended and it was onto exhibition. Chewy and I were safe since we traded one of us older guys to Williams Lake. I was feeling better and more confident, but my body was really sore. Not only the grafted areas, but my muscles were fighting back, begging me to rest.

Now that I knew I was staying with the Vipers, I met with Pimmer so we could chat about a plan. My body was beat up. Pimmer agreed I should take most of the exhibition games off. He knew I was hurting, despite how hard I was trying to hide it. If all else was equal, based on play alone, I'm sure I would have been healthy scratched for the home opener. But the coaches knew what my presence brought, and my return to the lineup would probably be a powerful emotional catalyst for the team.

September 9, 2005 – our season and home opener against Williams Lake. I was nervous, but jacked up, as the game approached. This crazy journey was finally coming to a head. I was about to make another one of my visualizations come to fruition. *How would my body hold up?* The League was mean back in 2005, not like it is now. Guys would do anything to win. There were cheap shots, lots of fights, and people hit to hurt.

We went out for warmups, and I could do nothing but smile. I did it. I'd made it to the season opener. My body was nowhere near where it needed to be, but it was good enough. I felt no pain as the euphoria took over. Now I just needed to get that scholarship to Brown so I could continue playing hockey for another four years and get an education.

I got the call for the starting lineup. We went out on the ice and lined up on the blue line. I took my helmet off and soaked up the electric atmosphere. When my name was called on the loudspeaker, the crowd erupted, and the cheering didn't stop. It felt like an eternity before the sound subsided. Most of the city knew what had happened to me, and at that moment I was flooded with emotion. I looked over to where my parents were sitting (they never missed a game) and saw them hugging. I broke down and the tears started streaming down my face. The rest of the team felt the emotion as well. A catalyst this was, indeed.

Four and half months before this, I had succumbed to the "fact" that my hockey career was over. I had been pushed to the absolute brink that summer. I proved everyone wrong and myself right. But I wasn't done yet. There was more work to be done and a lot more pain in store.

Chapter 20

Bears

—

I had an assist in that first game and played pretty well. I learned to work smarter since I was so stiff. I was also itchy as hell from the healing. Instead of resting between intermissions, I spent my time changing dressings and getting scratched by my teammates. The coaches gave me an opportunity to play more minutes, and I ran with it. I had six points in the first six games. This was more than I had in my entire rookie year. My confidence was sky-high throughout the month of September until I started having pain in my pelvis area.

Anytime I got bumped close to my hips, a paralyzing pain would shoot through me. It almost felt like I tore my groin, but I could stretch it without pain. It hindered me when I put weight on my legs and tried to push off – not ideal in hockey. Yet, through October I had twelve points in thirteen games and continued to play well. I never imagined I would be a point-per-game player, especially after my summer of hell. I even started talking to other schools besides Brown. *Maybe I would have my choice at an NCAA school!* Often, players would get recruited by several schools and have a decision to make about which one they committed to. Princeton and Holy Cross seemed the keenest compared to the handful showing interest. It was finally happening; I was almost there. I was so close to getting that scholarship.

I talked to our doctor many times about my pelvis issue, and he sent me to a specialist in Kamloops, a larger city about an hour and a half away. No one could put their finger on it. I hadn't pulled any muscle, but the consensus was since my thigh muscles had suffered such intense trauma, my muscles around my pelvis were all overworked and out of balance. I tried strengthening my core and smaller stabilizing muscles, but nothing helped. The pain got worse and worse as the season continued.

Eventually, this issue became so bad that I was on crutches coming and going from the rink. I was getting shot up with Toradol and Cortisone just so I could play. None of the schools recruiting me knew I was struggling until I started sitting out every other game. When I did play, it was usually just on special teams (penalty kill and power play). It got to a point where I could barely skate. The shots masked the pain enough for me to play, but I felt it the next day. Pimmer knew I was struggling in a bad way. Eventually I practiced less and less so I could rest.

I was so close to getting my scholarship and had gotten off to such a good start, and now I couldn't even get to the rink without crutches. I was holding on by a thread. I didn't know how long I'd be able to continue like this. The grafts themselves weren't my issue anymore. Maybe this was why the doctors said it would take years to fully heal. My third-degree burns were so deep that my muscles were compromised, and they wouldn't be able to withstand competitive sports. I thought back to the first time I saw my third-degree burns in the debridement room. The image of rotten cauliflower filled my mind again. *No shit your muscles have issues.*

Danny Brooks was coming to see me play at the end of October. Talks with Princeton and Holy Cross had fizzled out, so I needed to put on a show for Brooksy. That meant an extra dose of Toradol. I blocked the pain as best I could and tried to kill anything on skates, aside from the refs and my teammates, although they were possible collateral damage. It was time to tap into that place I had accessed in my mind for the months leading up to this moment. The place where that pain was forced to surrender to the greater task at hand. Push through. Stay in the fight.

The game started with Danny Brooks in the stands. I laid out a handful of big hits and scored a goal, while getting shot up between periods. After the game, I tried my damndest not to limp when I went to talk to Brooksy. I couldn't let him see me on crutches.

"Volpatti, brotha! Great fucking game. You were a force out there. I didn't know they called you the Patti Train. That's fucking great!"

"Thanks Danny, and thanks for making the trip."

"You're exactly what we need on our team. How'd you like to come for a visit to Brown?"

"That would be awesome. I'd love to!" I said, trying to play it cool and not wince from the pain I was in.

I was almost there...

He knew I had gotten some interest from a few other schools, Princeton being the closest rival. What he didn't know was that I would have accepted an offer right there since I could barely play.

A couple of weeks passed. Fly-downs were reserved for serious recruits. It was one thing to talk with an NCAA school, but if you were offered a fly-down, they wanted you on their team. Those official words hadn't been said yet, but I knew I was close. I called my parents, and they were so happy. But they were also concerned about what I was putting my body through. I never told them I was getting shot up to play. Not many people knew about this. But they saw me on crutches after every game, my face filled with doubt and pain. I only played four out of twelve games in November. Brooksy called me after he noticed I'd missed a few games. I lied and said it was a little tweak and that I was just trying to get back to one hundred percent.

My fly-down. Our goalie from the previous year, Mark Sibbald, was at Brown, so he was able to take me under his wing and show me around. The fly-down usually consisted of three things: meeting the staff and players, seeing the facilities, and drinking – lots of it. I welcomed the break from playing so I could get some rest. If I took a few days off of skating, my pelvis usually felt a lot better. That's what made it such a strange injury. I could feel pretty good going into a game, and as soon as I got bumped the wrong way, I could barely walk, let alone skate. So, I was walking around okay on Brown's campus.

My first taste of college life was amazing. Brown's campus was beautiful, with old Victorian buildings providing a picturesque setting. Watching the hockey team practice was very eye-opening. There was way more skill than in the BCHL. Everything was fast and crisp.

There was also a tussle involving a couple of guys on the team outside of the bar one night. When I saw another guy rushing in to grab one of our guys, I figured it was a good opportunity to get involved and "earn my stripes". So, I jumped in and grabbed the guy, throwing him to the ground. The melee got broken up within a couple of minutes and we were all left unscathed. Thankfully, I didn't have to throw any punches – that would have been interesting.

A couple of hours later, we were partying across the street at the hockey house when I started talking with this sexy brunette. She was a senior and didn't understand how I was the same age as her. She asked about the gnarly scars on my right arm, which, of course, led to a conversation about a lot more. I ended up back at her place to cap off a wild night. I'd gotten into a little scrap and met my first woman at Brown. *The scars might not be so bad after all.* It was a ton of fun; I needed more. The guys on the team were a great group and I knew this was where I belonged.

I flew back to Vernon and got a call from Brooksy a couple of days later.

My heart began to race when I heard him say, in that heavy Rhode Island accent, "Hey, brotha, how do you feel about becoming a Brown Bear?"

I tried to play it cool. "Really?"

"Yes, really big guy."

"Yes!"

I had done it. I called my parents and told them the news, and we all cried in happiness. To think back to where I was earlier that year, when my parents didn't know if I would survive, was a feeling I could barely put into words. As I reflected on the pain I had endured up to this point, I felt an immense sense of pride in my accomplishment. I thought about how I was so close to giving up all those times. *What if I had? What would my life have looked like?* I had reached my pinnacle; I was going to be an NCAA athlete. I was beyond ecstatic. I was going to be in elite company with some of the best young players in North America. I had achieved my dreams and reached my NHL. The fight was worth it. Now it was time to get healthy.

During a radio interview shortly after the Vipers announced my commitment to Brown, Pimmer said these words: "I think Brown made a good choice in signing Aaron. He can skate, is strong on the puck, and takes the body like no other player I have ever coached. What he's been through is something you could never fathom, and frankly, I don't think the NCAA and the Ivy League are ready for Aaron Volpatti."

He was right.

Chapter 21

Final Hurrah

—

It was almost the end of November. I played the next game when I got back from my fly-down and I was back on crutches after the game. Over the next week, I rested for five days and tried to play once more, but I could barely walk. After talking with Brooksy, Pimmer, and the doctors, we all agreed I should shut it down. My body had been through so much and just simply wasn't ready to play a full season. It was difficult for me to turn that internal switch off, especially after the way our last season had ended. I wanted to win a championship with this group of guys. But I had to give myself permission to take care of my body and rest now. I couldn't get shot up every game just so I could play a few shifts on special teams. I had done what I sought out to do. I returned to the game I loved and got my scholarship. My body was in ruins, but I did it.

My new mission was to get healthy for playoffs in March, and obviously for my rookie season at Brown the following year. I took the next six weeks completely off and focused solely on my rehab for my skin grafts. Eventually, I played a couple of games in January and February. The issue was still there. I continued working with specialists, but no one could give me an answer. They always ended up telling me to just rest. "It's no surprise you have these issues based on the extent of your grafts. Your body hasn't had a chance to fully heal."

So, I rehabbed and became the stat guy for our team, where I would sit in the media box and keep track of guys' hits, blocked shots, scoring chances, et cetera. At least I could still be around the team and the atmosphere of our arena while I allowed my body to heal.

Once playoffs rolled around in March, I was feeling pretty good. I was in the last phase of my rehab for the burns and my pelvis felt fine. But I had had little contact, so who knew how it would hold up in the grind of playoffs – where the game got a lot more physical. I was closing in on one year since the accident and everyone felt good about my return to the lineup, including myself. It was my last chance to win a championship with the Vipers.

We met Prince George in the first round and won the series relatively easily in five games. In game one, I got bumped into the boards pretty hard and my pelvis lit up again. I was back to square one. Fuck! This injury was so strange. I sat out game two in hopes it would subside. It didn't. I was back on the Toradol and Cortisone for the rest of the series. In hindsight, I should have shut it down for the season to get ready for Brown, but I wanted to win a championship. I was putting my health second again. Right or wrong, I couldn't fully turn that switch off.

Brooksy knew the situation and although he was hesitant about me playing, that was part of the reason they recruited me – I would do anything to win. I was a big boy and made my own decisions. None of the coaches or staff forced me to play. And because the doctors had no idea what my specific injury was, no one was sure if playing could make it any worse. I just needed long-term rest, something I didn't have the luxury of, in my mind at least.

We had a few days of rest before the second-round series

against Salmon Arm, our biggest rival. I rested as much as I could, but I was on crutches again for the entire series. I played the first four games, and we were down 3-1. By games three and four, I was only playing a couple of shifts a period on special teams. I met with Pimmer before game five, and we decided I shouldn't play. We had other healthy guys that could contribute way more. And I was finally starting to worry I could have permanent damage if I kept going.

I could no longer keep overriding that internal switch. My concern for my health started trumping that switch. I had achieved my scholarship; it was time to put my health first.

That was a tough night, watching our loss in game five from the stands. I was sad that my Junior hockey chapter had come to a close without a championship, but I was extremely proud and excited for the next four years at Brown. I was officially going to be an NCAA student athlete.

Chapter 22

Freshman

—

We had our weeklong bender to close out the season – minus the beer bombs, of course. I stayed in Vernon that summer for a few reasons. A handful of guys on the team, including Chewy, were hanging around. I could also skate for most of the summer once I was healthy. My billets said I could stay with them as well for basically no rent. Claire was also around, and we were still on and off all the time. Maybe the on and off was a sign we should move on, but we would always get together whenever we saw each other out on the town.

My car had finally kicked the can, so I had no choice but to use my bike for transportation. Well not quite, I did have an opportunity to buy a new car as my grandma had passed away in Mexico and left me and my sister three thousand dollars each. But instead of buying a new ride, I bought a beautiful new Takamine acoustic guitar. I wasn't dead set on this purchase until I played it in the music store. I would sometimes just go hang out in music stores and play expensive guitars, dreaming of owning one someday. The sounds that came from this guitar lit up my soul. Should I have saved it for college? Or bought a new car? Yeah, maybe, but I certainly don't regret it.

My perspective on life had changed since my accident. I realized how life could change in a split second and also chose to always listen to my heart. I did what I wanted and what made me feel good. And I wanted that damn guitar. Plus, as an added bonus, I could get in amazing shape from having to bike everywhere instead of driving. I had taken another month completely off and my injury was feeling better. I was now back in training mode. Since I hadn't had contact for a while, I seemed to be close to getting the old me back.

Every Monday to Friday that summer, I would get up at 5:00 a.m., bike five kilometers to the gym, do cardio for an hour, stretch and rehab, bike to my job (as a drywaller and painter) for 8:00 a.m., work until 4:00 p.m., bike home, nap for an hour, bike back to the gym and do strength training for an hour, bike home, make dinner, go to bed by 10:00 p.m. I was robotic. I had gotten a glimpse of the talent level at Brown, so I was going to make sure I was a machine when I arrived. But I liked to have my fun too. So, on the weekends we partied. Plus, I was now an NCAA athlete. I had made my dreams come true – made it to *my NHL!* That was something to celebrate.

Friday to Sunday every weekend – Chewy, Zinger (another fellow Viper), and I gathered our crew, pre-gamed at someone's house, shut down the bar, and found the appropriate after-party. In hindsight, I probably partied too much. But we were young, we recovered quickly, and I needed some balance with my intense training regimen.

I was in great shape and my pelvis issue was feeling fine. It was July, and I was heading east to Providence in a month. I was feeling good on the ice too. Maybe this pelvis injury was finally behind me. The burns were still stiff, but I knew this would be the case for a while.

My parents bought me a couple more burn suits, and I was off to the next chapter of my life – Providence, Rhode Island – for the next four years. I was stoked. I showed up at the airport with two hockey bags (one for gear, one for clothes), my sticks, and my Takamine guitar. I would have been better off buying a guitar when I got there because twice a year I would pay over a hundred bucks to ship the damn thing. But next to my hockey gear, it was my most important belonging.

I spent my first night on the couch of the hockey house, somewhere I soon realized you didn't want to be sleeping. As freshmen, we were supposed to room with a random student, but somehow I got paired up with Devin Timberlake (Timby) who was another freshman on the hockey team, whom I had played against in the BCHL for the previous three years. All these young eighteen-year-olds were getting dropped off in Jaguars, Land Rovers, Escalades, you name it, and here were me and Timby, with hockey bags, my guitar and two thirty racks of Natural Light (Nattys) each. He also looked like he was forty. The looks we received from everyone's parents were priceless. You could read their minds – *Who the fuck are they? My daughter is going to live in this dorm with them?? They have all that alcohol!*

We received the keys to our room and started slamming beers. We swapped stories and got to know each other. I knew right away we'd be getting along just fine. The RA (resident assistant) came by shortly after and questioned us about where we were getting the booze. She didn't fully understand how we were twenty-one-year-old freshmen.

Brown was an "academics first" school, which was fair. It was an Ivy League institution, after all. Plus, hockey was one of the least popular sports there and the average student didn't understand the concept of playing Junior hockey in Canada in order to get recruited to the NCAA. Sometimes, as in the case of Timby and I, it took a few years to get noticed – which is why we were just starting college at twenty-one.

The first month of school was just a big party because our hockey season didn't start until mid to late October. We partied almost every night. Providence was like a mini-Boston, with eight colleges and universities throughout the city and plenty of bars to service their students. We went to Fish-Co all the time, a great bar on the water. If you've watched *There's Something About Mary*, you've seen Fish-Co. Wednesday was Brown's night at Fish-Co, but every other night of the week was a different school's night. If you couldn't get laid there, you might as well just chop it off. We had early-morning workouts in an attempt to curtail the partying, but they didn't deter us in the least.

My fly-down had definitely been an accurate indicator of college life. The U.S. college party scene was pretty epic. We trained hard and partied harder. I had a reputation for being the crazy Canadian hockey guy who lit himself on fire and who could strum a mean tune on the guitar. This was both good and bad. Good with the women, but it got me into trouble with some guys at Brown, especially other athletes. When word was out that I could fight, and that I was a little crazy, challengers started lining up. As much as I didn't go looking for it, I didn't totally avoid it either. Eventually my fuse grew shorter and shorter as my ego grew bigger, which would later get me into more trouble off the ice.

My body felt pretty good. The pelvis issue still nagged me from time to time, but I had made serious progress in the nearly eighteen months since the accident. The scars remained leathery and the same deep purple colour. I still had to wear the suits during my freshman year too. Brooksy loved this. Timby told me Brooksy had said, "Wait til you see this Volpatti kid, he's fucking mental. He burnt his whole body and acts like a maniac." Funny enough, Brooksy told me the same thing about everyone else in my class, minus the burns, of course. I think he just enjoyed pumping us up.

Everyone on the team seemed to be chasing some type of

business degree, so I figured I should follow suit; however, I wasn't interested in business. I had always been a science guy. I'd thought about being a doctor or getting involved in sports science in some capacity. I knew hockey would come to an end after my four years at Brown, so I had to start thinking about my career. I knew if I got cut from the hockey team, they couldn't take away my education, which wasn't the case at other scholarship schools. We had a great mentorship program. I remember talking candidly with my mentor, Scott, about what to enroll in for my major.

"Take whatever you're interested in. The degree is a piece of paper. Some of the most successful people I know have degrees in random shit that has nothing to do with their profession. The degree just proves you can learn. It just shows you have the commitment to complete something. It's always who you know and how hard you work."

This was great advice. I thought about my Visualization practice that got me to Brown. I wanted to dig deeper into biology, psychology, and especially the human brain. So, I followed my passion and went for a Bachelor of Science in Human Biology. This meant my schedule would be a lot more hectic trying to balance hockey, four-hour weekly labs, and the extra work involved to get all my credits. Plus, I had to leave time for some fun.

Our freshman class was an amazing group of guys. I'm still tight with them to this day. We just bonded instantly – the six of us being locked in the basement of the hockey house with a keg probably didn't hurt. We weren't allowed out until it was finished – part of the rookie initiation. All the guys knew I had been burnt once they saw my body, but I kept things pretty close to the vest. That's just the kind of person I was. No one knew about the shit I had gone through to get my scholarship.

As far as they were concerned, I got burnt and recovered.

That was pretty much it. Everything was kept under the hood. I always kept it positive and upbeat. Off the ice, I liked the attention. But I never advertised or boasted about what I had been through and the roads I'd traveled on to get to Brown. This was almost, in a way, sacred to me. Very few people truly knew.

I was quickly humbled by how much better everyone was compared to Junior A. These were all the best Junior A players in North America. I didn't really have expectations for myself. I was just so thrilled to be a Division 1 athlete. I knew how tough it would be to crack the lineup. In college hockey, there are often close to thirty players on the team. Only twenty-one players dressed for the games, including two goalies. Timby and a few other guys were recruited ahead of me, and their skill level showed. I knew it was time to revert to what had made me successful. I wasn't going to get noticed because of my skill.

When our camp finally opened in October, I tried to kill anyone and everyone. I was respectful, but I knew I wasn't likely to make the starting lineup unless I got noticed.

I didn't care if the guys were a senior or a freshman. If they were in the trolley tracks, I was coming. There wasn't any fighting in college, but I was happy to oblige if anyone had an issue with me going after them. I knocked a couple guys out of practice the first week, then it was time for our scrimmage.

One of the seniors was wheeling around the net with his head down as I was back checking into my own end. I smelled blood. Right before contact, I planted my skate blades in the ice and dropped my shoulder. I hit him so hard that his cage collapsed and split his face wide open. There was blood everywhere. He ended up getting around forty stitches. He quit and hung up his skates for good the next day. Our head coach pulled me into his office, and we had a talk.

"What the hell are you doing? We're not going to have

a team left if you keep hurting everyone, especially our top guys. I like that you play hard, but I need you to let up a bit, save that for the games we have coming up."

"I'm just trying to make the starting lineup coach. I need to get noticed because I know how good everyone is."

"You'll be in the lineup opening night, don't worry."

That was all I needed to know – mission accomplished. I felt bad-ish that one of the seniors quit, but I was hungry. Fight back or get the fuck out of my way – or get your head up. I let up for the next week of practice and was ready for opening night.

Brooksy had told me about a conversation he had with Vandy. They still kept in touch even though Vandy was coaching in the WHL. I know Brooksy secretly loved how hard I was playing in camp. I would always catch his devilish smirk after I buried someone. He knew there was something special about the way I hit. That's what they recruited me for. Brooksy relayed one of their conversations to me.

Brooksy said, "Volpatti is a nut job! He just murdered one of our seniors!"

Vandy replied, "I told you, this kid hits like a freight train."

"No fucking shit! When I said murdered, I meant it. I thought the police were going to come and take him away."

We opened our season against Cornell at home – they were a powerhouse team. It was very surreal, and I took a moment before the game to reflect on my journey from that night up at Bluenose Mountain. *Look where I am now. I did it.* I was jacked up and ready for war.

Unfortunately, my first NCAA game didn't go well. During my first shift, I received a double minor penalty (four minutes instead of two minutes) for charging, and I only clipped the guy. But I really did try to kill him. I wasn't playing hockey; I was head-hunting. In my second shift, I received a five-minute major penalty for checking from behind and was kicked out of the game. Not the debut I was hoping for. We ended up losing the game, and my play certainly didn't help.

The coach tore me a new one. They wanted me to play aggressively, but not reckless like that. I couldn't singlehandedly lose us the game. I didn't play again for over a month. I started getting down on game days when Timby would head to the rink for the games while I sat in our dorm room. The weeks kept going by without me playing, and I started wondering if I had permanently tainted my college hockey career. I just hit the books, as I figured I might as well focus on school. I put my head down and worked my bag off in practice and in the gym. In Junior, if I wasn't playing well, I could always contribute by fighting. Now I was just fighting off the ice. My frustrations of being out of the lineup didn't help me in that regard.

I did finally get back in the lineup just before Christmas break. I never looked back and played every game thereafter. I didn't play a ton of minutes on the fourth line, but I played smarter. I still hit to hurt guys but picked my spots better. Unfortunately, my pelvis started flaring up again. The doctors at Brown couldn't figure it out either. It was so frustrating. I tried to get my hands on some Toradol, but that wasn't on the menu at college, only pills. The only thing that kept me playing was the fact that we only played on the weekends. And I rarely played more than ten minutes a game, anyway. I pushed through it like I always had. Our team was at the bottom of the standings, so it wasn't like we were set up to go on a deep run in the playoffs. I figured I could grind my way through whatever remained of our short season.

I was finally free of my burn suits at the end of my freshman year. Two full years. The scars had lightened up but were still noticeably darker than the rest of my body. It took about another year before they started matching my natural skin colour. I used to get some pretty interesting looks from people once I had these suits off for good, especially during the summer. I had to be diligent with sunscreen since the scars were very sensitive to the sun.

I could usually come up with several iterations of how and why I had all these scars. Shark attack was probably the best one. Or jellyfish. Or I would stick with the burns but say I ran into a burning house to save someone's cat. Part of me liked to see what people would believe and the other part of me was tired of telling the real story all the time.

I felt so naked without the pressure suits at first, which I guess made sense – they had truly become a part of me. But it didn't take too long to feel free and less constricted. My skin grafts definitely benefited from me following the two-year protocol. They weren't raised at all and actually felt quite soft.

To no one's surprise, we lost in the first round, and my freshman year came to an end. It was full of ups and downs, but one thing was certain – it was a blast! I had solidified my spot on the fourth line, which in my mind, was a success. I had five goals and two assists in twenty-three games. Nothing to write home about, but it was better than my first year with the Vipers.

Chapter 23

Role Playing

—

My next two years as a Brown Bear were very similar to my freshman year. I was the fittest guy on the team and solidified my role as a third, and fourth-line, grinder. I managed ten points my sophomore year and thirteen in my junior year, in just over thirty games each season. Respectable, but nothing crazy. I further established my reputation as one of the hardest hitters in the Ivy League, which I took pride in. My chin had stitches in it for pretty much my entire four years, due to pressure cuts. In Junior we wore a clear half- visor that protected just our eyes. In college, you had to wear a full-face covering. So, when I hit someone, the chin piece on my cage would constantly blow my chin apart.

I continued my recklessness off the ice and partied harder than ever. Looking back, I should have leveraged the power of Visualization I discovered in the burn unit. But I was too young and immature to think, *What's next? What else could I accomplish?* Since I had achieved my pinnacle in hockey, it didn't even register for me to think I had a chance to play hockey after Brown. I wasn't *that* good. So, I figured I would soak up every ounce of my college experience. I still worked harder than anyone on our team. Well, except for maybe Petey, another guy in my class. We would always go head-to-head to see who would reign as the fitness testing champion.

Life was fragile, so live it up. That was my motto. I would still focus on school and hockey, but everything in between meant having fun.

My pelvis issue completely disappeared for the start of my sophomore year. Just like that, seemingly out of nowhere. I finally felt like my pre-fire self. My burns were still somewhat stiff and itchy, and they looked wild, but I had recovered. Turned out the doctors were right. The recovery *would* take two years. I just refused to believe the limitations laid upon me during that time.

Claire and I continued our on-and-off status for my first two years at Brown, just as we had done in Vernon. We would start chatting, she would come visit, things would be good, but then one of us would end it. Our relationship was cyclical like that. We were like a drug to each other. We couldn't resist the urge for another fix, but deep down we knew it probably wouldn't work out. That led to commitment issues for both of us. I really did love Claire, but we were in completely different places in our lives, going in completely different directions.

Plus, the long distance made it extra difficult. We were always torn whether to give it another shot or just be single and free – something I also enjoyed about college. As far as I was concerned, I would probably live in Boston or New York after I finished at Brown. Or maybe go to medical school in some other big city, not go back to Vernon. And Claire had a family business in Vernon she was interested in continuing with. After our last breakup during my sophomore year, we decided to amicably call it quits for good. We had some amazing times and a ton of fun, but it was time to move on, for both our sakes.

It's often said we will have a few defining moments in our lives. Or even epiphanies. Moments that significantly alter the trajectory of our lives. This has been especially true for me. My first major defining moment was the phone call I received in the hospital from Vandy, who told me to call Brooksy.

My second defining moment came towards the end of my junior year at Brown, at twenty-four years old. It was just like any other day, but it was a day that would change my life forever.

Chapter 24

Lion's Den

—

Our junior year ended with another disappointing first -round playoff loss. The season was over, but we were still in school for another couple of months. We would still work out and play ball hockey once the ice came out. One of the assistant coaches pulled me aside one day.

"I thought you made some good strides this year. You know there have been a couple of AHL teams asking about you?" The AHL is one tier below the NHL and is considered to be the second- or third-best league in the world, depending on who you ask.

"Really?" To say I was surprised wouldn't do my reaction justice.

"Yeah, you know, I really think you could carve out a solid career for yourself if you put in the work. I could see you having a ten-year career in the AHL. And who knows, maybe even work your way up to the show one day. You're a big, strong kid and I've never seen anyone hit like you, ever. I know you can fight too, but you just have to work on the skill part of your game."

I responded, somewhat chuckling. "To be honest, I've never even thought about pro hockey."

I was almost twenty-four years old. I just figured I was too old, and not good enough, to pursue that path. Sure, maybe playing a year in the lower professional ranks could be fun to say I did it. But I didn't really love the idea of fighting to make a few hundred bucks a week. That's why I just figured I would go the school route and leverage my Brown education.

"Well, if I were you, I'd seriously think about it. Do you have an advisor?"

I laughed even harder. Only draft picks and top players had advisors. "No," I replied, shaking my head.

"I'll put you in touch with my old agent. He lives right in Boston."

"Okay, great thanks!"

Just like that, I had an advisor, Peter. An advisor was what agents in college were called because you weren't technically allowed an "agent" since that could mean receiving incentives. If you received any incentive, you would be ineligible to participate in the NCAA. This was why playing Major Junior hockey made you ineligible; you could receive small benefits and even make a bit of money.

I went home after this conversation and began thinking more about the possibility of playing pro hockey. *Wow, me, a small-town kid who barely snuck into Junior A, could possibly make it to the pro ranks. A kid who'd got cut from most summer hockey select teams. Who played house hockey at age fourteen. Who scored one goal in his first year of Junior A. I could potentially make decent money playing the game I love.*

The thought of that last statement lingered in my mind. I could make money playing a game. The game I loved more than anything. Hockey had given me so much, but maybe there was more.

Then, like clockwork, I started thinking back to my journey. About the burn unit, and what I had endured. I glanced at the scars on my right arm. A thought popped into my head right at that moment. *If I could overcome that type of injury and not only come back to play hockey when I was told I couldn't, but also achieve my scholarship to Brown, why couldn't I play in the NHL?*

I sat in silence for another minute. A massive smile spread across my face. Then I said to myself, *Well, let's fuckin' do it then.* I decided right there and then. I was going to play in the NHL.

I thought back to my Visualization practice when I was bedridden in Vancouver General Hospital. I remembered the power in overcoming insurmountable pain. I needed to go back to that. Be *that* version of Aaron Volpatti. I couldn't believe I had let my mindset go these first three years at Brown. *What if I had these thoughts earlier?* I quickly forgave myself and figured it was better late than never.

I needed to visualize myself in the NHL and visualize the process to get there. It was time to write the true ending for my story. I was prepared to work like I had never worked before. There was a deep, powerful purpose for me again. A purpose to set out and see what I was truly capable of. A purpose to honor and fight for this new dream. It wouldn't be easy, but I knew I could defy the odds again.

I called my parents the next day and told them I wasn't coming home to work at the mill or help my dad renovate their house like I had done the previous summer. I would find a way to make money. I told them I was staying in Providence to train and give hockey a shot. My actual plan was to play in the NHL, but I never told a soul. They would all find out once I accomplished it.

I had unlimited access to our rink and training facility, so my plan was to essentially live there. I also knew that if I was going to leave my senior year spring on an ATO, I needed to get my academics in order. An ATO is an amateur try-out contract that players signed either as an actual tryout or if they signed with an NHL team. The NHL contract typically wouldn't kick in until the following year, so the ATO was a chance to get your feet wet with the AHL affiliate team.

I needed research credits for my Human Biology major. These credits were kind of like a thesis but less work. By staying in Providence for the summer, I'd be able to get an early credit for this research portion of my major. Luckily, I had also taken five classes one previous semester. If I took five more in my senior fall semester, and if I could get this extra summer credit, I could leave during the spring of my senior year pretty much graduated.

I ended up subletting my room at the hockey house so I could move into the other house (shared by basketball and hockey guys) and share a room with two buddies. This decision was primarily financially motivated since none of us had any money. We moved into Scott Vanderlinden's room. We actually called him Steve-O. I legitimately thought his name was Steve for the first month of freshman year, and it stuck as his nickname.

We called our room the Lion's Den. I was dating a girl from California who was staying in Providence for the summer. Let's just say there were some nights with a lot of bodies in that room, especially if the other two guys had company. Not our best look, but most of us found some humor in it. I took Steve-O's futon, and Mull took the mattress on the floor. Mull was a basketball player who we'd become really good friends with. The hockey team and basketball team just got on really well. Mull was about six feet nine inches so I'm not exactly sure how he ended up on the floor, probably because he didn't fit the futon.

We had quite the crew in the house that summer. The three to six of us in the Lion's Den on any given night, another hockey guy who had graduated a couple years prior living in the attic, a track and field specimen, a wrestler, a brainiac who never left his room, and a couple of University of Rhode Island girls on the first floor. We were truly a unique bunch.

Since Steve-O, Mull, and I split one room's rent, we had to sneak into the house because the landlord's office was attached to the connected duplex on the other side. He wouldn't have approved of our arrangement.

Most people were working, but the track athlete and I were training full-time. I was glad to have someone on the same level as me. We would still have some fun on the weekends, but I kept it dialed in.

The summer of 2009 was the hardest I had trained in my entire life. My Visualization practice and mindset pushed me to put in the countless hours at the rink, in the gym, and on the ice. I manifested such a deep sense of belief that my journey would lead somewhere special. The more I visualized, the more I started imagining the movie of my life – I began to create an actual experience when I closed my eyes and lived this movie. I could truly feel every emotion that was part of this final ending. Sure, no one in the NHL knew who I was yet, but I was ready to let them know.

Chapter 25

Relentless

—

My training turned robotic, and I felt so energized and rejuvenated with this newfound purpose in my life – to make the NHL. I worked out twice a day, worked on my stickhandling and shooting for hours, watched videos, and further cultivated my obsession through Visualization. Mull and Steve-O were working their intern jobs, so I was the cook of the house as well. This was my daily schedule:

6:45 a.m. Wake up and visualize

7:00-8:00 a.m. Hill sprints or a long run

8:15 a.m. Breakfast

9:00 a.m.-12:00 p.m. Stickhandling and shooting

12:30 p.m. Lunch

1:30-3:00 p.m. Visualize, watch video clips of my games, shoot more pucks. Wait for Steve-O to get to the rink

3:00-5:00 p.m. Lift and plyometric field work with Steve-O. Focus on explosiveness

5:30 p.m. Make dinner, then hang with my girlfriend and the house crew for the night

11:00 p.m. Visualize, then bedtime

I would usually take the weekends off, with the exception of one long run and my Visualization practice – I watched my movie play in my mind every single day. The only other change to my schedule was going to the office for my research study on the odd day. And I had the odd side job to make some money. Guitar lessons and clam bakes – those were my means of living that summer. The clam bakes were a catering gig. The guy who owned the company would hire us hockey guys and pay us cash to serve at weddings and other events.

The research study struggled to get funding, so it turned out to be minimal work for me. This worked out well as it meant I could train more and work these side jobs. I was looking forward to the study; the mission behind it was to research the effects of exercise on the brain – through functional magnetic resonance imaging (fMRI). With my background and love of science, it was right up my alley.

The ice went in at the beginning of August. I was able to put on my gear and do all my skill work on the ice instead of on concrete and plastic sheets. It didn't take long for me to notice a huge difference in my shot and my hands. Months of practice, six days a week. We hired all new coaching staff in August as well. These guys really worked with me and specific areas of my game.

Jerry Keefe, our assistant coach, was especially great. If I asked him to work with me, he'd put his skates on and run me through drills. We would work a lot around the net, dialing in specific skills in order to bury loose pucks, which was largely based on body position. Before working with him, I had never really cared where the puck was. My game was solely focused on skating and trying to kill anything that moved. That was changing. My confidence was growing by the day. I was slowly adding that much-needed skill part to my game, and I was in the best shape of my life.

I now had my Visualization practice down to a tee and had even added a soundtrack to this movie I'd created in my mind

– "Hero of the Day" by Metallica. These lyrics ignited my inner fire. I had almost been broken, but I was now unbreakable. I was the hero of the day and the hero of my journey.

I would visualize my movie every single day. What I had been through, where I was, what I had to do, and the domination of my upcoming senior year. And of course, the ending. I would see myself playing in the NHL. I'd imagine what it would feel like to put on that jersey as I walked down the tunnel for my first NHL game – I could feel and smell the jersey. I would sit with this feeling, and it evoked such intense emotion in my soul. I would then imagine my parents' reaction in the stands watching their son play in the best league in the world after everything that had happened in 2005. I'd circle back to my purpose as I imagined skating in front of twenty thousand screaming fans. *I proved everyone wrong. I never gave up. I honored my ultimate dream.* The movie would end and I'd open my eyes.

This type of "story work" Visualization gave me such extreme belief and confidence in myself and my path ahead. The key was to not just change my thoughts, but to create a full experience in my mind. I felt like I was already living and playing in the NHL every day. It pushed me to become obsessed and train like I had never trained before. I knew there was absolutely zero chance that anyone in the NCAA had put in the work I had that summer. I put in the absolute max. It was extremely empowering to have this realization in my back pocket – a type of untouchable confidence. Whenever I looked across at someone, whether it be my own teammate or an opposing player, I knew for certain I'd sacrificed more than them.

Chapter 26

Putting the pieces together

—

I was named one of the three captains for my final year at Brown. Since we had a new coaching staff, our camp was a whole new tryout. Everyone had a clean slate. Brendan Whittet, our head coach, knew I was beyond determined from all the extra work with Keefer. Brendan gave me an enormous opportunity right from the start of the season, and I ran with it.

I logged a ton of minutes and played on the first power play and penalty kill units. I had packed on fifteen pounds of muscle and now weighed two hundred and fifteen pounds. I was bigger, stronger, more skilled, and relentless.

I got off to a hot start and never looked back. It was almost Christmas, and I already had more points than I did in the previous season. I'll never forget the feeling of wanting the puck all the time. I had never experienced a level of confidence like this; I wanted to be the difference maker. This is a trait all elite athletes share; they thrive under pressure in big moments.

I played with some great players that year as well. Our team still struggled, though. We could finally score goals but couldn't keep the puck out of our net.

Before every game, I would go through the same routine. I'd get my dynamic warmup in, loosen up my muscles, then find my seat in the stands and play "Hero of the Day". Then I'd close my eyes, and my mind would hit play on my movie. In the middle of the movie, I would insert all the details of the game that night. Everything from small plays in the corner, feeling the puck glued to my stick, delivering massive hits, scoring big goals, feeling my legs – fresh and powerful. Then, of course, sit with the ending of the NHL. That was my guiding star.

It didn't take long before NHL scouts started talking to me, and my confidence really started snowballing. I knew the process was working. *Holy shit, it's working. Just like in the hospital.* I could really feel it happening.

By Christmas, there were a handful of teams talking with me. The Vancouver Canucks, Nashville Predators, Edmonton Oilers, and New York Rangers.

I'd hit like a truck in Junior at one hundred eighty pounds, and even harder during my first three years at Brown at two hundred pounds. Now, at age twenty-five and weighing in at two-fifteen, I was really hurting people. Being a late bloomer, these four years at college really gave me time to become a man, which didn't bode well for some of the smaller eighteen- and nineteen year-olds coming into the NCAA. There were collapsed lungs, broken ribs, broken collarbones, lacerated spleens and kidneys, concussions – you name it.

Our trainer, Brian, would fill me in on some of the damage after his visits to the other team's dressing room. The really serious injuries were scary and were not what I wanted to see happen. I never set out to seriously hurt someone. But unfortunately, they happened to be collateral damage from the mission I was on. Whether anyone liked it or not, the reality was it brought the attention of NHL scouts. Intimidation was still a big part of the game. Plus, I now had added the skill element to my game – a pretty rare package. It was an amazing feeling going into a game knowing I was going to dominate and contribute to the score sheet.

After Christmas Break, the momentum kept rolling, and more teams were talking to me. After talking with Peter, I knew I was going to sign an NHL contract somewhere. There were now ten teams talking to me, with a few front-runners showing the most interest. Peter gave me some advice before the Canucks' scouts came to chat with me after one game. "Don't change out of your tight undergear. Let them see how built you are." I just laughed but figured, why not? I was in the best shape of my life, so it couldn't hurt. But he was right. Every little thing mattered and, of course, teams were interested in what kind of shape I was in.

My plan was being executed to perfection. I only needed two credits to graduate going into my final semester. One credit would come from my thesis project, and the other would be a course I could take pass/fail that wasn't even for my major. I didn't have any more four-hour labs, followed by another four hours of homework – a pleasant change. Some of these courses had taken up a lot of my time in the first few years at Brown.

Now, I could spend more time at the rink in the mornings before we practiced in the afternoon. I was going to sign a contract in a few months, so I needed to keep putting the work in. My research credit still didn't end up being that much of a time commitment because the struggle for funding continued. I mostly just read similar studies to keep me busy. Once in a while, I would get to join the doctors and look over the MRI scans from our limited participants, which I found really interesting.

The only people who knew I had so much interest from NHL teams were my coaches and teammates. I didn't even tell my family. There wasn't really anything to share yet. Not until I physically signed a contract, would I tell them. They obviously knew I was having an exceptional year since they watched every game online, but I just told them I was getting some interest from a couple of pro teams. I put my head down and went to work every day. When they came for their annual visit in March 2010, they were blown away. The difference in my play was huge.

Our team got hot towards the end of the year. We faced RPI, Rensselaer Polytechnic Institute, a technological research university in Troy, New York, in the first round of playoffs. We were underdogs by a significant margin. The playoff format in college hockey was greatly different from Junior hockey. The first two series were a "best-of-three" format and the winners from those series went to their respective division tournaments. To get into the NCAA tournament, you either needed to win your respective division or have enough votes to get in.

We upset RPI two games to one and were set to face Yale for round two. I was on the scoresheet every game and was the best player on the ice. Our goalie was playing well, and our team was firing on all cylinders. Yale was ranked in the top five in the country, and normally we didn't hold a candle to them. But the pressure was on them. We had nothing to lose.

More and more scouts came to every game. The farther we could make it in the playoffs, the more my value increased as a free agent. With Yale being such a powerhouse, I knew this was a chance not only for our team to do something special but for me to show the scouts I was ready for the NHL. I was an unrestricted free agent since I was older, so I was free to sign with whatever team I wanted for any amount of money.

We had no business beating Yale, but that's exactly what we did. We were outplayed, but our goalie was unbelievable, and some of our guys stepped up in a big way. In the third and deciding game, we won 1-0. I had never felt better, and it showed. Scouts were talking to me and Peter after every game. The pressure built, but I felt more and more comfortable.

We arrived in Albany, New York, for the ECAC tournament

the following weekend. If we could win this tournament of four teams, we were off to the NCAA tournament. We faced off against Cornell in the first game, another powerhouse. I always played my best games against them, except for that very first college game, of course. I was beyond excited to be playing on the big stage.

But our impressive run ended. They outplayed us, and it was one and done. No more series or second chances. We beat St. Lawrence in the consolation game 3-0. I scored the first goal and game-winner, my seventeenth goal of the season, which was more than my first three seasons combined. I finished with thirty - two points in thirty-seven games, again, more than my first three seasons combined.

Before this final game, it was brought to my attention that I was six penalty minutes away from breaking the record at Brown. I wasn't ever going to break any offensive records, but penalty minutes I could do! Most of these penalties came from hitting people too hard or roughing after the whistle, not fighting – it wasn't allowed. Well, it was, but you'd get suspended if you fought. I had already gotten suspended for a game my junior year for "fighting" but my gloves didn't even come off. Hard to call that a true fight.

Before the game, the ref skated over to me and said, "Hey I heard you're close to the penalty record."

I laughed, "Yeah, you wanna throw a ten-minute misconduct my way towards the end of the game?"

He laughed back and said, "Well just give me a reason to and it's done."

He winked, and we both smiled. In the last ten minutes of the game, I took a penalty. As I was skating towards the penalty box, we locked eyes and he gave me a look that said, *Well…. you gotta say something.* I can't remember exactly what I said, but it was probably something simple like, "Fuck you, ref, sweet call."

All the while, I had a huge grin on my face. He laughed and threw his hands onto his hips, signaling a ten-minute misconduct. I believe that's the only record I've ever broken. It was short-lived, though. Harry, a junior during my senior year, would break my record the next year before signing with the Philadelphia Flyers.

Just like that, my last season as an NCAA athlete was finished – what a ride! I was officially a free agent, and the offers started pouring in. I met with Peter the next day for dinner, which he could finally buy since my time as an amateur was over. He was no longer my advisor, but my agent. We had contract offers from six teams, and another six or so saying they would offer in the coming days. The contracts were all pretty similar in terms of length and money, except for one.

There were two factors in my decision-making process. One was opportunity, where signing with a worse team could mean a better chance to be in the NHL right away. The second was money, especially since I had none of it. I had made my final decision, unless anything else came to the table overnight. We agreed, and Peter said to sleep on it. We'd sign the deal the following day. I couldn't believe it. I was going to sign an NHL contract after everything I'd been through. I was one step closer to the dream I had manifested in my mind. Just like in the burn unit. The mental and physical grit that my journey and Visualization practice had equipped me with was remarkable. I was filled with pride, nervousness, and a ton of excitement. It all seemed surreal.

I couldn't wait to tell my parents. I called them right after I signed my contract on March 22, 2010.

"Hey Mom, Dad."

"Hey bud, how's it going? Are you still in party mode or resting up now?"

I laughed, "A little bit of both. But there's going to be more partying because I have some good news."

"Oh yeah, what?"

"Remember how I told you I had been talking with some scouts from pro hockey teams?"

"Yeah…"

"Well, by some scouts I meant a lot. And by pro hockey, I meant the NHL."

"Fuck off!" Dad said jokingly.

"Yep, guess who I just signed with for two years?"

"Who!?" I could feel their excitement through the phone.

"The Vancouver Canucks!"

"What!! Get out of here! Are you serious? You're fucking with us?"

I laughed again. It still didn't seem real.

"No, I'm serious. It's a two-way contract and I'll most likely spend some time in the minors to start, but I'm one step closer."

"Holy fuck, I can't believe it. We're so proud of you, Hub." I could hear both of them cry tears of happiness. I followed suit.

"You've been through so much and worked so hard. Congrats, bud."

"Thanks. I couldn't have done it without your support. Guess what they're going to pay me?"

"What?"

"Well, my AHL salary is two hundred thousand a year, and if I make the Canucks it's five hundred fifty thousand and I get a hundred-thousand-dollar signing bonus each July 1. So, if I do nothing, I'm guaranteed to make six hundred thousand over two years. If I'm with the Canucks, we're talking over a million dollars! To play hockey!"

"Dude, you know it takes me ten to fifteen years to make that kind of money?!"

"I know! It just seems so surreal still."

I had zero dollars to my name and was in some serious debt – a hefty line of credit and a twenty-five-thousand-dollar student loan. The amount of money this contract was going to pay me was completely foreign. Our family didn't make this kind of cash. My values weren't tied to material things, but I was still going to enjoy the benefits.

"I'm speechless," my mom said. "Good for you, bud, you deserve it. I can't believe out of all the teams, you signed with the Canucks – your favourite team growing up!"

"I know, it's so crazy. But they have been the most interested from day one and the money plays some factor too – who knows how long my career will be. I'm signing an ATO and heading to Winnipeg either tomorrow or the next day to join the Moose (the Manitoba Moose were the Canucks' AHL affiliate team where some of the prospects would play) for the rest of their season. So I'm gonna get my feet wet right away here."

"How long have you been talking with NHL teams?"

"Since before Christmas break."

They were shocked. "You've known for that long and didn't tell us?!"

"I wanted it to be a surprise, and nothing was guaranteed," I said, laughing.

They laughed too. "Wow, so cool. Well, go enjoy, Hub, and let it sink in. Call us tomorrow when you know what's going on!"

"Sounds good. Love you."

"Love you too."

I sat down, took a deep breath, and allowed an indescribable feeling of joy and pride to wash over me. I had just signed a fucking NHL contract.

Chapter 27

Moose

—

My teammates at Brown were ecstatic, probably because I would have to buy all the kegs when I got back from my stint with the Moose.

Just like that, a few days after our season was over, I was off to Winnipeg to prove I was worth the money the Canucks had signed me for.

What were the chances that of the thirty teams in the AHL, thirty different cities across North America, my first professional hockey game was going to be in Abbotsford, B.C.? From Nova Scotia to New York, to California or Texas, I could have ended up anywhere. Yet here I was a few hours from home. My family could drive to my first and second (we played back-to-back nights) professional hockey games. I called my parents as soon as I saw the schedule.

Sometimes I'm amazed how fate and destiny have played into my life. The universe has truly worked in mysterious and wonderful ways for me. Through the good and the bad; the wins and the losses. Everything has happened for a reason, like there was this grand master plan. I was just given the map, an opportunity. What I did with this map was up to me.

I arrived in balmy Winnipeg and got set up in a condo by the rink with another guy on the team. He was Czech and didn't speak English very well, so our conversations were limited. As I lay in bed that night, my mind was racing. I was excited, yet nervous, for my first practice the next day. *Would I look out of place? What are the guys like? I need to make a good impression.*

Most college players who turn pro sign with the minor league teams in the AHL, ECHL, CHL, or SPHL. If you signed an NHL contract, there was obviously more pressure. And my deal in the AHL put me near the top in terms of salary (even though I technically wouldn't make that until the following season when my contract kicked in). That meant, with my current ATO, I would take someone's job who was likely making forty thousand dollars on either an AHL one-way contract or a two-way AHL/ECHL contract. So obviously, I had pressure to perform.

The dynamic in the AHL is tricky because there is a balance of winning and developing prospects for the parent, or NHL team. Since I was a high-profile signing, the Canucks would have some say in where I slotted into the lineup. But teams like Manitoba, who were at the top of the AHL and privately owned, also prioritized winning. They didn't care who was on what type of contract, they just wanted to have the players in the lineup that gave them the best chance to win. Hence, the tricky balancing act of winning and keeping the NHL affiliate brass happy – sometimes guys on the NHL contracts didn't necessarily contribute more. I wasn't only a hockey player now; I was a business asset.

I was at the rink before anyone else, for a couple of different reasons. One, to show everyone I was eager, and two, to get set up in all my new equipment. All the equipment you could see – helmet, gloves, pants, and sticks – they all had to be CCM or Reeebok since the league was under contract with them. Skates were the only visible piece of equipment we didn't have to change. Most of this was fine, but I really didn't like the fact that I had to use a different stick. I had used an Easton stick in college and had grown to love it, especially after my senior year.

All the guys seemed great and welcomed me with open arms. But my first practice was a disaster. My nerves were too high, and I kept falling in pretty much every drill. My hands were terrible, and I really didn't like my new gear.

Peter called me shortly after I got home from the rink that first day.

"Everything okay?"

"Yeah, but practice didn't go too well. I was a little nervous, but I'll be better tomorrow."

"I heard that." The general manager had called Peter and asked why I couldn't skate. Skating was one of my best attributes. "No worries, shake it off. But this is a business now, so need ya to keep yourself on your feet, okay?"

"Ya, I got it."

The next day, I was much better. I couldn't believe how much bigger everyone was compared to college. I went from being one of the biggest players in the NCAA to average size – basically overnight. I was practicing on the third line, and one of my linemates was Mike Keane. This was a guy who had played over a thousand NHL games and was in his fifth AHL campaign. He was a true professional who had played hard and meant business. He was a forty-two-year-old grizzled veteran who really helped me out and took me under his wing.

We boarded our plane and were off to Abbotsford a few days later. Claire had messaged me on Facebook right after I signed offering her congratulations. It was a pretty popular story, especially in Revelstoke and Vernon, and although she was actually living in Vancouver at the time, I wasn't surprised she caught wind of the news. It wasn't every day that a team signed someone from their home province, let alone from a small town like Revelstoke.

Claire and I hadn't talked since we amicably called it quits for good. It was great to hear from her, but I honestly didn't think much of it. We naturally started texting and catching up. She seemed like she was doing great, and I figured I would see if she wanted to come to a game in Abbotsford with her friends.

I had no intention of changing my relationship status and figured her coming to a game with some friends seemed innocent. In fact, I didn't even think I would see her. We had a long history, and she was genuinely happy for me, but there wasn't much more to it. We had both moved on and maybe we could stay friends.

It was time for my first professional hockey game. Again, I was nervous, but I was confident I would settle in as soon as the game started. I also knew it was time to start chucking the knuckles again. The Canucks didn't sign me to be a goal-scorer, that I knew. I think we both had aspirations that I could turn into a solid third-liner and penalty-killer, though.

I started feeling the pressure of all the people that were going to be in attendance for these two games – about twenty family members, the Canucks brass, and the five thousand everyday fans.

Puck drop. I knew to just play my game – keep it simple, get in on the forecheck and throw the body. The difference now, compared to college, was when I hit someone, there would be a handful of pure fighters on every team that would come knocking on my door.

It was towards the end of the first period when the play was whistled down in the Abbotsford zone. I gave one of their players a little jab to stir the pot. He gave one back. "Who the fuck are you?" he said. I hadn't fought (on the ice) in four years, so I knew I'd have to shake off the rust at some point. "You wanna find out?"

I had no idea who anyone was in the AHL, who was tough and who wasn't, who was a rookie or a veteran. Of course, this guy obliged, and I was in my first pro fight. We squared off, and in true rookie fashion, I tripped over the back of the net before we even threw a punch. The crowd erupted with laughter and boos. The Abbotsford player had a smile on his face, as did I. I got myself up, shook it off, and we went at it. Only in hockey could something like this happen; two people about to beat the shit out of each other, having a laugh beforehand.

It was a pretty even fight until I switched to lefts and clipped him with a couple of good shots. He went down. I'd won my first fight.

My first game was capped off with a goal in the third period. I was driving the net on a rush and the puck bounced off my shin and into the net. The game couldn't have gone any better; a goal, a fight, a few big hits, and we won 5-2. I definitely left a good impression in my professional debut.

I met with Stan Smyl after. He was one of the guys responsible for recruiting me (and also a Canucks legend), and he concurred – I had made a solid impression. Then I met up with my family. They were all hammered and enjoying themselves. They couldn't believe I was playing pro hockey. It was so surreal, for them and for me – the difference being, I knew this had been my destiny for a while. I'd seen it for the past year, every single day. My confidence was high, and I was feeling great. I could smell the NHL. It was close. I wasn't done yet. I wasn't at the end of my movie. After visiting with my family, I went back to the hotel to rest for the game the next night.

The second game was a little quieter. We lost 2-1, but I was happy with how I played. We were staying the night and flying out the next day. I had dinner and some beers with my family before heading back to the hotel. Claire had texted afterward, thanking me for the tickets. We kept the conversation going and agreed to meet up to say a quick hi before she and her friends drove back to Vancouver. I told her to meet me at the hotel after I was done celebrating with my family, and we could all have a drink.

Maybe we should have known what would happen based on our history together. There was always this force that seemed to pull us back together. Who would have thought we would reunite in Abbotsford, of all places? It had been a long time since we talked, but as soon as I saw her, I knew I was in trouble. Those old feelings came rushing back. I could see it in her eyes, too. We all had a couple drinks, caught up, and shared some good laughs. After about an hour, I walked the three of them back to the car to say goodbye. I hugged Claire last. "It was good to see you."

"Good to see you, too. Let's keep in touch."

"Definitely," I agreed.

Our gaze never diverted. Her friends were in the car now, as we were both flooded with those old, familiar feelings. My mind raced as I debated whether to kiss her or not. Our eyes stayed locked, and she innocently smiled. I stopped thinking and just leaned in and kissed her. We were definitely in trouble now.

The three of them left, but Claire and I obviously kept texting. I figured this was a sign. If I would have signed my contract anywhere else, we probably would have never reunited.

I was chatting with the guys back at Brown often. Everyone wanted to hear how things were going. They had been enjoying the big spring week party on campus, which was a full week of mayhem. A small part of me was upset that I couldn't be there with them, but I was where I needed to be – continuing to make a name for myself in pro hockey.

We flew straight to Toronto from Abbotsford for my third and fourth games against the Marlies. Winning my first fight gave me some confidence and, sure enough, I found someone to tangle with in my third game. This time I picked a much tougher opponent – six foot five inches and around two hundred and forty pounds. I didn't fare as well, and he popped me in the face with a couple of heavy shots.

The refs broke the fight up and gave me the signal that I had lost the fight.

"Okay, Volpatti, you're gonna need to head to the dressing room for repairs."

I felt fine, so I thought, *Nice, I have a cut that needs some zippers. It's been a while.* I got to the bench and Mullet, our trainer, gave me a little smile.

"Oh boy, that's going to need some work. You really went after their biggest guy, eh?"

I got back to the dressing room to have a look. No cuts, but the tip of my nose was lying flat against my cheek. Broken nose number three. Mullet took me to the Marlies' dressing room to see the doctors so they could reset it. This brought back some memories. He put the tubes up my nose and gave me the three-second warning. I knew this wouldn't feel good.

"You ready?" he asked.

I just laughed; I couldn't believe I got my nose caved in in my second pro fight. At least he was bigger than me. I could take my licks when they happened.

"Yep, snap 'er back." I grabbed the sides of the table and with a quick crrrruuunch, he popped my nose back. My nose was never totally straight after the first couple of times I broke it, but it would have a significant hook after this fight. It was better than lying flat against my cheek, but it was still pretty fucked up.

I got back to the dressing room, and the guys gave me a round of applause and laughed as we headed out for the rest of the game.

I was really finding my way – playing on the third line, feeling confident, and penalty killing lots. I wasn't lighting up the score sheet, but I was happy just getting my feet wet and making a name for myself. And I was sporting some nice shiners from my broken nose. I looked like a hockey player again! We were playing in Hamilton for my fifth game. They had a really strong team, and we were losing 5-1 going into the third. That meant it was my job to stir the pot.

One of their defenceman was wheeling around the net with his head down and I popped him, knocking him out of the game. Another guy on their team quickly jumped me – or so he thought. This is what I called the reverse jump, and I did it many more times with the Moose. I'd throw a massive hit, and that meant someone would come to fight me. Well, this guy didn't think I saw him coming. I ducked his attempt to grab me and gave him a forearm to the face while I got my gloves off. I had him pinned on the boards and fed him three good shots before he collapsed.

Mullet and the trainers called this performance in Hamilton the double homicide. It would be my first of many. Two guys knocked out of the game, one from a hit and one from a fight. Now I was really making a name for myself.

I preferred these organic fights over the premeditated ones because I didn't have time to think. There was something different and raw about these fights. I actually felt rage and wanted to seriously hurt the guy. My wires would already be crossed, unleashing the Papa Jerry in me. The times I didn't do as well and generally got hurt, were the premeditated square-off fights. In these bouts, it wasn't always easy to have that killer mentality you so desperately needed as a fighter. I needed to flip that switch. Some guys could easily flip it, but it wasn't as natural for me.

As my pro career progressed, I eventually grew to hate the premeditated square-off fights because I had to wait to get punched in the face to truly get mad. But I wasn't there quite yet. I was a rookie and actually enjoyed fighting, especially when I got back to the locker room and the entire team was patting me on the back. Or when I stuck up for a teammate after a malicious hit or cheap shot. They would come over and tap my shin pads – as to genuinely say thanks. It wasn't an easy job, but I enjoyed being this guy. It was a familiar role I had with the Vipers, and I think there was an element of doing something most people didn't want to do. I didn't expect to be a one-dimensional player; I knew I could contribute on the scoresheet as well. But I still wanted to play a mean, hard game.

I finished my eight-game stint with the Moose with one goal, one assist, and three fights – not including the playoffs. I was feeling good and really felt part of the team. It wasn't always easy joining a team close to the playoffs, especially when I was coming out of college as one of the team's top signings. I wasn't a draft pick or anything, so no one on the team knew who I was; on the other hand, everyone did know what type of contract I had signed, so they expected big things. The coaches liked my play and enjoyed the sandpaper I brought to the lineup. At least that's what they told me.

We then lost in the first round to the Hamilton Bulldogs – in six games. I actually got suspended for game four because I instigated a fight with a guy in the last five minutes of the game. That was a dumb rule. I'm not sure if it still exists anymore. But I scored in game five and helped the team stay alive in the series.

The season came to an end, and I was headed back to

Brown for graduation. I would have loved to go on a deep playoff run with the Moose, but part of me was happy to see all the guys from Brown and enjoy graduation. The party was about to begin! I bought a bunch of kegs for our first party to kick off grad week, just as I'd promised after signing my contract.

I was quite hungover for graduation, but my self-induced illness quickly abated as I received my diploma – a Bachelor of Science in Human Biology – from an Ivy League school. All those countless hours of lab work and studying, often throughout the night until daybreak, had paid off. The most memorable parts of my academic study were the neuroscience and psychology courses, where I dove into the workings of the human brain and mind. I was just scratching the surface on this, but I found it very fascinating. I learned about the science behind the changes my body had experienced throughout my life – through recovery, and especially through my Visualization practice. I discovered why this type practice had worked, and how we can all rewire the circuitry in our brains to affect our psyche and physiology.

I had my degree, a two-year contract in the NHL, and a happy, healthy family. Life was good. No, life was great! I deserved it; I knew the amount of work I had put in to get to where I was. But I also knew the work had just begun if I wanted to put on an NHL jersey.

Chapter 28

Stoned Again

—

We all hung around campus for a few days after grad, then the guys started dispersing on their respective paths. I had just turned twenty-five. I started chatting with the player development team in Vancouver and they thought it would be a good idea for me to live, train, and skate there with a group of other prospects. My home base was flexible, and this seemed like a great opportunity. Claire was also living in Vancouver, which was a bonus.

It had been over two months since I saw her in Abbotsford, and we were talking more and more every day. I visited her on my way home to see my family before heading back to Vancouver full-time to train. It was very clear that our love for each other was still there; we wanted to be together. The long distance had been too difficult when we were younger, and now we wouldn't have to worry about that. After this visit, we decided to go all in and get a place together. Maybe this was a little trigger-happy, sure, especially based on our rocky past. But we were older and both ready to commit to this thing for good. We had agreed that if I started the year in Winnipeg, she would come with me. I had enjoyed all my single years, but no one had moved me the way Claire did.

I enjoyed a quick visit to Revelstoke with family and friends before heading to Vancouver for the summer. Everyone was stoked. I did what you're not "supposed" to do and bought a new truck with my signing bonus that summer. I packed it full and headed back to Vancouver.

Claire and I ended up renting a place about two blocks from Vancouver General Hospital. What were the chances? I would walk there a few times a week just to visit and reminisce. I loved walking in and out of those hospital doors. It had all come full circle. I'd hobbled through those doors five years prior, attempting to make the comeback of a lifetime. A comeback to get a scholarship to Brown, without a single thought about pro hockey. And here I was, walking through the same doors as a member of the Vancouver Canucks.

Chris Tanev, myself, and a few other prospects worked our asses off that summer. Three-a-day workouts – we would get to the rink in the morning and either do cardio on the bike or speed and agility exercises in the concourse. Then we would do an hour or so of strength workouts. We'd eat lunch, then drive out to Burnaby to skate with Dave Gagner and Dave Babych, the player development team. These guys were absolute gems. We had a blast while working on every little skill. These "skill" sessions were disguised as bag skates because we wouldn't get any reprieve, but I loved it; I knew it was fueling my purpose to become an NHL player.

My first development camp in July went well. This was a summer camp for all the top prospects. I think I made a lasting impression, but I was also a lot older than the other players. I had played with a handful of guys on the Moose, so it was nice to see some familiar faces. Some of these kids had insane skill levels, further cementing in my mind that I really needed to embrace my role in order to make the big club. I was still confident that I could contribute to the scoresheet from time to time, but I had to trust what had gotten me to this point.

The summer flew by, and I was in amazing shape. I'd actually lost about ten pounds. I was ripped, explosive, lean, and mean.

Rookie camp was in a week. Claire and I decided to go for a nice romantic dinner in White Rock one night. Things were great between us, and this definitely felt like the real thing.

I started having a sharp pain in my back a few hours before dinner, but I didn't think too much of it. It progressively got worse and by the time we sat down for dinner, I couldn't eat because of the pain. Claire looked at me and knew something was up. I could usually eat; I mean, *really* eat. So, when I wasn't chowing down, she knew something was up.

"What's wrong?"

"Nothing, I'm fine. I just have some pain in my back."

Then I started thinking, *No fucking way*. This pain felt similar to something I'd experienced five years earlier. I went to the bathroom and sure enough, I pissed straight blood. I came back out with a grin on my face.

"What?" Claire asked.

"I'm pretty sure I have kidney stones. I'm pissing blood."

"Oh no, again!? Okay, well, let's get to the hospital."

"We will, but finish your dinner and wine, then we'll go. I'll manage. There's no huge rush."

She thought I was crazy, but we stayed while she rushed to finish her food. I was slightly humored by it all. I grabbed a bowl of ice cream on the way to the car, as if to say, *Fucking try me, kidney stones.* Then we headed for the hospital.

My self-diagnosis was confirmed. Was this the last thing I needed heading into my first professional training camp? Absolutely. But I couldn't do anything about it at this point, except indulge in some sick humor and move on.

The stone was so big; I wouldn't be able to pass it. That meant I needed extracorporeal shock wave lithotripsy – a procedure where they blast the kidney stone with shock waves, allowing the fragmented pieces to pass through my system. I was going to be given a mild sedative for the procedure, which would take place the following day. I had to down a bunch of castor oil, a powerful laxative, hours before the procedure. They wanted to clean me out. I drank a full cup of this awful-tasting oil. I nearly vomited. A couple of hours went by. Nothing. I figured it was some hippie shit that didn't work. Man, was I wrong.

Stimulant laxatives cause the bowel to move, squeeze, and contract harder than they normally would. Suddenly, the feeling finally hit me. I'll just leave it at that. It wasn't pleasant, but thankfully the procedure was successful. My recovery wasn't too bad – just a few days of soreness. Back to pissing through a filter again. The stone more or less turned into dust, and I was done with it. The doctors said I was more susceptible to having kidney stones when I was dehydrated, something that made more sense with the summer of extreme training.

Stoned again. Another little test to add to the collection.

Chapter 29

The Double Homicide

—

Although I was twenty-five and old by rookie standards, I still had to compete in rookie camp. Training Camp was in Penticton, which was great because my family could come watch. Penticton was just over an hour's drive from Vernon. Rookie camp also coincided with the Young Guns tournament. Five teams – the Vancouver Canucks, Calgary Flames, Edmonton Oilers, Anaheim Ducks, and San Jose Sharks were to play in an eight-game round robin tournament. This was basically a showcase for all the young prospects. The best players would continue on to their respective team's main training camp.

I had a great tournament. I scored three goals, added a couple assists, beat up a few kids, and threw my weight around. Most weren't NHL-ready players, but they were some of the best young talent in the world. I knew I belonged, even though I was older. My confidence was sky-high. My ultimate goal was to make the big club, but I also knew they had their roster solidified before camp began. Between talks with Peter and some of the coaching staff, the plan for my rookie year was to start in Manitoba. I would have to really turn some heads to knock a regular out of the lineup, but it was possible. If I started with the Moose, I would put my head down and go to work. I figured that it would just be the long road – something

I was very familiar with. I'd fought through worse, and I was prepared to fight again.

I definitely suffered another concussion during our first game of the tournament. This big defenceman crushed me by our bench. I tried to shake it off, but I couldn't remember where I was or who we were playing for the rest of the game. This was still during a time when there wasn't enough awareness about concussions.

I did what countless guys before me did, and what we all continued to do. I lied and said I felt fine because I didn't want to be perceived as weak. I had a small headache the next day, but luckily nothing lingered much past that. Thankfully, college had given my brain somewhat of a break with the no fighting rule. I don't know how many concussions I had in Junior, but it was enough that I didn't need any more.

Main camp rolled around a few days after the tournament wrapped up. I was starstruck – being on the ice with the players I had watched on TV. The Sedins, Luongo, Bieksa, Kesler, the list went on. I continued my stellar play. I couldn't believe how fast the pace was, and how crisp everyone was with the puck. Guys didn't make mistakes like in college or the AHL. I remember being on odd-man rushes with the Sedins and scoring on almost every one. Henrik and Daniel Sedin were some of the best people I'd ever met.

NHL exhibition was a grind, especially when you're a bubble guy who's expected to bring that physical element. A bubble guy was someone who didn't have a guaranteed spot on the team. Someone who would have to make some serious "noise" at camp to earn a spot. If they did make the team, they often spent most of the season splitting time between the NHL and the AHL. I was a bubble guy.

Exhibition usually consisted of eight or nine games, and us bubble guys would play in almost all of them. The regulars on multi-million-dollar deals had their spots solidified and would play a couple of games towards the end of camp to shake the rust off. For us fringe players, it was basically an extended tryout. That meant fighting almost every game, sometimes multiple times a game. I was coming from college where we only played on the weekends with no fighting. This year, I went to development camp in the summer, rookie camp, the Young Guns Tournament, main camp, and played almost every exhibition game. It felt like I had played a whole college season before my first full pro season had even begun.

I ended up getting sent down to the Moose, which wasn't too surprising. I had made it to the last round of cuts. There were a series of cuts throughout training camp – typically starting with around sixty to seventy players and trimmed down to twenty-three when the season started. Being cut didn't frustrate me at all. I knew this would be part of the process and my journey. I was happy just to be a professional hockey player. But I damn well knew I was going to play in the NHL soon.

If I had been upset with my play, it would have been a different story. I played well and had a few good scraps under my belt. I continued visualizing my movie every day. I hadn't imagined what the AHL part of my journey would look like, but now I had an idea. I inserted it into my practice. The ending remained the same. It was still happening.

I was given every opportunity when I got to Manitoba. I started on the second line and was even playing some power play minutes. I wasn't a pure goon; I could play now. My last season of college showed that, and my new coaches knew I could contribute offensively. Plus, I had to live up to my contract. I got off to a great start in my first couple of games. I had two assists in my first game, was plus three, and hit the post in the slot on a power play.

We were in Rockford for our second game of the season.

I was driving the net and sprayed snow in the goalie's face – a big faux pas. A big defenceman – he must have been six foot five inches – gave me a shot in the face. I popped him back. The next thing I knew, I was in another scrap. I often found the big guys easier to fight because I could protect myself better in tight – I just had to watch for uppercuts. When they would extend themselves, I'd counter. It didn't work every time; I took my fair share of lickins from some big boys. But I had this slip move that served me well as a fighter. I'd switch to the left when the other guy was exposed.

I popped this big defenceman with a couple good rights and when I switched to lefts, he slipped and fell. I won the fight. We were skating to the box, and he started chirping me as I skated away.

"Fuck you, Volpatti, you better be ready to go again. I'm going to drop you as soon as we get out of the box."

I was ready to chirp back and oblige, but then I recognized he was Wade Brookbank. *Holy shit. I just won against Brookbank.* I used to watch this guy fight the heavyweights when he was with the Canucks. I quickly changed my mind. The last thing I wanted to do was square off with him. That's why I always did better with spur-of-the-moment fights. I was actually mad. If I were to square off with Brookbank, he'd likely string me out and wail away.

I needed to be smart, so I laughed and said, "Fuck that, I'm taking the win." He was fuming. He chased me around every time we played them that season, feeding me cheap shot after cheap shot. I probably would have been better off just fighting him again.

My offence started drying up, and next thing I knew I started playing less. I couldn't score. I hit a couple of posts but couldn't catch a break. I had a couple more assists in those first ten games, but that was it. I was fighting every other game and winning most bouts decisively, but it was tough to get out of this scoring slump. I had so much pressure to get that monkey off my back and score my first goal, but the slump dragged on.

Every guy goes through this in his career. I was just having mine right out the gate. I put so much pressure on myself to score that it just exacerbated the problem. I had to trust in the journey. My Visualization practice helped put me at ease through these struggles. I focused on the things I could control: relentless work ethic and dropping the mitts. I knew I could contribute with my body and my fists to bide time for the puck to start going in. I just wanted to bring the total package, like I did in college.

I look back and wonder what would have happened if those posts in the first couple of games were goals. I would have stayed on the power play, played top six minutes, and contributed more offensively. My confidence would have snowballed, just like my senior year at Brown. My dream might have been realized sooner. But again, the long way seemed to be the only way I knew. My time would come.

I was quickly labeled a fourth-line fighter. I'm not making excuses. That's just the way things shook out. The game was a business now. If I couldn't score, someone else would take my spot. I knew I was better than what my stats showed. But I was also a grinder at heart. And that was what the Canucks wanted from me. I wasn't going to be a top six guy there, so I went back to my roots: skating, hitting, and fighting. If I could be one of the best in the world at playing my role, then I knew I would get called up. I could add the offence after I solidified my roster spot. I embraced my role. It was what I needed to do to achieve my dream.

I had a blast in Winnipeg. We had a young team and partied hard. After getting sent down at the start of the season, Claire and I moved into a place in downtown Winnipeg. Every weekend the team wasn't on the road we would walk home from Whiskey Dix and the other bars after long nights of partying. On Monday nights we always went to the Palomino. Claire got along well with the other guys' girlfriends. They were all young as well and liked to have a good time. There was nothing like bonding over beers at the bar after a game. Some people might think I, or maybe all hockey players, partied too much. They might ask themselves why I would even drink or party if I hadn't reached the NHL yet. But, like many players, I was wound really tight. I was laser-focused and poured an immense amount of energy into every day. So, like many players, I needed to let off some steam once in a while.

It's important to have escapes from the demands of professional sports. Music and guitar provided some escape, and partying with my teammates was another. It allowed me to reset and show up with everything I had the next day. That didn't mean getting shitfaced all the time – more just socializing and bonding with the guys. Sure, we still picked our spots where we went full throttle too.

Eventually, I was a healthy scratch for a game in Hamilton. I was down. I had been such a big part of the team during my ATO and now I was watching from the stands. It didn't help that the coach during my ATO, Scott Arniel, had moved on. He loved my game and played me a lot. The new coach, Claude Noel, and I didn't see eye-to-eye. I actually didn't mind Claude, but we got into it often about my ice time, or lack thereof. I had my opportunity at the beginning of the year. I just wished I had gotten another look.

The season took a turn for the better when we were back in Abbotsford at the end of November. It was good to see my family and play in front of them again. My dad's brother, Shane, was there as well. He loved the fact that I was a fighter because he shared that trait with Papa Jerry too. My parents knew I was struggling. Maybe this would be a turning point.

It was. Not offensively though; it was the scene of another double homicide. *The* Double Homicide.

It was the third period, and I caught one of their players cutting across the middle. My shoulder connected with his jaw, and he was out cold. Unfortunately, since he was knocked out in midair, his face smacked the ice on his way down with a terrible thud. I was quickly jumped by another player. I slipped out of his grip with my left hand free and popped him in the face three times. His helmet went flying, and he collapsed to the ground. *Fucking right,* I said to myself. I yelled to the sky and felt like an uncaged animal. All the pressure I had been putting on myself released as the energy poured out of me.

For some reason, however, the crowd was silent. I got to the penalty box and quickly saw why. The guy I had beat up in the fight was slowly getting up trying to make his way to the bench. But the guy I hit was laying in a massive pool of blood and still hadn't moved. When I say massive, I'm not exaggerating. It had nearly filled the face-off circle and was getting bigger every second that he lay there, motionless. Another minute went by. He still hadn't moved. My raw, animalistic feeling quickly turned to one of sickness. *Shit, come on man, move. Please move something.* I took pride in the way I hit, and if I broke one of your bones from a thunderous hit, the sick part of me liked that. But I *never* wanted to see someone unconscious.

The game was also a lot different then than it is now. During this time, there were no penalties for hits to the head. There was minimal awareness around concussions and the long-term effects that could result from repeated head trauma. Destroying someone with a big hit was almost a rite of passage and something to be proud of as a hockey player. Now there is more onus on the player delivering the hit. If this was in today's game, I wouldn't have been able to make this hit without a significant suspension. But back then, the onus was on the player receiving the hit. It was up to them to protect themselves. The player I'd hit had his head down and I caught him. It was a clean hit, and I didn't receive any penalty.

I was also on a mission – similar to my Junior and college career. If you had your head down or picked a fight with me, I considered you collateral damage in the pursuit of my dreams.

Then there was the intimidation factor. If I knocked someone out of the game, I knew no one would go near me for the rest of the game, and potentially for the rest of the year. Think of guys like Scott Stevens or Jordin Tootoo; these guys made a living on intimidating and hurting people. Sure, they could play the game too, but this intimidation and toughness defined them. They scared the living shit out of other people. I was trying to be one of them.

I wouldn't make that hit today, for a few reasons. For one, it would be against the rules. Second, I know a lot more about the debilitating effects a serious concussion can have on someone. And last, I am a much different man today than I was at twenty-five years old. I still have that "killer" mentality in achieving my new dreams, but that doesn't include hurting people along the way. My experiences in life have softened me with more compassion and empathy. I am much more spiritual and emotionally in tune with myself and other people. But don't be mistaken – if I find myself in a situation where I have to protect myself, Papa Jerry will be the one showing up. I don't regret making the hit because of who I was and the mission I was on. But I regret the injury the other player sustained.

The trainers and medical staff were laying in his blood assessing the injury, as others tried to clean some of it up. Doctors and trainers had to follow tight protocols; they had to be very careful with head injuries. For all they knew, the guy I hit could have suffered a spinal injury. He didn't move for minutes, and I started thinking the worst. *Fuck, come on, man, come on, come on.* You could hear a penny drop. The crowd was so quiet. I felt like I was going to puke.

Finally, his leg moved. *Thank God.* By the time he got on the stretcher and the blood was cleaned up, twenty minutes had gone by. Those minutes of silence felt like an eternity.

If my reputation hadn't been cemented in the AHL, it sure was now. And the Canucks' brass were there to witness it all. Thankfully, the injured player was okay, although he had a long recovery and didn't play many more seasons. I felt terrible and was filled with remorse for that. I felt even worse when I saw my mom after the game. She was in tears and could barely get her words out. "I thought you killed that poor guy." My dad and uncle were concerned for the injured player too, but they had seen me deliver hundreds of hits similar to that one. They were also preoccupied with what had happened in the stands.

The Volpattis were fighting on *and* off the ice that night. The crowd started yelling at my family shortly after the double homicide. My family members were all sporting my jersey. "Volpatti is a piece of shit. He should have been left to burn in that fire," people yelled at them. My uncle turned around and threatened to put one guy on a stretcher as well. Apparently, it got pretty heated, and security had to get involved. Volpattis stick together.

I reached out to the injured player after the game to apologize – I wanted to make sure he knew that what had happened was never my intent. He seemed to accept my apology. I've never been on the other end of a phone call or text like this, so I'm not sure exactly what, or how he felt. Obviously, dealing with a serious concussion doesn't make you feel good in any way.

A few more games went by, and I got called into the coach's

office after practice. *What now?* I knew they wanted more from me in terms of offence; I heard about it every day. I had a chip on my shoulder when I walked in. Claude had a grin on his face. "You've been called up to Vancouver." I don't remember what I said exactly. I was expecting him to tell me I was going to be scratched again or something. There was a weird disconnect between the Canucks and the Moose staff. The Moose weren't happy with my play, but the Canucks were thrilled. I was bruising guys with massive hits and winning most of my fights. I remember talking to Peter about this issue.

"Do you want to play in the NHL or the AHL?" he asked me.

Of course, I replied with, "The NHL."

"Exactly," he said. "I'd much rather you keep the Canucks happy, not the Moose."

Obviously, I wanted to score more goals – everybody did. The Moose were paying my minor league salary, so they wanted me to produce offensively. But the Canucks signed me for toughness. If I could produce, that was a bonus. The NHL is composed of the best seven hundred hockey players on the planet. Skill wise, I wasn't in that seven hundred. But for my role, I was right up there as one of the best.

It was right before Christmas, and my first game was going to be against the Toronto Maple Leafs in Vancouver – Saturday night – Hockey Night In Canada! This was an iconic night every Canadian kid was familiar with. The marquee matchup of the night, and "Coach's Corner" with Don Cherry and Ron MacLean. People across the country would tune in for these Saturday games.

Holy shit. I did it. I'm really going to play in the NHL. I had visualized this moment so many times in my mind, so it wasn't a surprise. But it was still very surreal. It filled me with immense pride and excitement. I had made the movie of my life come true.

Chapter 30

Showtime

—

I flew in two days before my first game, which worked out well because I could shake off any cobwebs during practice. Thankfully, I wasn't falling all over the place like I had in my first practice with the Moose. My practice with the Canucks actually went great. I knew I belonged.

I also knew what they called me up for. They saw what I could do. They had witnessed it a couple of weeks prior in Abbotsford. The pressure to score wasn't there, at least for now.

The media frenzy associated with Canadian NHL teams was pretty wild. I couldn't believe how many reporters I talked to after my first practice. *Was this what fame feels like?* The guys on the team were amazing, and the camaraderie was impressive; it didn't hurt that we were one of the best teams in the league.

I might have slept for three hours the night before December 18, 2010. I was beyond excited and nervous. When I visualized that night, I couldn't wipe the smile off my face. I was at the end of my movie. I was actually living it this time. It was real. I paid a small tribute to all the adversity I had overcome. I felt like I could take on the world.

If it wasn't for my experiences, I absolutely wouldn't have ended up at this final scene in my movie. If I hadn't found that untapped potential deep within me, I would probably have been finishing up school or working as a carpenter. Of course, there is nothing wrong with that – my life would have just looked very different.

Claire and my parents flew into town the day of the game, but I wouldn't see them until after. I wasn't sure if I would be with the Canucks for one game or for the rest of the season, so I decided to take it day by day.

The day of the game went by at a snail's pace: pre-game skate, meetings, lunch, and pre-game nap (where I struggled to get some sleep again) – the game itself couldn't come soon enough.

After bouncing off the walls of my hotel room for hours, it was finally game time! I started thinking, *Who should I scrap?* I looked at their lineup. This was when teams still had true heavyweights, unlike today's NHL. The Maple Leafs had Colton Orr and Jay Rosehill – big time heavyweights. I was an average-sized NHL player at six-foot-one and two hundred and five pounds. Some of these heavyweights were over six-foot-five and two hundred and forty pounds. Squaring off with these big boys wouldn't be the smartest idea. Guys like Steve MacIntyre and Eric Godard – I had no business fighting them, nor was I expected to. I'd have my hands full with the middleweights, anyway. I decided to just go out and play. If a fight happened, so be it.

The feeling when I went out for the warmup was something I will never forget. I was shaking with nervous excitement – skating in an NHL arena about to play my first game. I couldn't stop looking around. My nerves were so high I could barely handle the puck, so I pretty much stopped handling them all together. I just skated around with a huge smile on my face, soaking up the electric atmosphere. I thought back to the Canucks' intermission games I had played as a young kid – meeting my idols like Pavel Bure, Trevor Linden, and Kirk McLean.

I thought back to when the Canucks had their training camp in Vernon in 2003. I was starstruck back then. Everyone was amazingly skilled, fast, and larger than life. I was so far away from even the slightest thought of pro hockey at eighteen years old. Now I was one of them. I shook my head in awe of my situation and kept smiling.

Showtime. The lights went out in the arena as we waited for the call to walk from our dressing room to the ice. Some guys were screaming and getting jacked up, others were intensely quiet, focusing on the battle that would ensue in a few minutes against the Maple Leafs. For me, this was it. I was living my movie. I had a moment to close my eyes and reflect before I officially stepped on the ice for my first NHL game.

I couldn't help but think back to my conversation with the doctors in the burn unit – the feeling of my soul being crushed with the thought of a life without hockey. In that moment, I could feel the same liberation I'd felt when I left the Vancouver General Hospital with a new outlook on life and a relentless determination. The treacherous recovery of returning to the ice. The overwhelming emotion during the national anthem of the Vipers' season opener. My conversation with the assistant coach at Brown. Climbing the proverbial mountain to chase a dream. The feeling of physically signing that contract with the Canucks. Telling my parents. Their stunned reaction. Fighting my way through the AHL. And now, here I was – at my ending. Maybe I had been manifesting this dream my whole life, even before the accident. I just hadn't realized it. We walked through the dark tunnel to the ice surface.

Except this time, as I stepped onto the ice for the first period of my first NHL game, the lights didn't go out. The credits didn't roll like they had in my mind so many times before. I was skating in front of eighteen thousand screaming fans. The wind was in my face as my skates cut through the fresh NHL ice. I was absolutely flying. My teammates were yelling behind me. They had all had their own special experiences with that first

NHL game. Wondering what the expression was like on my parents' faces, I felt an overwhelming amount of satisfaction and excitement. I was just getting my pro career started. A different movie, the sequel, was about to begin.

Once the puck dropped, the nerves quickly dissipated, and I settled in. In my second shift, I saw an opening to make a huge hit, but I would have to skate out of position. I didn't want to make a habit of it, but my adrenaline was running high. I couldn't help it. I crushed the defenceman and the crowd erupted. That was the energy they were paying me for.

I only logged six or seven minutes in total ice time, but my first game was in the books. Afterward, I met Mom and Dad, Brianne and Claire, and my billet family for a celebration – it was an amazing night. Peter even took care of my parents and set them up with a suite in the Fairmont Hotel.

We flew to St. Louis the next day, and I played my next game on the 20th of December. The first game against the Maple Leafs was a bit of a whirlwind. I felt much more settled for this game against the Blues. It was the best game I would play in my entire pro hockey career.

People don't realize that the AHL can often be a harder league to play in. It's more chaotic. Guys are trying to work their way up to the NHL, or not get sent down to the ECHL. And the players aren't as good, so there are way more mistakes. Every time I got the puck in the NHL, guys were always in the perfect position to receive a pass. And if you made a bad pass, they still picked it up off their skate. The pace of the game was still high, but it was more controlled.

Everything about my second game just felt great. I executed perfect plays on my wing. I felt solid on my skates, just as I had visualized. I was fast and made some big hits. My confidence skyrocketed.

To make things even more special, I scored my first NHL

goal in this game. Tanner Glass made a massive hit in the corner. Then my centreman, Alex Bolduc, found me wide open in front of the net. I got the puck in the slot, settled it, and fired it five hole (through the legs) on Jaroslav Halak, the Blues' goalie. It was one of the greatest feelings in the world. Time briefly stood still as I thrust my right arm into the air. My teammates embraced me, sharing the same reaction – screams of happiness and ear to ear smiles.

I would later play with Jaroslav Halak in Washington and never let him hear the end of that one. This goal really solidified that I belonged, at least for me. My game got stronger the more I played. I hit the post in the slot during the third period too. I almost had two goals in my second NHL game! The assistant coach talked to me briefly after the game and said how impressed they were. I was on top of the world.

We had two more games before Christmas break. I enjoyed a couple days off with family in Revelstoke and we were back for a game on boxing day. Before I knew it, I had played five NHL games. I still hadn't gotten into a fight, but that soon changed against the Philadelphia Flyers at home.

I made a nice play around their defenceman, Sean O'Donnell; I toe-dragged the puck to avoid his stick and got a nice shot off through his legs. He gave me the business when I went to the net. *All right, here we go! First tilt.* We grabbed on and as I hit him with a right, he fell to the ice. He actually lost his footing when he stepped on a stick. I fed him a couple more good ones as we fell to the ground. The last one was pretty late, which he wasn't happy about.

There was a code in fighting. If a guy was down or in a vulnerable position, you didn't keep hitting him. My adrenaline was so high against O'Donnell; I just kept going. He was obviously pissed, probably because it wasn't much of a fight since he fell. And because I hit him late. We got to the box, and it was like a flashback to my fight with Brookbank. He looked over and said, "We're going again, kid." I knew he was a tough customer who had been in the league for fifteen years and had his fair share of scraps. He was also about forty pounds heavier than I was. But I knew I had to answer the bell. I'm not going to lie – I was a little nervous. Mostly because I didn't want to lose in front of the home crowd and because I knew I didn't do as well when I squared off, especially with the big dudes. But the biggest mistake was to show weakness to an opponent. They would eat me alive. And I could get sent back down to Manitoba if I backed down from a challenge I should accept. So, I said, "You want more, old man? Bring it on, let's go." We stepped out of the box and shed the mitts.

As a fighter, I would go into such an interesting headspace before bare-knuckle boxing on skates in front of a packed arena. The crowd would be going crazy, but I couldn't hear anything. It was just me and the other guy, staring each other down and circling around, seeing who made the first move. Things seemed to move in slow motion. The punches didn't hurt because the adrenaline was so high. The face and hands would feel it the next day, though.

It was a pretty even scrap. We exchanged some good rights, and I snuck in a few quick short lefts. He got me off balance and landed a solid right before the refs came in. I was pretty cautious in this fight and didn't want to exchange big punches with a much bigger veteran. I stayed in tight where I could land some good shots.

A couple more weeks went by, and I was still playing with the big club. We were in Dallas for New Year's Eve. The guys had a party planned after the game at a hotel bar, so I was excited to let off some steam with everyone. My first NHL party.

I played my standard seven or eight minutes and was riding

the stationary bike after the game, excited for the party. One of the assistant coaches came up to me and said, "Hey, you gotta skate with the other scratches and injured guys in the morning before we fly to Colorado." I quickly said, "Okay, sounds good," but in my head I thought, *Damn, I was hoping to let loose and not have to worry about practicing hungover. Oh well, I'll still have fun and sweat it out tomorrow. Wouldn't be the first time, or the last.*

Well, I took it too far, though I still hold some of the other guys responsible. My alarm went off at 9:00 a.m. the next morning and I woke up in my desk chair. My face was in a puddle of my own puke and blood. *What the fuck happened?* I had totally blacked out. I struggled to get up but convinced myself I'd get through the day. I just had to suck it up. I brushed my teeth, looked in the mirror and saw a big cut on my forehead. *Huh, that's not from the game last night.*

I arrived at the rink and started putting my gear on. The guys were laughing as they looked in my direction. "Fun night last night, Patti?" I smiled back, but I was holding on for dear life. I rushed to the bathroom to puke right before we went on the ice. I'd been hungover for practices many times before, but this was by far the worst. As soon as I stepped on the ice, I knew I was in trouble. I was still drunk and could barely stand. I fell on my ass every drill and couldn't handle the puck. It was a disaster.

Glen, our skills coach, came up to me and said, "Jesus Patti, you're still drunk?"

"Sorry, Glenny, the night got away from me. I'm fucked."

Thank God the other coaches weren't around – just Glen and our goalie coach. It was a long forty-five minutes. I felt like shit, physically yes, but I was also ashamed because I thought for sure I was going to get sent back to the Moose after. Guys getting injury treatments slowly started piling on the bench to watch. I'm certain word got out that I was a complete disaster.

Every time I looked over, half the team was dying in laughter at the display I was putting on. I was literally like Bambi on ice. I couldn't help but laugh. We finally finished, and I got to the dressing room. The guys started showing me some footage of the party. "You fuckers!" They'd gotten me shitfaced on purpose. Pouring vodka down my throat, handing me shot after shot. I mean, not that I couldn't have said said no, but they went out of their way to see how drunk they could get the rookie. Damn initiation. They were probably licking their chops, knowing I had to sweat it out on the ice too.

I wanted to make a good impression and I liked to have a good time. I'm sure there came a point in the night where I just rolled with it – letting the small town boy from Revelstoke take a hold of me. There was one video of me cruising down the street where I headbutted a stop sign. *That's where the big cut on my forehead came from!*

We landed in Denver, and I passed out for about sixteen hours, hung to the gills. I was worried they would send me down that day, but it didn't happen. Either the coaches found out and didn't care, or they never found out, or the captains went to the coaches and told them how it all went down. Either way, I don't know. I'm just glad I stuck around, especially after receiving my first paycheck.

In two weeks, I had netted nearly twenty thousand dollars (forty thousand before taxes and escrow). Some guys were taking home three hundred thousand every two weeks, *after* taxes. This amount of money was unbelievable to me, even at my league minimum salary. We were flying chartered planes with all the food you could imagine (the infamous acronym for the NHL was the Never Hungry League). We were eating at five-star restaurants, staying at the nicest hotels in the country, frequenting well-known bars and clubs, cruising around big cities, seeing the sights, and meeting other celebrities. It all happened so quickly. The difference in travel, accommodations, and lifestyle between the NHL and the AHL (the Always Hungry League) was drastic. The NHL was the best of everything. I thoroughly enjoyed Manitoba (we had it very good there), but once I got a taste of "the show" I did not want to go back.

The Canucks organization was a well-oiled machine. We had every resource you could imagine, and we worked our asses off. We worked out every practice day and had access to sleep coaches, sports psychologists, physical therapists, you name it. I had to pinch myself after every home game and practice, where fans would line up outside for autographs. I loved signing autographs and mingling with fans. Around town, I started getting recognized.

We also had our rookie party that year, which was a blast. I don't know why we had it in Minnesota of all places, but we did. Usually, teams would try to have their rookie party in cities like Nashville, Vancouver, LA, or New York (and now Vegas). We rookies had to dress in women's clothing while going curling for a couple of hours. Then we went for a nice dinner where the rookies had to split the bill. At every rookie party, the veterans order the nicest bottles of wine and most expensive shots on the menu to rack the bill up. And of course, a feast like no other. Thankfully, there were a decent number of rookies, so we only had to dish out five grand or so each. I've heard stories where some guys had to pay a lot more, so I considered myself lucky. We ended up at a club early into the morning. I was functional at practice the next day, especially compared to that night in Dallas. Days off after rookie parties were usually rare – the coaches preferred if we sweat out all the booze with a long bag skate.

I was a little complacent in my second fight against Brad Staubitz. He fed me some of my own medicine by switching to lefts. I got off balance and he gave me a good shot on the way down. A clear loss.

The good thing about fighting in the NHL was that we played almost every other night. If I lost a fight, I could get right back in the saddle and redeem myself quickly. On the other hand, this could also really wear on a guy, not just physically, but mentally.

I was always thinking about the next fight, or the mere possibility of the next one. There was no reprieve, like there is in boxing or the UFC. This didn't really affect me during my first couple of years, but eventually it would start to weigh on me. I don't know how fighters in the NHL do this for ten-plus years. It's a grind. I have mad respect for everyone that has embraced this role. Most people don't understand the grind and anxiety that comes with the territory.

As a few players started returning from injury, I started playing less and eventually got sent back down to the Moose in the middle of February. I was up for two full months. I wasn't disappointed. I figured I just needed to put my head down and work to get called back up. Making the NHL is one thing, staying there is a whole other animal. There was always someone in the minors or overseas ready to take my job. As a fourth-line player, I was easily disposable.

I had lived the ending of my movie. But now I had the wherewithal to think, what else could I accomplish? Next time, I'd be back to stay.

Chapter 31

Stanley Cup

—

In my fifth game back with the Moose, I delivered another double homicide in Toronto against the Marlies. Similar to the Abbotsford one, I caught one of their guys with his head down as he skated around the net. He didn't see me coming and paid the price. Luckily, he wasn't injured as badly as the Abbotsford player, but injured enough that he was on the ice for a couple of minutes. Once again, I didn't have time to process the devastating hit since I was fully aware someone would be coming to fight me. I reverse-jumped the guy who came after me and laid a beating on him, too. I had him down by the boards, picked him up with my right hand and fed him a string of lefts. One of them missed and I smoked my hand against the boards. It wasn't broken, but it was in rough shape for the weeks following.

The refs escorted me to the penalty box. I had to step over the two guys laying on the ice as the trainers came to help them. At this point in my career, I was laser-focused on getting back to the NHL. I cared more about that than any injuries I inflicted on my opponents. I wasn't letting up if someone had their head down. Again, the onus was on the player receiving the hit, not the one delivering it. Get out of the way or be prepared for me to run you over on my way back to the big leagues.

Rick Rypien came to join the Moose about halfway through March of 2011 after a leave of absence with the Canucks. I wasn't completely aware of the situation. I just heard he had been battling some inner demons. At the time, there wasn't enough awareness surrounding mental health. Not just in sports, but in life as a man. Being vulnerable and talking about your struggles was perceived as weakness. Thankfully, the landscape has changed in today's world, but I believe we still have a long way to go.

Ryp was such an amazing guy – humble, quiet and funny with an infectious smile. He seemed like he was in a great place. This, of course, wasn't an accurate representation of what was really going on. Ryp and I were linemates, along with Garth Murray. Garth was another tough journeyman veteran, and Ryp might have been the toughest pound-for-pound fighter to ever play in the NHL. He seriously hurt a few guys with the Moose that year and eventually, no one wanted anything to do with him. We had the scariest line in the entire league. It was great. We could do whatever we wanted. If anyone came for Garth or me, we wouldn't hesitate to drop our gloves. But when Ryp was on the ice, there was a unique element at play. He absolutely terrified the opposition. But, like most fighters, away from the rink he was a humble teddy bear, and the nicest guy I had ever met. I loved Ryp's charismatic personality, and we quickly grew close.

Our line was unstoppable in the playoffs. We beat Lake Erie, located in Cleveland, in game seven of the first round. I was suspended for games five and six because I laid a monstrous hit on a young Russian rookie in game four. He went back to Russia and never played in the league again. I was pissed that they handed me a suspension for that clean hit, but there was a silver lining – I was able to visit the Rock and Roll Hall of Fame. I spent the better part of two days reading up on the history of all my favourite bands. I wanted to be on the ice, but this was a very nice alternative.

I was back for game seven and we won 4-1. It was one of the most exhilarating hockey games I've ever played. Game sevens are what dreams are made of. Sure, it wasn't the NHL, but it was damn good hockey and loads of fun. Unfortunately, in round two, we lost to Hamilton in triple overtime of game seven. It was one of the longest games in history, and another amazing experience.

With our season ending, that meant I got called up to be a black ace with the Canucks. Black ace was the term used for the handful of players that came up from the minor league team to join the NHL team for their playoff run. Little did I know, I would be chasing the Stanley Cup. Just being around the team and the city was intoxicating. I was very close to playing in game seven against the Boston Bruins because one of our guys was hurt. They ended up putting in Alex Bolduc, who was a centreman. If I would have played that game and we would have won, my name would have been on the cup! I probably would have only played two or three minutes, but that didn't matter in the least. I would have been as close as anyone could get to raising Lord Stanley's Cup.

If we thought the energy in Vancouver was next level, the atmosphere in Boston was even wilder. They put us black aces in the stands with the rest of the families. Terrible idea. The Boston fans ripped us apart. They called us, and the wives, every name you could imagine. Boston fans are fucking crazy – in a good way – I love it. But I seriously thought I was going to have to protect myself at one point if things had escalated further.

Many people might remember our loss in game seven of the Stanley Cup Finals and what ensued after in Vancouver: the citywide riots. For obvious reasons, the team laid low that night. I remember getting escorted back to my apartment with Claire. We grabbed a few cases of beer with the other black aces and their spouses and took in all the madness from our balcony.

What a rookie year it was. I couldn't have asked for a better experience. Did I see myself putting up more numbers offensively? Of course. But I had seventeen fights that year, winning well over half of them. We won the Presidents' Trophy, the award for the best regular season record. We were one game away from winning the Stanley Cup. I played fifteen games in the show and was ready to solidify myself full-time the following season.

The dynamic between the Moose and the Canucks still sticks out for me. The Moose wanted more from me, but the Canucks were totally happy. They didn't want me to change a thing. They needed more of that toughness in the lineup, especially after losing to the Bruins, and I could provide that. The consensus was we needed to get tougher. Obviously, if I could add that offensive element back to my game, that would be a bonus. My feet were nice and wet with NHL experience. I was making great money and had a good woman by my side. Life was great.

Unfortunately, the summer of 2011 was unimaginably tough for everyone in the hockey world. First we lost Derek Boogaard from an overdose, then came Ryp's suicide in August, shortly followed by Wade Belak's suicide. I was devastated and in complete shock. I had grown really close to Ryp in such a short time. I had some of the best times in my career playing on his line. The confusion this left me with was something I still think about to this day. He seemed so happy. He had just signed a new deal with the Winnipeg Jets, who were returning to the NHL. *Was there something I could have done? How is his family dealing with this tragic loss? What was he truly going through?* I felt like I should have been there for him in some way, or maybe I could have gone out of my way to ask him how he was really doing. I found it hard to comprehend what Ryp must have been going through. RIP Ryp, we miss you, brother.

I'm not going to lie – this tragic summer got me thinking. I thought about all the concussions and head trauma I had received in my life. *Was there really a connection between this and mental health? To what degree could this have affected these guys? Could I possibly suffer from CTE (Chronic Traumatic Encephalopathy) later in life if I kept fighting all the time? Maybe I should watch my off-ice habits more.* I thought back to how reckless I'd been in my younger years and wondered if I was more susceptible to mental health issues. Several of my extended family members had drug and alcohol addictions. I really sat with this for a while and thought about how lucky I was for my health. That summer was another stark reminder of the fragility of life.

Thankfully, mental health awareness has improved. As hockey players, we were always taught to play through injuries, including concussions. We never felt comfortable getting help if we weren't in a great spot mentally. It was never ok to be perceived as "weak". Now, people are considered strong if they ask for help. We have made tremendous strides over the last decade, but there is still room for improvement. I spent a lot of days throughout this summer thinking about Ryp and how I could change my life for the better.

Chapter 32

Knockout

—

$\mathbf{W}$e moved back to Vernon for the summer, and I trained like a madman. I was on the stone prevention diet this time – no milk and plenty of water. No more kidney stones before training camp!

The competition at camp the following season was fierce. There were about seven guys competing for two spots on the fourth line. The Canucks signed veterans Owen Nolan and Todd Fedoruk to tryouts. I was a little rattled because I felt like the spot was mine. *Had the team lost trust in what I could bring?* I had to remind myself that there was always going to be healthy competition.

The exhibition grind began and I was ready to make some noise. I won my first fight in Edmonton and then laid down another double homicide in San Jose a few games later. It wasn't my traditional double homicide. This time, the fight didn't happen until a few shifts later. But both of the guys were finished for the game. When I dropped Brad Winchester with one punch, I knew I had made the team. They had no choice but to keep me around. I was a younger, faster option than some of these veterans, and no one could ignore this game I had in San Jose. We needed to get tougher, and this game showed what I could bring. I remember seeing Stan Smyl after the game. He gave me a wink. A wink that said, *Welcome to the team, kid.*

I solidified my spot on the fourth line and played the first twenty games. Then an extremely interesting event happened.

Mason Raymond was coming back from injury, and I knew I was going to get bumped out of the lineup as the extra forward. I always wanted to play, but I knew I would be the odd healthy scratch. At least I was still making my NHL salary if I was up with the big club. I had injured my shoulder against the Kings in LA a few weeks prior, and it had been getting progressively worse. Part of me was happy to give it a bit of rest. It started slipping out of the socket almost every game and was causing me a lot of pain. Luckily, it never stayed dislocated, but my rotator cuff started to tear.

We were playing at home, and I was going to be scratched against the Nashville Predators with Mason's return to the lineup. I did my morning bag skate after our practice, then worked out. During the game, the scratches would come to the rink and ride the bike for another workout.

Timby was living in Vancouver, so I figured I'd see if he wanted to meet up during the day. I called him as I was leaving the rink.

"What's up, man? Have time to grab lunch at Cactus Club? I'm not playing tonight, so it would be good to let off some steam. Let's have a few beers and a burger if you're free."

"Beautiful!"

We met at Cactus Club at 1:00 p.m. The beers were flowing as Timby and I reminisced about our Brown days. Before we knew it, it was 4:30 p.m. I wasn't drunk, but I was definitely on my way. I figured I would just sweat it out on the bike during the game. I had just finished a burger and ordered a fresh pint when I got a call from Alain Vigneault, our coach.

"Patti, Mason's paperwork got fucked up coming off the injured reserve. We need you to play tonight."

I hesitated for a second. *Shit. I can't tell him I can't play because I've been smashing beers all afternoon.* So of course, I said nothing.

"Okay, sounds good. See you shortly."

Timby said this was the only time in his life he's seen me visibly rattled. He said it looked like I'd seen a ghost. "What's going on?"

"You're not gonna believe this. I gotta go. I'm playing tonight!"

He laughed, "Are you fucking kidding me? I'm not missing this." He called some buddies and bought tickets right away. We shared a laugh as I stared at the remainder of my beer. *Fuck it.* I finished what was left and paid. I ran to my condo to throw on my suit and slam a bunch of water.

Typically, guys show up to the rink between 4:00 p.m. and 5:00 p.m. for a 7:00 p.m. game. I showed up at 5:30 p.m., half an hour late, but obviously I had a free pass on that one. The guys gave me a quick clap as I joined in on the meeting. I just kept thinking, *I'm about to play an NHL game half-cut. More than half cut!* This must have been how the guys felt back in the old days. I didn't tell anyone except one of my linemates because I knew he would love it.

I was slightly apprehensive about playing. I debated getting into a fight every period so I wouldn't have to play. I could get my rematch against Jordin Tootoo. He gave it to me pretty good about a month prior. My shoulder was still in bad shape, so I was trying to avoid the premeditated scraps if possible.

So, the result? I played phenomenally and scored my first goal of the year. Once the game started, I seemed to sober up – maybe it was the adrenaline.

For the remainder of my career, I always debated having a beer and a burger for my pre-game meal. I never did, but maybe I was onto something there.

Unfortunately, I received an awkward hit towards the end of the game and my shoulder came out again. I cried out in pain as it finally went back into the socket.

The medical staff decided we should look into the injury more. I had some tests done the next day. I basically had no labrum left. It was eighty percent torn and my rotator cuff was twenty-five percent torn. The labrum keeps the ball of the joint in place, hence the reason my shoulder kept slipping out. My rotator cuff was strong enough to hold my shoulder in place when the subluxations happened, but it was tearing because of the constant trauma. If I kept playing with no labrum, I would eventually need rotator cuff surgery too, which was not a fun recovery. As it stood, my rotator cuff would heal on its own. After talking with the doctors, we decided that I should shut it down and fix the shoulder. The problem was only going to get worse if I kept playing. If it was repaired, I would be one hundred percent healthy for the following summer of training and there was even a possibility of returning towards the end of the current season.

I was bummed. This was my first season as an NHL regular. I wasn't putting up many points, but I was still doing my job. Our line was creating a lot of energy. I went for surgery a few days later and was looking at a four- to six-month recovery.

We lost in the first round of the playoffs that year. I was getting close to being able to play towards the end of the year, after a successful rehab, but it didn't happen. It was a big disappointment after being in the Stanley Cup Finals the year prior. Since my two-year contract was up, I was a free agent again. It was always poor timing when you missed most of the season the year you were set to become a free agent. If you could put together a good season, you could sign a life changing, multi-million-dollar contract. I had to take another two-way contract and a pay cut to boot. I knew the circumstances, though.

I could have tested free agency, but Vancouver still wanted me. Since I missed most of the season, I had little bargaining power. I signed a one-year deal with the Canucks after the season.

That fall, going into my third pro season, was the start of the lockout. The NHL and the team owners couldn't come to an agreement with the NHLPA and its players on the Collective Bargaining Agreement. Shitty timing, but luckily I was on a two-way contract so I could play games in the minors. Or so I thought.

I had my bags packed in August for Chicago, where the Canucks' minor league team had moved to. But I received a call from Mike Gillis, our general manager, telling me they weren't sending me down. They didn't want to lose me on waivers. Waivers is a transactional process required to move a player who has met certain playing or experience requirements to be sent from the NHL level to the minor league level. When players are put on waivers, any other NHL team may put in a "claim" for the player and place him on their own roster.

It pissed me off and made me happy at the same time. Pissed off because I hadn't played a game in almost a year, and I needed to get some games in. The other part of me was happy because this meant they didn't want to lose me to another team. They saw me in their lineup. However, I had a hard time believing guys would get picked up on waivers during a lockout. I stayed in Vernon, desperately waiting for the lockout to end.

The lockout dragged on into December, and it was looking less and less likely that we would play. I was skating with the Vipers in Vernon with a handful of other NHL guys, which got old quickly. I started cross country skiing (skate style, not classic) to get some variety in my training. This was a nice change of pace, and one hell of a workout. At one point, I was really close to heading overseas to play in Belfast, but it never shook out.

I proposed to Claire that fall too. Things had been great for over two years. I knew I wanted to spend the rest of my life with her. After our on-and-off history, we had finally committed to each other. We started making wedding plans for the following summer. We were living a great life and didn't have a care in the world – a fact that would prove to be problematic in the future.

Chewy, my friend from the Vipers, was getting married in Jamaica that January. Once Christmas hit, Claire and I booked our tickets since there was no news on the potential end of the lockout.

It was about 3:30 a.m., 6:30 a.m. EST. We were at Big White Ski Resort in Kelowna on the last night of Chewy's stag. I had been training my ass off for months in anticipation of a redemption season. But since it sounded like we might lose the entire season because of this lockout, I decided to really let loose at his stag. I had a bottle of Jack Daniels in my hand, and we were partying with a bunch of people back in our condo.

Suddenly the guys started cheering, "Woooo Patti! You're going back to work, buddy!" I was in the middle of a big pull of whiskey when I looked over at the TV. *LOCKOUT OVER.* Camp would be in a few days, and I thought, *Fuck, I just went on a three-day bender and now I have to get ready for camp?* Obviously, I was thrilled to get back in action, but the bender wasn't ideal. I missed Chewy's wedding and couldn't get a refund on the trip, so I gifted the trip to Brianne and her husband, Tally.

Camp went surprisingly well, and the season started shortly thereafter. They scratched me for the odd game, but that was part of the deal with being a fourth-line grinder. I never liked it, but it was important to keep spirits high and still be a positive, fun presence in the locker room.

Alain Vigneault was my favourite NHL coach. When I was a healthy scratch, he always made sure he took the time to communicate the reasons why. Sometimes it was because he wanted a little more skill in the lineup, and sometimes it was because I wasn't playing well enough. As much as I didn't like his decision to scratch me, I respected him for communicating with me. That's more than I can say about some of the other coaches I had.

A few weeks into the shortened season, I finally got the letter. A letter telling me to find a place to live. This was an enormous deal. They were clearly happy with my play. During the previous couple of years, I was either in a hotel or a condo that the team paid for. Rent wise, this was a win since I paid nothing, but it also meant I wasn't enough of a mainstay. They hadn't felt comfortable enough for me to find a place to live. So, every day prior, I came to the rink wondering if I was still going to be in the NHL. I'd gladly take the rent tradeoff, not only for the fat paychecks but for the peace of mind knowing there was more stability in being a full time NHLer.

Claire and I eagerly found a place to rent and signed the lease. A week passed, and I was a healthy scratch again. I got called into the coach's office after the game. That was never a good thing. They told me they were putting me on waivers. Oh innocent, naive me – how could I think this letter guaranteed stability.

Why would they tell me to go find a place to live, then put me on waivers now? I was especially mad that they had kept me from playing hockey in the minors during the lockout, and *now* they were sending me down. They explained that they wanted me to play more, which was totally warranted. It was a business, and I understood that, as players, we were just assets that could get moved around. It was hard not to dwell though. I wished they had just sent me down to Chicago during the lockout which would have allowed me to do exactly that – play more.

The Canucks royally screwed this up, in my humble opinion, because they should have known Ryan Kesler had a broken foot from blocking a shot in the previous game. There are usually constant conversations between the medical staff and coaching staff – which players have been injured and the severity of those injuries. Something either got missed here or there had been a communication issue. I went on waivers before they were aware of the broken foot, but it was too late. You can't rescind putting someone on the waiver wire. And they may have wanted me to play more, but what they really were after was to give Steve Pinizzotto a look on the fourth line. He played a similar style to me but had more skill. Again, totally understandable. If he was an upgrade from me, they *should* send me down. But they could have put Kesler on the IR, given Steve a look, and kept me on the team too.

I was talking with Peter the next day, voicing how pissed off I was. Not necessarily because of the waivers, but because of the way it went down. I had other people in the organization calling me, telling me they didn't agree with the decision to put me on the waiver wire. It was a mess. But these types of miscommunications happen all the time in pro sports. I just happened to be on the wrong side of this one. There were headlines in the paper stating how the Canucks wished they could have "pulled back" their decision.

Peter quickly put me at ease. "You know I've had calls from almost every single team? They're all putting a claim in for you. You're staying in the NHL, so don't worry."

I enjoyed my time in Vancouver, playing in my home province. I was grateful for everything the Canucks organization gave me. But I had a sour taste in my mouth from the way things shook out. Similar to my other experiences of adversity, this one would also be a blessing in disguise.

Out of all the teams that submit a waiver claim, the team with the worst record is awarded the player. I spent all night and the next day wondering where I was going to go. Part of me was still pissed off, but I was excited about starting a new chapter. I finally found out I was headed to Washington, D.C., to join the Capitals. In response to this transaction, the Canucks then claimed another fighter saying, "After we lost Aaron, we wanted to find that element as quickly as possible."

Chapter 33

The Capitals

—

Interestingly enough, I met the Capitals in Winnipeg. NHL teams could sometimes relocate to other cities, and the Winnipeg Jets had relocated from Atlanta. This meant all the Moose staff I had known had simply moved up with the big club. I skated on my own the day before the rest of the Capitals arrived. I got to bullshit with all the old Moose trainers. I hadn't seen them in a couple of years, so it was great to catch up. I went for dinner that night at my favourite Italian restaurant in downtown Winnipeg.

I took the worst beating of my pro career in my first game with the Caps. I figured I'd get in a tilt to make a good impression with the team. After all, they didn't pick me up to score goals. Anthony Peluso strung me out and had his right hand free to lay bombs on the back of my head. I knew I was in trouble and had to "turtle" (protect myself instead of punching back). His reach was so much longer than mine. He exposed me when I was in a bad spot. I may not have won every fight, but I showed up and could take a punch. I would have been better laying someone out with a quintessential Volpatti hit and getting in a quick, heated scrap, but I was trying to make a quick impression. I spent the whole second period getting close to thirty stitches in my head before coming back to play.

Mullet, the current trainer for the jets, and my trainer with the Moose, came into the room. We shared a good laugh. Peluso broke his hand on my skull in the fight, so I guess, technically, that means I won, right?

This trumped the most stitches I'd gotten at one time. Earlier in the season in Vancouver, I took a puck to the face during practice – from point blank. Many people don't realize that the pucks are frozen, so it's like getting hit with a rock traveling up to a hundred miles miles per hour. It hit me right above my top lip, but luckily it was high enough that it didn't knock out any teeth. If it would have been a half an inch lower, it would have cleaned my teeth right out. The puck did, however, blow my lip apart, fracture a bunch of the roots of my teeth, and make a mess of my maxilla (the upper jawbone). There was a big hole where my lip connected to my maxilla, so the doctor could stick his finger up into my cheek. It was a mess, and I had to go see a plastic surgeon. I spent hours getting twenty-plus stitches. It's impressive how good the scar looks now, considering how bad the damage was. Every time I got a cut sewn up playing hockey, I considered it an addition to the extensive collection of scars all over my body. But all my scars from these cuts differed from the burn scars. These cuts almost seemed more like acute nicks on my face (although they definitely didn't appear that way) compared to my burn scars – these appeared vastly in random places all over my body. The dark purple colour had faded, but they were still very noticeable. They also felt different from the rest of my skin – like a very thick piece of leather was covering my flesh. I couldn't feel any light touch but could feel firm pressure. When the cuts healed, it almost felt as if there was a little twig buried beneath the skin as the scar tissue formed.

Joining new teams was always interesting for several reasons. I'd get to meet new people from different countries, and usually there would be one or two guys that I'd fought at some point prior. Those were the best encounters; past enemies always seemed to hit it off as new teammates. Navigating around a new city was new and interesting – experiencing the different cultures and meeting new people. But perhaps the most intriguing aspect of joining a new team were the looks I'd get in the change room and in the shower. I would get a mixed bag of reactions when I told the summarized story of why I was battered with all the gnarly scars. Some would shake their heads in disbelief, some would laugh, and some didn't know how to react. But all they really knew was that I had suffered a severe burn injury, recovered, and played hockey after. I never shared the *true* journey.

Washington was a nice refresher. The guys were really close, and we hung out all the time. It was a little like a country club at first – too much so. Guys worked out only when they desired, and practices were definitely more relaxed than in Vancouver. This accountability piece eventually changed and a different culture was instilled in the organization – an emphasis on getting better every day, and a goal of working towards the Stanley Cup. It was no surprise when they won the cup years later. The talent was always there, but it was about adding some of those intangibles and instilling that winning culture.

Adam Oates was the coach for my first two years in Washington. He was obviously an extremely skilled player and had an insane mind for the game, but he wasn't my favourite head coach. He expected all of us to have eyes in the back of our heads like he did. He was one of the best passers to ever play in the NHL and was inducted into the Hall of Fame in 2012. I was really grateful for the skills he taught us and agreed it was important to add them to our game. But I wasn't going to be a Hall of Famer like him.

Oates was obsessed with everyone's stick. Pretty much

every guy on the team used the same curve, except for Alex Ovechkin and Nicklas Backstrom – heard of 'em? If we didn't use the curve Oates wanted, he would blame the stick for any mistake that was made and often bench guys for using the "wrong" stick. I was shocked. How did this shit happen in the NHL?! He essentially forced the best players in the world to use a specific curve. If you didn't use his curve, he wouldn't play you. If you looked around the league, you would see the vast variety of curves, tape jobs, and knobs on everyone's stick. Players refine their stick over the course of their entire career. I had used the same curve since I was ten years old, and I was just trying to stay in the league at this point. No chance I was changing my whole stick at this point in my career. A new stick would mean a completely different feel for the puck. I would have been open to suggestions, especially in the off season, but mid-season was not an option. So when he got on me and told me to change, I said no.

Another week went by and I came to the rink in the morning just like any other day. But there was one major difference. All my sticks were gone, and in my stall were five of Mike Ribeiro's sticks. The Ribeiro writing (every stick had the player's name on it) had been sharpied out and my number twenty-four was written beside it instead. Oates actually just took my sticks and replaced them. I couldn't believe it. I wanted to walk into his office and ask him what the fuck he was doing. But I decided against this since I couldn't afford to be out of the lineup.

The first few games were a bit of a struggle as I tried to adjust to this new stick. Receiving passes on my backhand was the biggest change. But as a professional athlete, I could adjust to new equipment reasonably fast. I became used to the new stick and finally settled in. I debated going back to my old stick a few times but knew I would probably end up watching games in the press box. Since I was trying to earn a new contract, being scratched wouldn't help me create value in negotiations. So yeah, that happened – in the NHL.

I started playing some great hockey and brought a ton of energy to the lineup. My confidence with the puck was growing every game. Again, I wasn't lighting up the score sheet, but I was playing my role well. Oates did give me a chance to play, so I respected the opportunity – even if it *was* because I reluctantly switched my stick. I remember one game I even started on the first line with Ovechkin and Backstrom, one of the best duos in the history of the NHL. I definitely had to pinch myself before that game. It only lasted a couple of shifts, but it was amazing – for me at least – they might not have been as thrilled to have a fighter on their line.

Towards the end of this shortened season, Peter called and said the Capitals had offered me a two-year deal. Even better, it was a one-way contract – my first one. Meaning I was guaranteed to make my NHL salary even if they sent me to the minors. It took about one second for me to say yes.

My life couldn't have been going any better – yet another climactic moment. I had inked a new two-year deal, and Claire and I were getting married in a few months, during the summer of 2013. I had the career, the money, and the woman – everything I figured I would ever need.

D.C. had been a refreshing change. I loved the city, I loved the guys, and I had solidified my spot on the fourth line. Not that I didn't enjoy my time in Vancouver, but this unexpected waiver pickup turned out to be the best thing for me and my career.

This was the first season I truly felt like a full-time NHL player. I struggled to add that offensive element still, but I hoped I could add it the following year. There were three factors limiting me from adding this layer to my game. First, I wasn't as naturally skilled as most guys in the NHL. Second, it was really tough to pick my spots to try new things. If our line made a mistake in the first few shifts of a game, we often wouldn't see the ice again – similar to Vancouver. As grinders, we were expected to get the puck behind the other team's defencemen and pound them into the boards. And if someone tried to fight us, we threw down our gloves and went at it. Our leash on the fourth line was really short. I had a hard time balancing offensive attempts with the puck versus not getting scratched, or even sent down if I made a mistake. And third, the demands of fighting finally started taking a toll on me. Not just physically, but mentally, too.

This was the only aspect of my life that wasn't going well. I had been in a lot of fights, and there was a big part of me that enjoyed being the protector. The grinders and fighters were really loved by the rest of the team and the fans. But I constantly thought about that next fight, or more the possibility of that next fight. I wanted to be a hockey player too and contribute in other ways – not just with my body and my fists. The anxiety started to infiltrate my mind. We are naturally wired to think about what could go wrong and what could hurt us. Without my Visualization practice, I would have been a complete mess. When I closed my eyes and imagined all the great things in my life, as well as the performance I desired on the ice, it acted like an internal reset. But the battle was constant.

Sleep started becoming an issue as my body was constantly filled with adrenaline and cortisol, thinking about the possibility of getting into a fight in front of twenty thousand people. Once the fight happened, I could finally relax and play the game. But once that game was over, I would quickly move onto the next game and wonder about the next fight. *Who was I potentially going to scrap? What were his tendencies? Does he throw lefts? I have a bit of a headache from the last game. Should I tell the trainers? Would I get sent down if I sat out a game? The cuts on my hands could use a break.*

My anxiety started increasing to a point where I couldn't sleep without having a few beers. And then this turned into a few more plus the odd sleeping pill. I started feeling guilty for having this anxiety. *I'm playing in the NHL. What could I possibly have to worry about?* I started thinking about my mental health more, knowing I shouldn't let this beast grow in my mind. I had to get my mind right, before it got me.

Don't get me wrong, I still loved playing in the NHL and was having a blast living out my dream. And I would have done it over and over again. But it's not always smooth sailing like people may think. There was a ton of pressure to perform, and I knew if I didn't, I was very disposable as a guy making league minimum. When I squared off with a guy five inches taller than me and forty pounds heavier, I not only didn't want to get knocked out in front of twenty thousand people and suffer a concussion, but I also didn't want to get sent down to the minors because of that loss.

The odds of making it to the NHL are around one in four thousand. I made it to the NHL and I don't regret my role or my path in pro hockey. I'm extremely grateful to have even played a single game. Fighting and hitting not only got me there, but kept me there, and I'll always remember that.

I didn't play every game, but I felt settled and really enjoyed being a Capital. I had a couple doozies for scraps that year, too. My fight with Mike Brown might have been the best one. He was ferocious, and we went toe to toe in one of the best fights of the year. He took the win in the end, but I caught him with some bombs as well. My face was in rough shape after this one and I added another broken nose to the collection. Blood poured out of my face and onto the ice as I skated to the bench.

One of my biggest regrets was letting up on Steve Downie. He was a scrappy and skilled player, and he played his role well, but he was also one of the dirtier players. We shellacked

Philadelphia 7-1 in their arena. I made a borderline hit on one of their players and Downie came in to jump me. We grappled for a while and then I successfully made my shimmy shake transition to the left hand. This had been a successful move (honed in the minors) in many of my fights – I'd caught Kevan Miller with a few good lefts earlier in the year from this same move. I would take my right arm across the guy's body and grab his upper right arm. Then I would be in control. If he wanted to trade lefts, that was fine by me. Because of the angle after I gave the right handed shove, I could usually unload lefts without repercussions. I could throw left handed just as effectively as my right my whole life. If the guy was a southpaw, things would get a little more interesting.

I kept Downie strung out with my right, and then timed a quick punch perfectly. I pulled him in with my right at the same time as I twisted my whole body and landed a big left. In real time, you could barely see the punch – it happened quickly. I knew I had popped him good, and he was yelling at me to stop. "I can't see, I can't see! Stop!" His left eye was in awful shape, with blood pouring out of it. I yelled back, "Go down then!" As we were yelling at each other, the refs came in and I pushed him away. He missed a few games after this because of an "upper-body" injury.

Towards the end of the season, those double homicides finally caught up to me when we were playing against the New York Islanders. I received a nasty hit from behind. Matt Carkner had four inches and forty pounds on me. It happened so fast I don't remember if I turned at the last second or if he made a hit he shouldn't have. I flew headfirst into the boards after this huge collision. I turned my head at the last second as it jarred sideways, with my body slamming into the boards. My right arm and hand felt like they were on fire after I felt an intense pinch in my neck. That subsided after a good ten seconds as I laid on the ice. The first thought that raced through my mind was, *Can I move my legs?* Thankfully, I could, but my arm was completely numb. I couldn't move it. Normally, I would have dropped my gloves after a hit like this and went after the guy. But I couldn't feel my arm. I probably dodged a bullet because Carkner was a big, tough dude. I went off to the dressing room and things subsided a little bit. The burning sensation was gone, but my neck was really sore, and my hand was still numb.

I don't look back with disgust or resentment at Carkner. I'd made countless hits similar to this leading to other players injured. I didn't know him personally, but having played against him a few times, I knew he was an honest, humble, and tough SOB. I don't recall him delivering countless cheap shots in his career. The game happened quickly, and injuries were part of it.

We were in the middle of a ten-day road trip. I knew I was lucky my injury wasn't worse. I easily could have broken my neck if I went into the boards differently. I figured I just had a bad stinger, or pinched nerve. Well, that's exactly what it was, but it ended up being much worse. Career threatening worse.

Chapter 34

Fusion

—

Once we had returned home from the road trip, I told the trainers I still hadn't gotten the feeling back in my thumb and index finger. They were totally numb. Some red flags were raised. Aside from hockey, my guitar playing was also affected. I had worked up quite a collection of guitars by this time – twenty to be exact. I'd really been leaning on this escape due to the demands associated with being an NHL fighter. It was extremely awkward playing the guitar when my thumb and index finger of my fretboard hand had no feeling.

The injury got to a point where I couldn't keep my head in a neutral position without having nerve pain shoot down my arm. When I was driving, for example, I had to look at the road with my head tilted slightly downward. If I got bumped the wrong way in practice, my arm would light up just like it did from the original hit. It would cripple me for ten seconds or so. Once the pain subsided, my entire arm and hand would stay numb for minutes.

I was trying to grind through the end of the season, but once we knew we weren't making playoffs, I decided to talk more with the doctors. They ran a bunch of tests. I was shocked at how little strength I had in my left arm. I would hold my fists to my chest, and the doctor would pull my arms down. Under normal circumstances, there was no way someone should be able to pull one of my arms down. But he could move my left arm with very minimal force. My fingers on this hand also had zero strength, which explained why I was having so much difficulty holding my stick.

Once I had the MRI done, it showed that the disc between my C-5 and C-6 vertebrae had ruptured. The discs in your spine absorb shock by dispersing pressure and movement throughout the gel-like mucoprotein, which is encased by a harder shell made of collagen. These discs also allow for slight movement throughout your spine. If the movement or shock is too traumatic, the soft gel-like protein can rupture through a tear in the harder collagen shell. There had been enough force from this hit to severely rupture my disc, hence the ongoing nerve pain. This displacement of my disc was putting pressure on the nerves innervating my left arm and hand.

The doctor explained it like this: each vertebra has four "windows" or openings where nerves flow through and innervate specific parts of the body. Disc degeneration, disc herniation, or both, could cause these windows to become blocked, thus putting unpleasant pressure on the nerve. He told me two of my windows were totally blocked and that's why I was feeling this constant nerve pain and numbness. I couldn't get any relief no matter what I tried. In my mind, there was only one month left in the season, so I figured I would just tough it out. I had battled through many injuries before. After coming back from my burn injury and battling constant pain, I figured nothing could stop me.

I had a couple of steroid injections to help relieve some discomfort, but the issues quickly returned within a couple of days. Since it was a spinal injury, I was pretty worried. I decided to put my stubbornness and invincible mindset aside. I went to see a specialist in D.C., who said the best action would be surgery, based on how severe the herniation was. *Fuck, what does spinal surgery look like?* He recommended disc replacement surgery, where they essentially remove the disc and replace it with an artificial one. This type of surgery allowed the spine to retain most of the natural movement because the artificial disc acted like the real thing.

After talking with my family and the team doctors, I decided to get a second opinion. If we were talking about spinal surgery, I wanted to make sure I was doing the best thing for my future and the rest of my hockey career. I went to LA to see one of the top spinal surgeons in the country known for working on professional athletes.

I met with him and his team, and after another MRI he agreed I needed surgery. He not only recommended spinal fusion (the full name of the procedure is anterior cervical discectomy and fusion), but he also advised against the disc replacement option.

"You need this area of your spine to be strong. You don't want more movement that will come from the disc replacement." That was the one downfall of the replacement surgery. The artificial disc actually allowed for more movement. And since I played a high contact sport, especially with my role, the last thing I wanted was my spine to move *more*. This could result in catastrophic consequences.

The doctor walked me through the spinal fusion surgery. They would make a one to two-inch incision in the front of the neck, move the esophagus and trachea to the side, exposing my spine. From there, they would remove the ruptured disc and replace it with a bone graft. This bone graft had a cadaver shell with a piece of my bone, taken from my hip, inserted in the middle. They would insert this hybrid bone into the space left from the removed disc, allowing new space for the nerves to pass through. Then, they would immobilize this whole section of my spine by putting a titanium plate over the area; with four screws drilled into my surrounding vertebrae to secure it. During the six plus month recovery time, the bone graft would fuse to the adjacent vertebrae, creating one big vertebra.

It sounded terrifying. I quickly thought about my burn injury. The pain I had experienced with that was far greater than what I was currently dealing with. My neck was in severe discomfort, but I didn't have debilitating pain. The thought of this invasive surgery – where someone was going to rearrange my spine – scared me more than my skin graft surgery. I was also rattled and mentally drained with all these injuries that were piling up in my young career. I had pretty much missed the entire season with my shoulder injury in Vancouver and now I was going to likely miss the first few months of the next season with such a long recovery.

I had two different options at this point – disc replacement or spinal fusion. I got back to my hotel and called the Capitals' medical team. I told them I wanted a third opinion. Since I had connections in Vancouver, they lined up another appointment there with a specialist. I changed my flight and headed there the next day. *What if this doctor tells me I don't need surgery and I can just continue getting these shots and rehab the injury?* I'd have three different opinions and a tough decision to make. Luckily, he agreed, with conviction, that the fusion was the best option for me. The disc replacement might have been the best option if I had a sedentary office job, but obviously that was far from my reality.

The technology around the disc replacement was relatively new and was continuing to evolve (there have recently been players who have gotten the disc replacement surgery done, most notably Jack Eichel). The fusion has been around for over one hundred years, with high success rates. But there is also a risk of adjacent disc herniation and the possibility of another fusion in the future. With the fusion, doctors agreed that there was a high chance I could return to play after my spine was completely fused, so I felt comfortable proceeding. Well, let me rephrase that, I wasn't comfortable, but figured it was my best option to continue my hockey career at the time. I would get the surgery, recover in LA for a few days, fly home, recover with a halo around my neck for another six weeks, and begin the long rehab process.

I flew back to D.C., slugged a bunch of beers with the boys and said goodbye (the season had ended). We loaded up the truck and started the four-thousand three hundred and seventy-two-kilometer trek home. We usually spread it out over four or five days with stops in Columbus, Fargo, and Medicine Hat. Driving wasn't the most pleasant thing with my neck discomfort, so Claire was the primary driver on this trip.

About six weeks after the hit, I was going under the knife in Marina Del Rey – about forty kilometers west of LA and right on the water. Too bad I wouldn't be able to enjoy the beach after my surgery.

The procedure was a success, and I recovered for a few days at a hotel. My neck was quite painful, especially when I moved around to go to the bathroom or eat, but Claire looked after me. At least she got to enjoy some sunshine by the water while I slept the days away.

We flew home and tried to settle in for the summer. I wasn't able to stand for long stretches of time without my neck getting really stiff and sore, so I pretty much just rested and watched TV.

Once the end of June rolled around, and I was seven weeks post operation, I could go to the gym. Light rehab and stationary bike workouts made up the bulk of my summer. Although I wasn't able to take part in training camp that fall, it was good to be back around the guys. We had just hired Barry

Trotz, our new head coach, and I was looking forward to a fresh start. By this time, I was skating on my own and getting in some good workouts. Contact was still strictly prohibited since the doctors wanted me to wait a minimum of six months before returning to the lineup. I had to ensure my fusion was one hundred percent healed.

The end of November came, and I flew back to LA to meet with the doctors to see where I was at. Things looked great, and I was fully fused. I was given the green light to ease back into contact in practice for a couple of weeks. If that felt good, they would clear me for games. I was a little apprehensive about the first couple of practices, as were the rest of the guys. They knew the extent of my injury and wanted to go easy on me.

Unfortunately, I was left really sore after I started contact. A week into practice and I could barely get out of bed in the morning because my neck was so stiff. I could barely shoulder check driving to the rink. Deep down I knew I wasn't ready to play, but I knew if I didn't my career in the NHL was likely over. I was in a contract year. If I didn't play any games, I was unlikely to sign another deal. I thought about the possibility of heading over to Europe if that was the case. If I could just get in the lineup, who knew, maybe I would start rolling and ink another contract. It wasn't so much the big hits, when I was braced and ready, that aggravated my injury. It was the small pushes and shoves, like cross checks in front of the net that I didn't see coming. My neck wasn't braced in these moments and when my head jolted forward, it crippled me.

The coaches and management wanted to send me to Hershey, the minor league team, to get a couple of games under my belt. Test the neck out and get my game to where it needed to be. I figured this was a logical step to get back in the lineup, so I made the drive to Hershey. It was mid-December, and I would get a couple of games in before the short Christmas break. I was apprehensive based on how my neck felt, but I decided to see it through. I told myself I might just need another month to heal, and things would hopefully get better. I was wrong.

The surgery was successful in that it had rectified all my nerve pain. I knew I would have limited range afterward, but I didn't think it would be this stiff and sore after contact. I was reluctant to fight based on how sore my neck was. For the most part, I played pretty well in Hershey, but I wasn't the junkyard dog I used to be. That killer mentality was lacking because my neck now restricted me. I struggled to even leave the hotel in the morning.

I returned to Washington after this stint for the short Christmas break. The season would start up again in four days. I could barely lift my head off the pillow the next morning. I was beyond stiff and extremely groggy from all the pain killers I was consuming. Luckily, with the holiday break, I could give my neck some much-needed rest.

I was putting my mission ahead of my health, just as I had done in the burn unit. Now my mission was to successfully return to the lineup and secure another contract. Claire and my family became worried. Claire had really only known me as a fighter, literally and figuratively. I was always injured. I got burnt shortly after we met. Now, as an NHL player, she was the one at home with me, behind the scenes – through the shoulder surgery, the neck surgery, the countless black eyes and broken noses, all the sprains and tears, the stitches, and hands that looked like they had gone through a meat grinder. It wore on us all.

It was one thing to push through pain from my burn injury or other war wounds from hockey. But with my neck, everyone, including me, started worrying that if I re-injured it, it could be life altering. I knew I could play through pain and push my body to the limits, but I also wanted to be able to pick up my future kids one day. I wanted to be able to throw them on my shoulders. I wanted to be healthy and active after I retired. The life I imagined after hockey might have been in jeopardy.

With my burns, I knew I couldn't make them worse. I was fine with the pain and the risk of infection. My grafts couldn't become more stiff from playing. I was also much younger then and in a different place in my life. I never really thought about a family when I was in the burn unit. It was just me, my dreams, and this massive wall standing in my way. Now, I knew I could make my neck worse, with the risk of another fusion. So, every day, I had this constant battle inside my head about what the right thing to do was. Fight through the pain like I had always done or give myself permission to put my health first and let my body heal.

I told the trainers how sore my neck was, and they put me on the short-term IR (injured reserve) to rest up. The team was rolling, so I didn't get back in the lineup for another couple of weeks, anyway. I was more careful in practice, and started feeling a little better in January. I finally got into a game and the same issue continued to plague me. I was crippled the next morning. I was frustrated and wondered if it would ever feel better. During the last few months of the season, I was on and off IR. I only ended up playing one more game, which was on the father and son road trip.

I met my dad in LA with a brand new Takamine acoustic guitar I'd picked up on our previous road trip to Nashville. This was one of eight guitars I had bought that trip. Dad had no idea, and I was pumped to surprise him with it. The other seven were for my collection.

He was speechless when he picked up the guitar. We shared a couple of beers in the hotel room and jammed for a while. This brought back many great memories of us jamming to our favourite songs.

Most NHL teams do a father-and-son trip once every year or two. In Vancouver we did a siblings trip, so Brianne got to tag along, which was great. There have been more mothers' trips in the league now, but unfortunately they didn't happen in my years with Vancouver and Washington – sorry, Mom.

Dad got to see me play against the Kings in LA, but though he was happy I was back in the lineup he could tell I wasn't even close to a hundred percent. He was quite concerned. I had a hard time opening up and kept my thoughts bottled up. I just told him it was bothering me, but I was just trying to make it until the end of the season and secure a new contract.

When we boarded the plane after the game, Dad couldn't lift his carry-on bag into the overhead bin. The fathers had hit the town pretty hard the night before, so I just made fun of him. "Hope you had fun last night, old man." I grabbed his bag and tossed it above us. We made the quick hop over to Anaheim. I didn't play in that game the following day, so I just hung out with Dad and the rest of the fathers. The whole team went out for dinner after. Then Dad went home with his brand-new guitar, and I flew back to Washington with the rest of the team.

A couple of weeks passed as I continued to battle the physical state of my neck and the mental warfare between my ears. Barry Trotz approached me one day in the locker room.

"Patti, did Mac (Brian MacLellan, our GM) talk to you?"

"No," I said.

"I think you're on waivers."

"What do you mean, you think?"

"Just talk to Mac."

I'm sure Trotz knew I was on waivers. He was the coach, after all. That's the last I heard from him. I wished he would have just given it to me straight. Something like, "Patti, you've been working hard to get in the lineup here with your injury, but honestly, we just don't see you in our plans going forward." I wouldn't have liked it, but I would've respected the decision and how it was handled. I have no hard feelings towards Barry, and I know the team loved him. I would have just handled it differently.

I talked to Mac, and he told me they wanted me to get some consistent games in Hershey. This may have been true, but again, the painfully obvious point was that I just wasn't in their plans. I was recovering from a major surgery and still dealing with symptoms. And the team was rolling, so sending me down was understandable. I was obviously pissed off. It was a contract year, and I had only played two NHL games and two AHL games all season. I needed to go down to Hershey and grind my way back. My neck had been feeling better because I hadn't played a game for a few weeks. I had been rehabbing like a madman and thought I might have to deal with a little more pain before I was fully healed. Wrong again.

Claire and I agreed that she would drive our stuff back home with her dad while I went to Hershey. The regular season was nearing its end, so she would just fly back out to visit in a couple of weeks. And there wasn't exactly a lot going on in Hershey anyway.

I grinded through the next three games. I was right back in the struggle to merely get out of bed. In one game, I received a blindside hit that left me stiff for days. I knew I needed to talk to the docs. The worry of permanent damage became greater and greater. I told the coach and started seeing some physiotherapists at Penn State University. Eventually, I went back on IR and flew out to LA to see my surgeon. He did an assessment and another MRI before delivering my final blow.

"I'm strongly advising you to not play with your current

symptoms. It might take a few more months or even years to feel better. The fusion is still fully intact, but because you have so much restriction and slight adjacent degeneration, the risk of an adjacent herniation and potential for a double fusion is too high."

"So, are you telling me my career is over?"

"Well, not necessarily, I can't make that decision for you. But you definitely shouldn't be playing with these symptoms. It's highly unsafe."

It had been almost one year since my surgery and my neck still felt terrible. I had only played a few games the whole year. I could take another few months or a year off, but I knew if I did that, no one would sign me. I left the clinic trying to process this information.

I called my parents and opened up about my struggles. Claire and I wanted to start a family soon. Health or hockey? I couldn't have both. I had to make a decision. I could have risked playing and possibly secured a nice contract, but I also wanted to live a normal life after hockey. There could have been major complications if I injured my neck again.

It was time. My career was over.

When I heard this decision echo in my mind, I thought of four things. First, I was crushed: my hockey career was over, after all I'd been through. All the pain I had overcome to not only make it to the NHL, but to stay there. Second, I respected the surgeon for being honest with me. He could have advised me it was okay to play to better the goodwill of his practice. Most of his surgeries were performed with the goal that the athlete would return to play. Third, part of me was relieved I wouldn't have to deal with so much pain and discomfort daily. By the end of this season in Hershey, I just sat in my shithole hotel room and drank. I didn't feel strong like the old Aaron. Deep down, I knew this injury was not something I should fuck with. Fourth, and final, I had to come to terms that this chapter of my life was closed. I had planned on playing professional hockey for at least five more years, potentially heading to Europe for a couple of years and seeing the world. Ideally, I would have left the game on my own terms.

Now I had to let all of that go. I needed to find the positives in my life. After all I'd been through, I'd played in the best league in the world for five years, albeit missing the majority of two full seasons because of injury. Not to mention the missed games from the lockout and being healthy scratched.

I only ended up playing one hundred and fourteen NHL games. But that's one hundred and fourteen more than 99.99% of hockey players in the world, and it filled me with pride knowing I was never supposed to play any type of pro hockey, let alone play in the NHL.

My wild hockey journey had ended in what seemed like the blink of an eye. I felt sad and scared, yet relieved. A weight lifted off of me, knowing I didn't have to lie anymore about what was going on. And I was looking forward to actually giving my neck rest without the dread of another, more serious, neck injury. But I didn't know what was next, and that scared the shit out of me. What did I even want at this point? I started thinking of different paths I could pursue for another career, but I didn't realize that over the next couple of years I would just be trying to survive.

Part II

"We must be willing to let go of the life we planned so as
to have the life that is waiting for us."
Joseph Campbell

Chapter 35

Calm Before the Storm

—

W hen I retired from the NHL, I thought my days as a fighter were over. I wouldn't be trading blows on the ice, but life would continue to throw punches at me in a big way. Claire and I found out she was pregnant a few weeks after we returned to Vernon. I wanted to be a dad more than anything and create a family like I had growing up. This gave me some light in a dark time when my identity as a hockey player had been stripped away.

I decided to just chill out and take the rest of the year off before exploring my next career move. I used to love fishing as a kid and had just gotten the family tin boat, The Buzzard (Papa Jerry's nickname). This was a third-generation hand-me-down. I spent a lot of time on the lake reflecting on my life, enjoying the picturesque landscape, refreshing mentally and physically, and reeling in some trophy-sized rainbow trout. The previous year had been tough on me in every aspect, so this was a nice reset. I also worked on our cabin throughout the summer. I'd fish all morning, work on projects during the day, and head out fishing again for the night bite. I slowly started to feel some sense of peace about what the future might hold in store for me and my family.

I also bought a motorcycle as my retirement present. My

neck was still pretty stiff, so I wasn't able to go on long rides at this point (I still struggle with this). I had secretly obtained my motorcycle license in D.C. during my second season there. We weren't contractually allowed to ride motorcycles, along with some other risky activities like skiing, bungee jumping, and skydiving. I kept this activity pretty well hidden from everyone else. Having stipulations like this in our contracts didn't mean guys didn't do them.

Obviously, it was only a problem if I got hurt. I remember chatting with one of my teammates on the Capitals that rode dirt bikes.

I always asked him, "What if you get hurt, break a leg or something?"

His reply was simple. "I would load myself up with painkillers, walk into the gym the next day and as soon as I got under the squat rack I would crumble."

This would allow him to still earn his paychecks since he would have gotten hurt during an "acceptable activity". Seemed like a foolproof plan to me!

We also bought a new house right when we got back to Vernon. It needed some work, so when we moved in toward the end of summer, I started knocking down walls. I completely remodeled the one end of the house, which took me a couple of months. I'd always loved working with my hands. Plus, I needed a man cave to house my twenty guitars and my hockey jerseys.

Having my first-born on the way seemed to pull my life back on track. I was still bummed about the way my hockey career ended. Moving into a new house, along with the anticipation of the baby arriving, really excited me for the next chapter. I really wished my new son or daughter could have seen me play in the NHL. But if I knew one thing, it was that life rarely went as planned. Time flew by, and before we knew it, winter had come – the baby was on his or her way. That's when everything went horribly wrong.

One morning Claire woke up really swollen, especially her face, legs, and feet. I poked fun at her, and we both laughed. Her pregnancy had been pretty smooth sailing until this point. We figured it was pretty normal to feel extra swollen during the end of pregnancy. But the swelling got worse this day – we knew something might have been up. We called our midwife and were able to see her the next day. The first test was to check her urine, which revealed she had proteinuria – high levels of protein in the urine. This was abnormal. Naturally, our stress levels quickly rose. *Was the baby okay?*

We drove up to the hospital to get a stress test to ensure this was, in fact, the case. I was so nervous going into this appointment. After an ultrasound, it was determined that the baby had stopped growing. Claire was diagnosed with preeclampsia, and we were scheduled for an emergency cesarean the next day. She was thirty-four weeks along. Luckily the baby was fine and healthy, but he or she needed to come out. The cesarean had already been a strong possibility because the baby had been in the footling breech position for a while. We just didn't realize it would be an *emergency* cesarean.

The onset of high blood pressure and a significant amount of protein in the urine are characteristics of preeclampsia. Abnormal blood vessel formation in the placenta typically causes this condition because there is an inefficient exchange of nutrients and waste products between baby and mother. Therefore, this inefficiency can make the mother sick. We were obviously worried, but apparently the delivery of the baby and placenta removal was a quick cure for preeclampsia and its symptoms.

There we were, in the hospital the next day, ready to meet our first born. Our due date was at the end of December, so the baby would come a few weeks earlier on December 9. We were just thankful this issue didn't pop up any earlier.

Claire went with the doctors to get situated. She received her epidural as I waited for the call outside the room. This was when the night from hell began. Because Claire's blood work was abnormal (her platelet count was low), the epidural wasn't able to be placed in the ideal spot. Or something along those lines. I just remember there was a complication with the epidural and her preeclampsia. Thus, it left one side of her body numb and the other side totally normal with full feeling. Imagine how that felt as they started making the incision. She screamed in pain. We asked for more freezing, but they couldn't administer more. I felt so bad for Claire; my heart wrenched. Going into the procedure, they said I could watch the baby being "delivered" but that all went out the window when Claire was writhing in pain. It was all a blur and there was a definite urgency to get the baby out of her sooner rather than later.

Finn Anthony Volpatti was born at 11:39 p.m. on December 9. At three weeks early, he weighed five pounds eleven ounces. I didn't realize it was a boy at first because I was so worried about Claire. She had almost passed out from the procedure and didn't look good at all. When I heard the cries, I figured the baby was healthy. Once I knew Claire was okay and being tended to, I went and held our baby boy. I was able to cut his cord and bring him over to Claire briefly before she went into recovery. The procedure wasn't what I had envisioned by any means, but I finally felt the pure joy that comes with bringing a life into this world. The three of us shared a special, yet brief, moment as a new family. Then they wheeled Claire away to recover from the surgery.

Finn and I moved to our room, and I placed him, this tiny little human, my little human, on my bare chest. I could hear my family outside the doors of the maternity ward. My mom's voice barked, "We know you're in there! Let us in!" But they didn't know what had just happened with the chaos of the birth. So, I took some time to just enjoy the moment. For twenty minutes, I closed my eyes with Finn sleeping on my chest, trying to reset after the craziness in the delivery room. I squeezed him and gave him a big kiss.

Finally, I let my family in to meet the newest addition to the Volpatti clan. I explained to them what had happened, so they waited until Claire came back to the room, gave her a quick hug, and let us be. By this time, it was almost 2:00 a.m., so we all drifted off to sleep. Everything seemed to be fine.

But Claire woke up a couple hours later with a pain in her chest that she described as terrible heartburn. We didn't think too much of it and the doctors gave her some medication since heartburn could happen with pregnancy. Again, we all slowly drifted off to sleep after Finn had a quick feed.

Another two hours later, she woke up again. I leaned over in the dark.

"You okay?"

She could barely get her words out.

"S-Something's wrong," she mumbled. "My head, I c-can barely see."

By the way she told me that, I knew something was definitely wrong. I rang the call bell for the nurse to come in. She flicked on the light as I said nervously, "She's really not feeling well."

The nurse took one look at Claire and ran to the edge of the bed to press a button. I heard "code pink" as she ran out of the room. I was in a state of confusion. "What's wrong?! What's code pink??" As the nurse ran to get help she yelled back, "Look at her neck!" I was now left alone with Claire as I quickly shot a glance at her neck. Her carotid artery was throbbing so hard, about to explode. It looked as if there was a tiny fist forcefully trying to push through the skin on her neck. I ran over to the edge of the bed, helplessly waiting for the nurse to return.

Chapter 36

Hellp

—

Code pink is the signal for pediatric or obstetrical emergencies. The nurse returned with more nurses by her side. Claire's blood pressure was 210/120. A hypertensive crisis is diagnosed when blood pressure is above 180/120, so we had well surpassed crisis territory. I was starting to fucking panic. I didn't even know blood pressure could get that high. One of the nurses said, "We need to get her blood pressure down NOW or she will stroke!" There was panic and desperation in the room. *Stroke?! Holy fuck.* I felt so helpless. There was nothing I could do except watch the nurses work on Claire. She was still coherent, but her eyes were forced shut, trying to deal with everything. She had a terrible headache and was having difficulties seeing.

They gave her a bunch of medications to bring her blood pressure down. About ten seconds after she received the meds, she tried telling me something as I held her hand. I couldn't hear her, so I put my ear right next to her mouth. Her voice was faint and fearful, but I could make out the words.

"My tongue, I can't breathe."

I quickly shot up and saw her struggling to get a breath. The look of dread and confusion on her face is forever etched in my memory. I was about to yell something, but the nurses already knew what was happening. "She's going into anaphylaxis!" Then I noticed a deep, red rash forming all over her body. During anaphylaxis, blood pressure typically nosedives, but Claire's blood pressure hadn't budged. It was still in crisis range. Her heart was racing, but it looked like the rest of her body was shutting down. Maybe her body couldn't handle these conflicting crises. That was when I saw the light start to leave her eyes. I thought I was about to watch my wife die right in front of me. All I could do was watch in complete shock.

It didn't take long before a handful of other doctors and nurses entered our room. Alarms started ringing and buzzing, further exacerbating the dread of the situation. "Stay with us hun," one nurse said to her. I remember screaming, "No, no, no, please." Her eyes rolled back and right as it looked like she was having a seizure, they injected her with the epi-pen. Before I knew it, she was being rushed down the hallway. I ran right beside her, totally oblivious to the fact that Finn had been in the room the entire time. I yelled at one of the nurses as we sprinted down the hallway. "Can you please watch our son?"

The doctors worked on her as they rushed her to the ICU. By this time, they had her shirt cut open and the defibrillator ready. I assumed they were expecting the worst. It seemed they didn't know what would happen first, a stroke or her heart flatlining. I'll never forget the image of Claire getting wheeled up to the ICU. Her eyes shut, her bare chest exposed, the pads of the defibrillator hovering and ready to shock her back to life, and the oxygen mask over her face as the nurses scrambled to get IVs hooked to her. The helplessness and shock completely froze me. I ran beside the bed, totally silent and terrified beyond my comprehension.

After what felt like an eternity, we were in the ICU and Claire was finally conscious, but barely. I knew she wasn't out of the woods by any stretch because the internists were having a very urgent debate about what treatment to give her. No one knew the full story yet. They just wanted to get her stable first before running tests. I remember hearing the words severe preeclampsia, eclampsia, help syndrome (which I soon found out was called HELLP syndrome), liver failure, anaphylaxis, nitric oxide, and a bunch of other dialogue I didn't understand. All the while, I was sitting beside Claire, squeezing her hand as hard as I could. I hadn't felt a squeeze back in minutes.

Within another minute or two, the internists had made their decision and started administering a bunch of different medications. Her blood pressure came down to about 180/100, which was better, but still pushing the red zone of a crisis. The ultrasound technician came up quickly and found what looked to be a large clot in one of Claire's organs. The doctors relayed to me how serious this was. They would need to add potent blood thinners to the cocktail of medications she had in her body. Apparently, she had many other small clots as well, which was one of the symptoms of HELLP syndrome.

I don't know how much time went by before they deemed Claire stable, maybe an hour or two. She was conscious, but not coherent, as they had her heavily medicated. The internist finally came to talk to me. I still hadn't processed everything that had just happened. It was about 8:00 a.m. I don't remember the exact words he relayed to me, but this is basically what I recall (and what I later learned from several tests and follow-ups):

Claire was stable, but not out of the woods yet. She had severe preeclampsia that was very close to escalating to eclampsia, seizures, and a stroke. Typically, with preeclampsia, the birth of the child and the placenta is usually a quick cure. But in some rare cases, the major onset of symptoms can happen post-delivery. Unfortunately, Claire quickly developed other very rare complications related to postpartum preeclampsia, including thromboembolism and HELLP syndrome. Thromboembolism is the blockage of a major blood vessel by a clot (which they saw on the ultrasound) and can prove very dangerous, if not deadly. They gave her Heparin, which is a potent intravenous blood thinner. This would ensure the clot didn't get any larger so the body could then reabsorb it. HELLP syndrome stands for hemolysis, elevated liver enzymes, and low platelet count. Her red blood cells were rupturing, and her liver had started shutting down.

To make everything even more complicated, she experienced a severe allergic reaction to one of the medications during this severe hypertensive moment. When I asked more about this, the doctor was pretty certain she wasn't actually allergic. Her body probably just went into severe shock and rejected the medicine. At this moment, their biggest concern was the blood clot and monitoring that. Unfortunately, she would likely lose a lot of blood because she had just undergone a cesarean and was now on Heparin. There would need to be some sort of drainage inserted to help with the blood that would seep from her wound.

I tried to digest all of this. All I cared about was whether she was going to survive. I expressed my concern over her bleeding so much, but the clot was the highest threat to her health, not losing blood. That could be mediated with blood transfusions, something I had remembered from my stay in the burn unit. The chances of developing HELLP syndrome are 0.24% in first pregnancies, let alone all the other rare complications culminating in this grand shitshow. This was truly a perfect storm scenario – an extremely rare cascade of events.

I sat on the edge of Claire's bed, still in shock over everything that had just transpired in the last couple of hours. She had endless tubes and IV lines hooked up to her. There must have been twenty bags of intravenous medicine hanging from bags on her IV tower. As my shock wore off, my emotions started pouring out. I broke down and started punching the bed by her feet in anger. The tears started pouring out of me and I couldn't control the flood of emotions. She continued to just lie there as I watched her lifeless body. As much as I tried to fight these feelings back, I was no match for them.

I didn't want to leave Claire, but I needed to get back to Finn in the maternity ward, one floor down. I was worried sick. *What if she has another crisis or goes into anaphylaxis again?* I opened the doors and called my parents.

They answered the call as I tried to gather myself and remain strong. My parents had driven the two hours back to Revelstoke after the quick visit just eight hours prior. They were very familiar with the drive because they made it to every home game when I played for the Vipers.

"It's Claire..." I fought back more tears and couldn't bring myself to say anything more.

"Bud? What's wrong?"

"She- she almost died."

"What!? What happened? Is she okay now?"

Another ten seconds went by as I tried to get myself together. "She's stable, but not awake. It was so scary to watch. I thought I watched her die right in front of me."

"Oh my god, I'm so sorry, bud."

There was silence for a while as I could feel the emotion through the phone. "We will be there in a few hours, okay?"

"Okay."

"See you soon, Claire is strong, she will be okay."

"Yeah, okay see you soon."

I came back to the maternity ward to find Finn sleeping. The nurses all gave me a look of sincere empathy. I asked how Finn was doing and they said he had been sleeping happily for the most part. Now it was time to talk about feeding him. Claire wasn't in a position to do so, and it was important for both of us that he breastfeed for the first year. Luckily, there was a bunch of milk available in the maternity ward and in the milk bank for situations like this, or situations where the mother simply couldn't breastfeed.

One of the nurses coached me on how to feed Finn with a tiny plastic tube taped to my pinky finger. They connected this tube to a test-tube-like container that held the milk (warmed up beforehand since it had been refrigerated). Since Finn was small and premature, he needed to be woken up every couple of hours to feed. I picked him up, laid him on my lap and put my finger and tube in his mouth while I held the tube of milk in the other hand. The trick was to not hold the milk too high because gravity would force it into his little mouth. I was supposed to hold it level so he would have to suck, similar to breastfeeding. I couldn't believe it – it worked. I felt so many things. I was full of happiness and joy while I watched Finn fill his little belly. But I was also consumed with fear, anger, and disbelief as I knew Claire was laying right above us in a nightmare she didn't even know she was living.

I called her family next and filled them in on the situation. Everyone was so scared, but this would only get worse once they saw her lifeless body. For the next two days, I put on a lot of miles, moving from floor to floor. I would feed Finn, then my family or Claire's would take turns watching him as I went and sat by Claire's bed. I coached them on how to feed Finn during the night so I could be with Claire. I'd come down every few hours to check on him. If he was sleeping, I'd just rub his little head and give him a kiss.

Claire finally woke up on the second day in the ICU, but she couldn't speak. She just opened her eyes briefly but couldn't stay awake.

The tears filled my eyes. I whispered in her ear, "I thought I lost you. You are a strong woman and you're going to be fine, okay. Finn is doing great. He is downstairs with our families. I love you so much."

Her eyes stayed closed, but tears started rolling down her face. I knew she could hear me. I felt sick, especially because she couldn't hold her son. But her tears also reassured me as I figured this meant she was going to be okay. I couldn't imagine what was going through her head at that moment.

There weren't many visitors allowed in the ICU, so both our parents were allowed to visit her briefly – that was it. After this initial visit, I was the only one allowed to move back and forth, so I was constantly relaying how she was doing. Claire wasn't a pretty sight, so it was hard for me to be real with everyone.

I tried catching small bits of sleep next to Claire but couldn't. I just held her hand all night and watched her, hoping her blood pressure would come down. I stared at that fucking screen for three straight days, wondering what the coming hours would bring. Her blood pressure held strong at 170/100.

By the third day, Claire was more alert. She still had a terrible headache. The doctors weren't totally sure why her blood pressure wasn't coming down, but at least it wasn't climbing. The clot seemed to get smaller but still posed a threat. The Heparin was causing a lot of bleeding and they actually had to cut open the one side of her wound to relieve the pressure. She was continuously getting her dressings changed and the wound drained. They packed the wound to mitigate the bleeding, but the gauze was saturated every time they changed it. It reminded me of being in the burn unit – dressing change after dressing change.

"Can I see Finn?" Claire croaked. I knew he wasn't allowed in the ICU because of the risks posed to him and other patients. But I pleaded my case to the ICU doctors, and they agreed to let us bring Finn up for a quick visit, just this one time. I sprinted down to grab him.

Claire had so many IV lines going into both arms. There were countless nodes on her chest and she couldn't really grab Finn. I opened her shirt, moved all the lines and cords out of the way as best I could, and set Finn down on her. She hadn't seen him in days, and even though she wasn't aware for the first couple days, I knew it was heart-wrenching for her to not be around Finn. She started crying, and I immediately followed. We both shared this feeling of helplessness, but there was finally the first inkling of a reprieve knowing she was awake. Claire then asked if she could feed Finn. The answer, however, was a definite no because of the medications pumping through her veins. Especially the nitric oxide, a potent vasodilator.

I felt sick taking Finn away from her, but she was falling asleep, and we weren't allowed to stay long, anyway. At about 10:00 p.m. that night, Claire asked me, "Have you slept?"

I hadn't. It had been three days.

"Why don't you go home and get some sleep? I'm okay."

"I don't think I'll be able to. I don't want to leave your side."

"Just try. I'll be okay here."

I'm not sure if she fully understood how serious her situation was at this point. Her blood pressure hadn't budged, and the clot was still there. And she had an open wound on her stomach that continued to bleed.

I was reluctant but knew I couldn't stay awake forever and the doctors assured me she was stable. I grabbed our dog Rufus from her dad's house, went home and headed for a walk around our ten-acre property. I walked into our barn and my emotions took over. I fell to my knees and wept like a baby. I relived the moment when everything went awry – when Claire was fighting for her life. I don't know how long I cried for, but it felt like hours. I'm not religious, but I prayed that night. I prayed that Claire would be okay. I thanked God for the nurses and internists that acted so fast and diligently. It was amazing how calm they were during such an intense crisis. I vowed I would be forever grateful if she returned home healthy.

As my crying subsided, I laid against a hay bale with Rufus curled up next to me. I closed my eyes and felt the exhaustion set in. I thought about getting up and going inside, but there was something peaceful about just laying in hay with Rufus. I was dressed warmly, so I kept my eyes closed and drifted off to sleep. I woke up a few hours later. When I looked at my phone, I saw I had a missed call and a voicemail.

It was Claire. She was crying. They had to cauterize her wound because she was bleeding so much. She described the torture and said she wished I had been there. I couldn't imagine how much cauterizing an open wound would hurt, even with freezing. The missed call was over two hours ago. I felt terrible. Claire needed me, and I hadn't been there. *I knew I shouldn't have left.*

I rushed back to the hospital. Claire was asleep as I talked to the nurse. "It's been a tough night," she said. "That's a very painful process she had. But we needed to slow the bleeding." That was the problem – she still needed the Heparin, but it was causing a lot of bleeding through her open c-section wound. This led to the necessity of cauterizing the wound.

I went to check on Finn. He was in good hands with our families. Claire's sister even breastfed Finn a few times since she'd had a baby a few months prior. Finn had a bit of a smorgasbord in terms of milk from different women – from the boob and from multiple donations from the milk bank.

I returned to Claire's side until she woke up in the morning. "I'm so sorry," I said.

"It's okay, I'm happy you're here now. It hurt so much. Did you get some sleep?"

"A little."

Claire was in the ICU for a week. Once her blood pressure came down to about 150/90, she was allowed to return to the maternity ward. She went off Heparin because the clot was finally gone and she could now take the blood pressure medications orally. Unfortunately, she still had a lot of pain surrounding her wound. The wound had been essentially open and bleeding for a week, even with the cauterization. The discomfort became worse, and after another ultrasound, it was determined she needed to have surgery to essentially perform the cesarean again. There was a large internal hematoma that was the primary cause of her pain. Claire broke down. She was defeated. We were both frustrated and just wanted this nightmare to end. The only positive thing was that Finn seemed totally healthy.

Claire recovered for a couple more days and they finally discharged her on the tenth day. After ten days of hell, we were finally home. We were ready for her to recover and for us to start life with our new son.

Chapter 37

Go Live Your Life

—

It was almost Christmas, but we were planning on just laying low. Claire was still recovering, and we were both trying to unpack the entire experience from the hospital. Our parents both popped in for quick visits. Aside from this, we just chilled out for a month. I have to give Claire credit. She pumped and dumped her breastmilk for weeks until she was off her meds. A lot of women would have said fuck it and just given up. She was determined to make it work for Finn and have that bonding she never got with him in the beginning. I thought it was a miracle she was able to breastfeed at all after what her body had been through. I was just so happy I had my wife back and that our family was intact. As our son lay beside us in his bassinet, I squeezed her as tightly as I could.

The next two months flew by, which was surprising since we weren't doing much except going on long walks as a family. It was almost the end of February when I made a quick trip to Vancouver. I had my motorcycle custom-painted several months prior, and the parts were finally ready to be picked up. My parents were also in Kamloops for a little shopping getaway. That's what they had told me, anyway. It worked perfectly for a brief visit since I drove right through there. When I left Vancouver, I called my mom. "We're still good to meet up for a late lunch?"

"Yep! Sounds good."

As I pulled into Kamloops, I called her again. No answer. Once I got to the restaurant, I discovered they weren't there. Another thirty minutes went by, and another phone call was unanswered. I was getting a little worried.

Finally, my mom called me. "Hey, bud, sorry we can't hide it anymore. We're at the hospital. That's the reason we're in town. Dad's been getting some tests done. I'm sure it's nothing, but we just want to be sure."

"Okay..." I didn't really know what to think. "You're sure everything is fine?"

"Yep. You can meet us here and we can head out for a bite after?"

"Sounds good. Where do I go?"

"We're in Neurodiagnostics."

My worries escalated after hearing this. "Okay, see you soon."

I battled my terrible sense of direction and finally found my way to the Neurodiagnostic area of the hospital. An hour went by. Then another hour. I texted my mom a couple of times but heard nothing back. That couldn't be good.

Finally, just Mom came walking out. She was shaking her head as tears filled her eyes. "Mother fucker," she said. I knew it was bad. Right away, I figured it was cancer or something.

I didn't know what to say as she hugged me.

"Dad has ALS."

The only thought that infiltrated my mind in that moment was a brief image of Dad in a wheelchair, unable to care for himself in any capacity. He was such an athletic and powerful man with a true zest for life. *How could he possibly have such a devastating disease? How much time does he have?* An incomprehensible future contaminated my every thought.

My mom and I embraced harder now as the tears started

flowing. Then I was overcome with worry for her and her future. At fifty years old, she was still so young. What would the rest of her life look like without Dad? He came walking out a few minutes later. I saw defeat in his eyes. I hugged him and didn't want to let go. "I'm sorry," I said.

"I didn't want you to find out like this, Hub."

"How do they know? Could it be something else?"

"They're sure."

ALS is also known as Lou Gehrig's disease, or Amyotrophic Lateral Sclerosis. After the Ice Bucket Challenge a year earlier, more people became familiar with this terrible disease. This was the worst-case scenario. A terminal illness where the average survival time is two to four years but can be as quick as one year. With ALS, the motor neurons stop communicating with the muscles and one is left to atrophy and waste away to nothing. Think of Steven Hawking – a brilliant mind trapped in a lifeless body. The doctor basically told my dad to enjoy the next six months, because the disease could progress rapidly. Dad was only fifty-four.

We didn't go out for food. We just sat in the parking lot trying to cope with everything. Dad was going to die, and most likely sooner rather than later. I still hadn't fully unpacked the trauma surrounding Finn's birth, and now this. My dad was the best father on the planet, and we were best friends. The thought of losing him shattered my world.

Chapter 38

The Power of Choice

—

After I retired from the NHL, life hit me harder than any of the shots I had received on the ice. I wasn't prepared for the emotional toll it would take on me. I had gone through physical and mental adversity in the past, but this emotional and spiritual adversity was a completely different beast.

Looking back, we realized Dad most likely had ALS a year before this diagnosis. The incident with his suitcase on the father-and-son road trip with the Capitals made more sense now. He was too weak to lift the suitcase overhead because he had been experiencing the symptoms of ALS. His speech slurred when he was cold at work, and one day he couldn't lift the tailgate up on his work truck. He was less than a year from retirement with CP Railway, but officially retired the day after the diagnosis. CP honored his full pension.

The initial shock of the diagnosis subsided a couple weeks later. We realized that the days were still passing by, and Dad was still here – still alive and well. We all dealt with the grief differently. For me, I felt a lot of anger, fear, and sadness. The emotions surrounding grief came in waves. Dad was adamant that he would not let ALS rob him of living an amazing life while he was still alive. He and my mom went traveling throughout Asia for a month that summer and had a blast.

They were definitely living like he was dying.

As the months passed, he had truly accepted his disease and worked to not let the stress affect him. We had some deep talks where he shared his thoughts. He said he had lived an amazing life, experienced everything he could have imagined, married the woman of his dreams, and created a beautiful family. And Brianne and I were all grown up with kids of our own. He didn't have to worry about us. The one worry he had, however, was about my mom. She had a lot more life to live – was she going to be okay? I admired my dad even more throughout these initial months after diagnosis. He was honest and raw.

Aside from the worries regarding Mom, he seemed at peace – content to bring love and joy to the world every day that he woke up. I couldn't imagine trying to live life with a looming death sentence. There were so many unknowns with ALS. When would he lose function in his arms? When would he need a wheelchair, a feeding tube, or a ventilator? We were all consumed by these thoughts, and I'm sure Dad was as well. But he didn't talk much about his disease. We all tried to continue on, just as we'd done before the diagnosis. He truly lived for the present, before and after life with ALS.

Personally, I had some great trips with Dad that summer. We rocked out at a ZZ Top concert and partied into the morning after a Guns n' Roses show in Vancouver. We went on a couple motorcycle trips with my brother-in-law, Tally, and a couple of my dad's friends – one trip to Whistler and one to Washington State. Dad was still able to ride with us on his beautiful, bright red Victory cruiser.

I wanted him to see Finn as much as possible. Maybe Finn wouldn't remember Papa, but either way, the three Anthonys were going to create as many lasting memories as we could. We all shared that name – Anthony. It had been passed down for generations. Finn was the fifth-generation Anthony Volpatti, even though Anthony was his legal middle name. I go by Aaron, my middle name, since Dad went by Tony.

Claire and I started drifting apart after all the trauma and adversity. We didn't agree on much and were constantly bickering with each other. When I was playing in the NHL, we never went through any real adversity in our relationship. We had no cares in the world and lived it up. I had my difficulties with hockey, but she and I just simply had fun. We were able to cultivate a loving relationship after our tumultuous past. But we hadn't really dived in to what kind of people we were, what our values were, what kinds of parenting styles we would have, or what we wanted the future to look like.

As it would turn out, we were on very different sides of the spectrum regarding all of these points, and the adversity we went through post hockey exposed these misalignments in our relationship and who we were as people. I didn't understand this at the time. It never crossed my mind to think if Claire and I were truly a great match for each other. We just both moved forward by how we felt. And we felt love. I figured that was all that mattered. But we were deteriorating more and more as time passed by, no matter how hard we tried to work on things.

Before I knew it, a year and a half had passed since I retired from professional hockey. Like many other retired pro athletes, I struggled with what I wanted to do next. What was my next career going to be? Between dealing with the lingering symptoms of my neck injury and early retirement, my identity crisis, the trauma of Finn's birth, my dad's diagnosis, a struggling marriage, and raising a child, I had a lot going on. The relentless chatter in my head stressed me out. *What are you going to do? You're only thirty-one years old. I'm just trying to fucking survive right now, spend this last bit of time with my dad, and get my relationship back with my wife.*

I'd made enough money to take some time off, but not the

kind of money a lot of NHL players made. League minimum was great cash, but not the kind you could retire on, especially after just five and a half years. I explored the idea of working with the NHL or NHLPA on concussion awareness. Few NHL players had an Ivy League degree in Human Biology – if any. I thought about going back to school to become a doctor, but I'd be forty by the time I'd finish everything, so I opted not to go down that road. I looked heavily into real estate development, starting my own business, and running a gym to train hockey players. You name it, I researched the shit out of it.

From the time I started making real money I became interested in investing. Now, I started heavily researching companies and trading stocks online. I decided to enroll in the Canadian Securities Course. If I enjoyed it, I would pursue a career in wealth management.

Claire and I essentially became roommates for the last year we were together. Eventually, there weren't many good days, if any. We pushed back against each other when our values clashed, and we both felt totally unsupported. The wedge between us kept growing and growing. I constantly thought back to that night in the barn and remembered the promise I made to myself. I had gotten Claire back, just like I prayed for. Now we were on the brink of divorce.

I really enjoyed the Canadian Securities Course, so I took a job in wealth management in the summer of 2017. I was initially excited, but after a few months I realized the passion wasn't there. I was really struggling with my identity. I had been a hockey player for thirty years and now I was working an office job that didn't ignite my soul in the least. Was this what the rest of my life was supposed to look like? It didn't help that my world around me was crumbling with my dad's illness continuing to progress and my wife and I living as contentious roommates. Every day I thought to myself, *How the fuck did I get here? How did this all happen so fast? Just two years ago, I was playing in the NHL, and I was happily married.*

Any married couple knows that marriage can be one of the most challenging, yet rewarding, journeys in life. As my friend Chewy once said, "Marriage is like a bath. You have to keep adding warm water." As hard as things may be, warm water is available when there is still love, respect, and loyalty in the relationship. The water may be murky with disagreements, fights, or lack of passion, but warm water is still added because there is love hiding somewhere below all the shit. Claire and I hadn't added warm water for a long time.

After a short separation, things finally blew up, and we agreed to divorce in 2018. I don't want to take away from the love that Claire and I once shared. It was very real and raw, like young love can be, but we weren't a great match for each other. A deeper level of connection was missing, something I would only realize later in my life. Maybe we should have dug deeper into why we were always on and off. Regardless of all of this, I was still crushed. I felt a tremendous amount of guilt because I thought I had failed Finn as a father. If anything, Claire and I were meant to reunite in order to create such a magical little boy.

I had strived to be the kind of dad my own father was, and now I felt like I had failed my family. On the flipside, I didn't believe in staying together just for the sake of Finn. What would this teach him about relationships? At least if Claire and I both had a strong partnership with someone else, Finn would be exposed to loving relationships from both of us. Having two homes wouldn't be ideal, but I knew that him being surrounded by love trumped everything.

Deep down, I knew I would find someone else, but that didn't soothe the initial pain of divorce. The next few months were probably the darkest of my life. I was completely lost. I often sat at my office desk lost in thought and depressed about what my life had turned into. I was soon to be divorced. When I didn't have my son, I missed him so fucking much. I felt like a failure. My dad was dying, my neck fucking hurt, and I was working a job that was sucking the life out of me. I tried to numb the pain with as much sex and booze as I could in the summer of 2018. That provided short-term gratification. But as the months went on, I was only dragged deeper into the reality of my situation – or what I perceived to be the shitty reality of my life. I was weak and pathetic, not curious and resilient. I wouldn't show Finn a loving relationship if I kept on my current path.

I reached my breaking point by the end of the summer. Another light bulb went off. I was awoken with another powerful realization – a new fork in the road. Finn was two and a half years old.

I was hungover one day, again, from partying the night before. Finn asked me to go play outside with him and I replied with, "Sorry, buddy, Daddy isn't feeling good." I put on a show for him and then it hit me. *You've never turned down an opportunity to play with Finn. Look at you, you're not even showing up for your son anymore. You're a bum. This is exactly what you said you would never do.* I always took immense pride in being a wonderful, attentive, and active dad. I wanted to create the same relationship my dad and I shared. At that moment, I decided that I had had enough. "Come on, dude, let's get out of here." I gave him a big hug and from that day forward, I made a choice to untie the shackles around my feet. I would no longer let that weight pull me down. It had sucked the life out of me, and I had rolled over and died. I needed to get the old me back.

There is great empowerment when we make a definitive choice. Remember, we always have a choice, no matter the circumstances. How we think, act, and react – what we choose to believe in or focus on. There is always a choice to be made. These choices, or forks in the road, have initiated the most impactful changes in my life. So, after this latest fork in the road, I reflected on all the lessons I'd learned about Visualization and manifestation.

Instead of thinking about what was wrong with my life, I started thinking about all the great things surrounding me. Having gratitude instantly helped initiate change. I started visualizing what I wanted every day: an amazing woman, a tight-knit family, a fulfilling career, that unstoppable inner drive, and a curiosity for life. I manifested it every day. I was going to walk around as the person I wanted to be and live in that reality. A life full of love, abundance, and happiness. I was still here and ready to fight again. Ready to fight for the life I wanted, not roll over as a victim of the perceptions of my reality. And just like every other time in my life, as soon as I flipped that internal switch to visualize what I wanted, everything changed.

Chapter 39

Birdie

—

I decided to take a leave of absence from work. My office was leaving my soul empty and draining my energy. I needed purpose again, and I knew it was out there for me to find. I was craving some sort of self-discovery and some physical adversity. I had discovered who I really was and what I was truly capable of in that burn unit, so I started thinking, *What's the hardest thing I can do?* After some research, I discovered the Ironman triathlon. It was perfect. A 3.86 kilometer swim, 180 kilometer bike, and a 42 kilometer marathon to finish. I had never swam (I didn't drown but was an overall terrible swimmer), never been on a road bike, and never ran more than ten kilometers at a time. It would be a challenge indeed. I decided to raise money for ALS in the process and spend more time with my family in Revelstoke.

I also opened up to the idea of dating again. I wasn't looking for a commitment this early after divorce, but I wasn't going to keep myself closed off to that possibility like I'd done after my split. I figured I would give the dating apps a shot. I was more of a traditionalist when it came to romance, but something new could be fun. I gave myself permission to just have some casual relationships and maybe something more down the road if it made sense. I was in full training mode for the Ironman and was feeling way better physically, emotionally, and spiritually.

After I consulted some of my old college buddies on how to set up a dating app profile, it didn't take long to meet this stunning brunette. I was actually driving through New York City on the way to a friend's wedding when she messaged me. The banter started flowing effortlessly. Right away, I knew she had a great sense of humor and was clearly very attractive from her profile pictures.

Michelle and I met at Gallagher's Canyon golf course in Kelowna a week or so later. I was at the counter of the pro shop when she walked in. It felt like a scene out of a romcom movie. The wind blew her long brown hair over her shoulder as she opened the door. She looked around and met my gaze. She was even more beautiful in person, and I could see her amazing blue eyes from a distance. I gave her a hug as we met and formally introduced ourselves. We held a long gaze and smiled, as if to say, *Shit, she/he is even better looking in person! Ya never know with these dating apps.*

Michelle and I instantly clicked. She seemed so free, and she exuded this unrelenting zest for life and adventure. We continued to share some stories as we headed to the first tee box. She could crank out a mean drive but she ended up losing a couple of friendly bets over the next few holes. This resulted in her playing barefoot and showing off some dance moves. Unbeknownst to me, she had danced professionally, so this was another pleasant surprise.

It was so easy and refreshing being around her. The more we talked, the more we realized how crazy it was that we were on this date. Of all the places on this earth we had been, and the completely different paths we had gone down, here we were at a golf course in Kelowna, B.C. I mean, I didn't advertise that I had a son (that came up on our second date when she climbed in my truck and saw a car seat, surprise!), but I said I had gone through a divorce earlier that year. I told her how I had played hockey all over North America and settled down in small town Vernon. I wished I had the opportunity to go play in Europe, but it never worked out because of my neck injury.

Turned out it was her first date on a dating app as well. She was from Calgary and had left a corporate oil and gas job to move to Spain and work for a start-up. She had worked in commodity derivatives at a major Canadian bank and now worked in Finance for a tech company, remotely. She slowly started checking off every box. Not that I was keeping track, but it was hard not to notice. Michelle was beautiful, funny, free, curious, smart, and had a love for travel. She lived abroad for a few years, but wanted to return to Canada. She moved back to Kelowna – a tech hub – which was about forty minutes from Vernon. After her latest relationship, she was on the verge of moving back to Calgary but figured she would give the app thing a try as well.

She had been busy pursuing her career and exploring the world. I had been playing hockey and settling down with a family. Everything in our lives had to unfold exactly as it had for us to come together on that day.

I still can't explain it, but right from the get-go, I had this feeling like I had seen Michelle before. Or even met her briefly somewhere. Maybe it was in a different lifetime, in our younger days, or at the Calgary Stampede. I couldn't put my finger on it, it was just this feeling I had. Like we had met when our worlds weren't ready to collide. There was this very strong energy present when she was around. As if our energetic fields were greatly amplified.

Of course, it was still early on our first date, but I couldn't ignore this energy. We were about six holes into our round, and I figured I would make my move. Maybe a little early, but I wanted to kiss her badly. Our flirting had escalated with every passing hole. As we walked up to the par three tee box, I looked at her and said, "Since you keep losing these bets, how about a shot at redemption? KP (closest to the hole)?"

She walked closer in her bare feet, "Okay sure, what are we playing for?"

"Well, I really want to kiss you, so if I'm closer than you, well… I'm going to kiss you." She hit from the closest tee box, and I was at the back, so this seemed relatively fair.

"You're not going to get closer," she said playfully.

"We'll see," I smiled back.

It was a foolproof plan because I could tell she wanted to kiss me too, or at least I thought so. I stepped up to the ball and hit it about five feet from the pin.

"You must really want to kiss me, eh?" she said.

"How can you tell?"

I'm about a ten handicap so it wasn't completely out of the ordinary to have the odd great shot. She clearly shanked her ball on purpose when it was her turn. I made my birdie and let the tension build until we reached the cart. I was mesmerized by her amazing blue eyes again. I slowly went in for the kiss. Our lips locked and stayed locked until the next group was coming up to the green.

A fire was lit inside both of us. There was something about this woman. I barely knew her, but everything seemed so right. Our date lasted late into the night after trivia night at a local pub. I got back to my tiny apartment later that night and couldn't wipe the smile off my face. I couldn't wait to see her again.

Chapter 40

Amor

—

The beginning of a relationship is always edgy and fun, with a lot of unknowns. Since we went into the date with no expectations, we were able to just be free. I had thought about her every second since I kissed her goodnight, so I called her the next day to arrange another date.

I also wasn't working (just training full-time and raising money for my Ironman race) and she had a fairly flexible schedule with her work. I think this allowed us to bond on another level. We kept it pretty casual for the first few months as we both did some traveling, but there was something so captivating and intoxicating about Michelle. We started spending more and more nights together, and I missed her when she wasn't around. I knew I was in trouble, Michelle was unlike any woman I'd met that entire summer, and as I'd find out over the next few months, unlike any woman I'd met in my entire life.

We had a fun inside joke as well. When people asked how we met, we would tell them it was at an open mic night: I was playing at a local pub or brewery, which I had actually done many times, and she came up to request a song. I agreed to play her song under one condition, that she sing me a song at the bar over a beer after. She smiled and agreed.

Michelle and I joked that it would have eventually gone down like this, and that the dating app, Bumble, just expedited our meeting. There is sometimes a stigma around meeting on dating apps. I think there is probably an aspect of sifting through some less-than-ideal partners and the tax that comes with that but it doesn't mean the good ones aren't out there as well.

We knew some people spent years on these apps with little luck, so we considered ourselves lucky in that regard. Both each other's first and last Bumble date.

We made trips to Vancouver and Washington, D.C., went on overnight motorcycle trips and slept on beaches, attended some fun costume parties, and she even trained with me. Turned out she was a great swimmer as well.

Aside from my feelings and deep connection with Michelle, there was something else that stuck out to me when we were out in public. Something I had never experienced before. Not that I needed vetting for our relationship, but I could not believe how many people went out of their way to pull us aside and tell us that we had something very special. We could be at a restaurant, at a bar, at a friend's house playing games, or at the grocery store. I mean people would literally grab our hands, or come up and interrupt us, and say things like, "I rarely approach people like this, but I felt a strong urge to say how amazing you two are together, and that you have such an intense connection. I can literally feel it." Complete strangers, time and time again, would say things like this. Since other people could feel our intense energy too, how could I not think we had something special? This was exactly what I had manifested, except it was so much more.

We went to Spain in the spring of 2019, which was such an amazing trip. Since Michelle had lived there and in other Spanish speaking countries, she was completely fluent. We were in the Parc de la Ciutadella in Barcelona when our tour guide started talking about the Roman goddess Aurora. Her and her golden chariot stood in marble stone at the top of the cascada, or waterfall. She was the goddess of dawn and would fly across the sky, turning darkness into daylight. Hence the term Aurora Borealis, or dawn of the north – also known as the Northern Lights. Depending on the cultural group, the lights could have different meanings. This instantly ignited something inside of me. *No matter how dark the night was, Aurora always brought daylight. No matter how dark the night, the light will always break through.* I started thinking about the darkness I had overcome on my journey to the NHL. I thought about the darkness I had experienced over the last couple of years, and how I was here now, where there was light. *The light will always break through.* Right then, I looked over at Michelle as she looked back and smiled. Her intoxicating blue eyes took hold of me, as they always did. I knew I had been falling for Michelle before our trip, but that was when it really hit me. I wasn't just falling anymore, I was madly in love with this woman.

I told Michelle I loved her a few days later on a river in Girona, Spain. It was all happening again. My life changed as soon as I made the choice to visualize and manifest the life I wanted. To fight for what I loved. And I loved Michelle with all my being.

Now there was only one minor problem about this. It scared me. I was afraid of getting hurt again and going through another heartbreak. My divorce had tainted me. I couldn't get over this fear that things wouldn't work out, regardless of the fact that I had never felt this deep of a connection before. So I only gave Michelle ninety percent of me. I kept the other ten percent locked away as protection for myself and Finn from future heartbreak. This ten percent mostly reared its ugly head when we were around Finn. I wanted to fully succumb to my feelings when the three of us were together, but it was extremely difficult for me. When it was just me and Michelle, I felt like that guard was let down. We could just be free and live in our love. Keeping this wall up wasn't fair to me, but more importantly, it wasn't fair to Michelle. This was incredibly hard on her as time went on, and it's a regret I still carry. But I, like her, was just trying to navigate this new life with another little human, Finn. Our love still trumped any hardships, and our ability to communicate about the hard stuff became vital.

I wanted to show up better for Michelle, so I started talking to other people, including a counselor. We dove into my fears and the trauma I had experienced. I still hadn't fully unpacked the last few years and the emotional toll it had taken on me. I also hadn't talked with anyone about my dad, who was still battling ALS. It didn't take long for me to come to a powerful realization.

Emotional adversity or trauma differed from the physical and mental adversity I had been through on my journey to the NHL. Although there was a small element of emotional adversity in the burn unit, I hadn't experienced this kind of emotional turmoil until much later in life. The hockey culture had also taught me to never show weakness. Now I realized that opening up and talking about trauma was a sign of great strength, not weakness.

I had a great childhood and was very supported in anything I did, and it wasn't until my thirties that life had really hit me. I was a mature man, but my therapist pointed out that I was still that young boy in many emotional aspects. I was a very determined, resilient, and gritty man that used to fight for a living. But when I was dealt this hand of extreme emotional adversity after retirement, I didn't know how to cope with it. I didn't have the tools. We talked more about how Visualization had impacted my life and how I had let it slip the last few years, only to revisit it before I met Michelle. This was a technique that she agreed would help immensely.

I had been focusing on all the negatives surrounding the adversity before I had met Michelle. As soon as I flipped my internal dialogue, the universe brought us together. Now, I had this unparalleled connection and love with her. This would be the last time I ever discounted the power of the mind and manifestation. It had proved so true to me time and time again.

I was scheduled to go back to work after my long leave of absence, but to be honest, I was dreading it. Going back to sitting in the office was not appealing. I remember talking to my dad and he really helped put things into perspective.

"Do you see yourself doing this job five years from now?"

"No," I replied. "Then I think you have your answer."

I quit that day.

Life was too short. My dad reminded me of this. Thankfully, he could still speak with his slow-progressing ALS. He was the epitome of someone that lived for each and every moment. I was thankful for my time at the bank, and I learned many great skills. I kicked open a door, and it wasn't the right one. I would just kick open a new one. It was all part of *my* journey.

In the summer of 2019, I completed the Ironman and raised over twenty-seven thousand dollars for ALS. It was a rewarding feeling, and it was a special day for my family. I missed the process of the daily grind of training towards something meaningful, of finding purpose like I had with my hockey career.

As time went on, Michelle and I were able to have more raw conversations about the fears we both had. The beautiful connection we shared was always there, but for me it was about giving her that last ten percent. And for her, it was communicating her fears about how our family would eventually exist in this blended dynamic.

If there was one thing I had learned about life, it was that adversity was inevitable. And even though I had found so much light through the darkness, there was much more adversity fast approaching.

Chapter 41

False Hope

—

When the Covid-19 pandemic hit in 2020, Michelle and I moved in together. We hadn't openly talked about it yet, but it had been on my mind for a while. I wanted to wake up beside her every morning and take the next step in our relationship. I felt giddy and nervous asking her. The mandatory lockdown also provided a perfect opportunity. This would only be for a few months until we moved into the house I was building in Lake Country (between Vernon and Kelowna).

I continued to fall more in love with Michelle with every passing day. We had successfully moved into the new house and enjoyed starting a new chapter together. And I knew I wanted to spend the rest of my life with this woman. We were so aligned with everything – our values, curiosity, and zest for life. We talked about the future and what it would look like. Or at least what we hoped it would look like. After two years together, our love had grown stronger than I ever thought possible. She was the one. I was so thankful every day that the universe had led me to Michelle. It was time to hunt for a ring.

Not long after I began my hunt, we found out she was pregnant. It was right before Christmas 2020. We were both shocked but couldn't be happier with how quickly it happened. I was one step closer to creating the family I had always dreamed of, with Finn included. There was a baby on the way, and I was going to propose in the new year.

Unfortunately, because of the pandemic, Michelle had to go into the eight-week ultrasound alone. I waited in the parking lot. Then waited some more. About twenty minutes later, she came walking out. *That's strange.* I was supposed to get a call or text when I was allowed to come in. As she got closer, I could see she was crying. "There's no heartbeat," she said in a defeated voice.

What a blow. Miscarriages are quite common, but we hadn't even talked about this being a possibility. I grabbed her and pulled her to my chest.

The plan was for Michelle to take Misoprostol, which stimulates the uterus to expel the pregnancy. Because her ultrasound was just under eight weeks, we wanted to wait to hear from the Obstetrician (OB) to confirm it was, in fact, a miscarriage. We had heard of stories where there was a misdiagnosis and the baby ended up totally fine.

But sure enough, our OB called the same day and said, "There is in fact no heartbeat. I'm so sorry, but this will miscarry. You can wait if you like, but I recommend taking the Misoprostol whenever you're ready."

We agreed to wait a week for Michelle to take the pill. Maybe she would miscarry naturally. There was also that small sliver of hope that the baby could be fine, and it was a misdiagnosis. A few days later, the OB called again.

"Have you taken the pill?"

Michelle answered, "Not yet, no."

"Okay good, don't take it!"

"Okay, what's going on?"

"I'm just waiting to hear more on your results. I will let you know as soon as I find out."

"Okay…" Michelle replied hesitantly.

Did they misdiagnose her? Maybe they just couldn't find the heartbeat. There were feelings of relief and happiness, but also frustration. She was very close to taking the Misoprostol. This would have aborted the fetus. We didn't know what was going on and were very confused by the phone call.

A few more days passed, and the angst built up. We finally heard from our OB again. The news was worse than expected. We had a partial molar pregnancy. Either two sperm fertilized one egg or one sperm had two sets of chromosomes. In both cases, and in a full molar pregnancy (where a sperm fertilizes an empty egg with no genetic information), the fetus can't survive. In fact, it never even has a heartbeat to begin with.

Michelle and I both felt awful. I felt especially guilty because I was giving her a hard time about how quickly she was showing. That was actually one of the symptoms. I kept telling her she had twins in there. As it turned out, I wasn't far off. Basically, since there were three sets of chromosomes, the fetus was surrounded by a bunch of growths and, in fact, wasn't really a true fetus. There was too much genetic material and the cells were growing out of control.

This was the reason the OB didn't want Michelle to take the Misoprostol pill. She needed to have an emergency dilation and curettage (D&C) procedure, where they manually go into the uterus and facilitate the miscarriage by gently scraping the uterine lining. This wasn't ideal because there was a risk of scarring. We also found out we would have to wait a minimum of six months to get pregnant again. There was a risk that the molar cells could start growing again and possibly lead to cancer. Scary shit.

Dealing with a miscarriage is extremely difficult. We thought there was something we could have or should have done differently, when almost every time it happens due to chance. For anyone that has dealt, or is dealing with a miscarriage, know that you aren't alone, and even though they are quite common – one in every four pregnancies – it doesn't make it any easier.

Michelle was always surrounded by kids. Between Finn, who had just turned four, my niece and nephew, Michelle's nephews, and all of our friends – pretty much everyone had kids. Michelle was amazing with them all, especially with Finn. From the beginning, the two of them shared a special bond and I could truly see how much she valued family. She never hesitated for a second to play fishing, dinosaur, or hockey games with Finn – she always made him a priority. He started calling her Miss Mo, which she and I really loved. She'll never replace his mother, but Finn and I are both grateful he has her as a stepmom.

I was very cognizant of how he was handling the divorce. Interestingly, he did great for the first year after the split, but he really started processing everything when he turned four. He asked many questions and struggled with the transition from house to house. He was trying to make sense of this double life he had, and why he had it. It was a tricky conversation because he was still just a young boy, but he was very intuitive. His verbosity shocked many strangers as well. He could have full on conversations with adults at two-years old.

I was pretty open with him in our discussions. Again, I believed that love and support from each household would trump any hardships for him. And I would eventually prove to be right. Although Claire and I had our differences, she has always been a great mom. I knew Finn was in a great environment with her.

Now here Michelle and I were trying to grow our family, and were being told we had to put it on long-term hold. It was difficult, for me of course, but especially for Michelle.

The night of the D&C, I dropped Finn at Claire's house for the night. My emotions overcame me, and I broke down when I hugged him goodbye. I felt like I was reliving the trauma the night Finn was born. That Vernon hospital triggered a lot of grief and angst for me. All those feelings resurfaced. The D&C was a pretty standard procedure, and we expected Michelle to be fine after. But I couldn't control my emotions. I had to keep reminding myself that she was going to make a full recovery. That's what was supposed to happen.

Chapter 42

911

—

Michelle got back to feeling relatively normal after a couple of days following the D&C. Some bleeding was expected after the procedure, but it got worse after a couple of weeks. She also still felt bloated, which was concerning because that's how she felt before the D&C.

In her follow up ultrasound, it was determined that the D&C hadn't removed all the material. There was still a three-centimeter long growth in her uterus. We expressed our frustration, but this was out of anyone's control. They didn't want to excessively scrape her uterus because we wanted to get pregnant again. There had always been a small possibility that some of the growth would hang on or start forming again.

The OB gave us two options: take the Misoprostol or have another D&C. Another D&C was the last resort in our minds because of the invasiveness. The OB agreed it was safe to take the pill. We just wanted to get this nightmare over with. Unfortunately, it was just beginning.

Michelle finally took the pill, and it took four hours to start working. I had picked Finn up from school, and shortly after we got home, Michelle started feeling the cramps. Everything seemed to be going as planned. She had to run to the bathroom a couple of times when her uterus contracted and expelled what was left of the mole (the term that was used to describe the remaining growth that resulted from the partial molar pregnancy). But the bleeding started to escalate, and she was passing what looked to be large pieces of fibrous tissue. We assumed these were placental or molar pregnancy tissues, not clots. We knew if she started passing golf-ball-sized clots, then we should take her to the emergency room. Heavy bleeding was sometimes expected with this pill. We weren't doctors, so we thought everything was okay and her uterus was doing what it was supposed to do.

She was in the bathroom while Finn and I watched a movie. I checked in with her every couple of minutes. She seemed okay and was now sitting in the bathtub rinsing herself. The next time I walked in the door, however, scared me. There was a lot of blood. There was water mixed with the blood, which made the bleeding look worse, but this amount didn't seem normal. It was also bright red, which I knew wasn't a good sign. It stopped after a few minutes or so, and we were monitoring it closely. She still felt okay, but if this volume of bleeding started again, we would have to take her to the hospital. I should have listened to my instincts and just taken her in when I saw how much she was bleeding. But she kept reassuring me she was fine.

We put Finn to bed, read him a story, and I got Michelle some food. But before she could eat she started feeling really nauseous and went to lie on the couch. She didn't look good at all. In the span of ten minutes, she went from looking totally normal to ghostly white. I rubbed her back and tried to comfort her. She felt more bleeding coming on, got up, and started walking to our bedroom.

"K, let's go to the hospital, babe." I was starting to really worry now.

But it was too late. She went down to her hands and knees

because she was so faint. She mumbled something I couldn't really make out. I got on my knees so I could hear her.

"I need to get to the bathroom," she repeated faintly. As soon as I helped lift her off the ground, she went totally limp and collapsed in my arms. *Fuck.* "Michelle! Michelle! No, no, no. Wake up!" I dragged her limp body onto the toilet. That's when I noticed the trail of blood all over the floor and running down her legs. I scrambled to get her underwear off. Then I saw the stream running over the side of the toilet. It kept coming out of her.

I don't know how much time had passed, but it felt like an eternity. Things went into slow motion, just as they had when I was on fire, when I fought in front of twenty thousand people, and when I had watched Claire's body shut down. This was the body's response during extreme or dangerous situations. An extreme rush of adrenaline and other hormones causes the perception of time to slow down.

I was in full panic mode now. I knew I had to get my phone to call 911. But if I left Michelle, she could face plant onto the bathroom floor. *Do I carry her into the kitchen with me? Do I pick her up and lay her on the floor?* I felt so paralyzed. *Do fucking something!* She was sitting upright but totally limp, with her head slung back. Her mouth was agape, and her lips were blue. More blood started running into the toilet. I decided to rest her upper body over her knees. She wasn't conscious, but this position seemed steady enough that she wouldn't fall over. I sprinted to get my phone and dialed 911. For anyone who's had to call 911, you would probably agree that the operator seems to move way too slow. I knew they sent the ambulance right away, but I wasn't thinking straight.

"Is she conscious?"

"No."

"Is she breathing?"

"I think so, yes she is."

"How much is she bleeding? Walk me through what happened."

I was panicking and started raising my voice.

"Just send a fucking ambulance!"

I didn't know what was normal in these circumstances or how much blood was too much. There was a lot on the floor and on the toilet, and it scared the shit out of me.

I'd learned that there were two ways to experience trauma. I directly experienced physical and mental trauma when I was burnt. But my parents had to deal with the emotional trauma of wondering if their son was going to survive. Two very different ways of experiencing a life-threatening situation. When you're the one in it, when the trauma is happening to you, it elicits a very different response. There's this odd calmness about it. Like you're just along for this terrifying, yet somehow peaceful ride. As I ran through the woods on fire that night, I was in an extreme state of panic, yes, but there was this calm peacefulness present too. Maybe that is what dying feels like.

When you're the one watching the trauma happen to a loved one, the helplessness is paralyzing. Michelle looked dead and there was blood everywhere. Her breathing was shallow, but present. She had a pulse, but it was also faint. I couldn't do anything until the ambulance arrived. I was totally and utterly helpless. *Was she going to die?*

Finally, after a few minutes, she came to. This wasn't like a typical fainting episode, though. I had seen people faint before. I had even fainted before – after getting pneumonia in high school. And when I came to, I felt fairly alert. When Michelle came to, she was making these terrifying mumbling sounds and her eyes were still rolling back in her head. I felt so sick. "Babe, wake up. Please, please." I slapped her face in desperation.

I couldn't believe I let her get to this state. *Why the fuck didn't*

I just take her in to be safe? She seemed fine until those last ten minutes before she collapsed. The doorbell rang finally. I folded her over her knees again and ran to the door. The ambulance came in. Her eyes were finally open, and she was slightly more alert. She had no idea what was going on. She started puking into the small garbage can next to the toilet. We got her onto the bed. The bleeding seemed to subside, at least for the time being. I was still terrified, but very relieved that she was awake as we talked to the paramedics.

Of course, the chances of severe bleeding associated with Misoprostol are around one percent, another one percent freak chance. This was becoming a common theme in my life.

Michelle had taken a picture of one of the tissue masses and I grabbed her phone to show the paramedics. "Those are clots, not placental tissue," he said. *No wonder she had passed out.* I felt responsible for all of this. *We should have known those were clots. But they were so massive.* The paramedics did some tests. We needed to get her to the hospital.

Poor Finn, he had heard all of this. Me sprinting around the house, yelling at Michelle, talking to the operator when I called 911. Thank God he didn't come into our room and see all the blood and Michelle on the toilet unconscious. I went into his room to grab him. He was leaning over his bed with a look of terror on his face. "It's okay buddy. Everything is okay. Daddy just had to call the ambulance to make sure Michelle was okay. But she's fine. Want to go see the paramedics?" I was trying to paint a much nicer picture than what had actually transpired. Most kids are fascinated with police, ambulances, and fire trucks, so he seemed to enjoy that. But kids are more in tune with our energy and emotions than we sometimes realize, and he was still very scared. I cleaned up the blood on our bedroom floor and simply shut the bathroom door as it presented a much more terrifying scene.

Michelle looked better after getting some attention and was much more coherent. The paramedics said it was fine for me to drive her to the hospital. I would have been following right behind them, anyway. I was apprehensive based on what I had just seen, but Michelle reassured me she felt better. She had more colour in her face, so I agreed. I gathered some of her things and Dogger (Finn's favourite stuffy) and we were off.

Being in Lake Country, the hospital in Vernon was almost thirty minutes away. I was trying to keep Finn at ease while watching Michelle closely. She seemed okay, but about ten minutes into the drive, she started feeling faint again. I kept squeezing her hand and thankfully she stayed awake until we got her admitted into emergency.

Because of Covid, I wasn't allowed to be with Michelle. I sat in my truck waiting for an update. Luckily, by the time she had an IV hooked up, she was able to text me. A couple hours went by before it was determined she needed another emergency D&C. She was devastated and even had to agree to a hysterectomy if it was a matter of life and death. She told the doctors that we really wanted a baby. But she ultimately agreed. If it meant saving her life, they could remove her uterus.

It was now after midnight as I waited in my truck. Claire had come to the hospital to grab Finn. I told her everything was okay, downplaying what had just happened. I could tell she was genuinely concerned, and she wished us the best. She, of all people, could relate to complications associated with pregnancy. Michelle and I were amicable with Claire, but we didn't have a deeper relationship beyond that. We generally stayed in our own lanes, but there was more of a team mentality with all of us whenever it came to Finn or anyone's health.

I got a call from the OB around 1:00 a.m. Everything went well, and she was in recovery. Hopefully, we would be in the clear after all this.

"She will be in recovery for a while. You can expect to pick her up around 5:00 a.m. or 6:00 a.m.," the OB said. I figured it was worth driving home to catch a few hours of sleep. I got home, crawled into bed and broke down, trying to process everything that had just happened.

I slept for maybe an hour. My phone pinged at 3:30 a.m. It was Michelle. "I'm awake and you can come get me whenever," her text read.

3:30?! That was way earlier than expected, but I was glad she was awake and feeling okay. I jumped in my truck and made the snowy drive back to the hospital. I stood at the door as she got wheeled out in a wheelchair. When she stood up to greet me, I squeezed her and cried some more.

"That was so scary."

I know," she said.

"I'm sorry babe."

"I love you," I said as I put my hands against her cheeks.

"I love you too."

She was still weak, so I helped her into the passenger seat, and we were headed home. I was still emotional, but there was a sense of relief as we went home to rest.

Chapter 43

Hell

—

Michelle closed her eyes as I drove home in a blizzard. We had almost made it all the way to the house when suddenly, as I made a turn, she went limp and crashed into me.

"Babe! Michelle?! Fuck!" I bucked a U-ey and hammered on the gas.

"Michelle!!" I was yelling now. "FUUUUUCK!"

Now I was both scared shitless and angry as hell. *Why did they let her out of the hospital? I knew it was way too early. How was she unconscious again?* Sometimes I thought this shit didn't even seem real. I hit the steering wheel as hard as I could to diffuse some of my anger.

I almost crashed a handful of times because of the icy roads and pummeling of snow on the twenty-minute drive, which would normally take thirty if I hadn't been speeding. I kept yelling at Michelle and shaking her. Nothing. Then her body started violently jolting, like a natural response to try to revive her or something. It wasn't a seizure, I didn't think, but it was terrifying nonetheless. Finally, we arrived at the hospital again. I ran to the passenger door and slung Michelle over my shoulder and ran into the hospital.

The receptionist simply said, "Hi, is she okay?"

I fucking lost it. "Okay? Does she look okay? No, get her

some help! You guys discharged her less than an hour ago and now she's been unconscious in my fucking car again! Why'd you let her leave?"

"Sir, calm down. I know nothing about her case. So, we admitted her earlier?"

I went off again and then she threatened to call security. She calmly repeated her question.

I shot back. "Yes! She had another D&C and you guys just let her go." Obviously, it wasn't her that let Michelle leave but I was fuming by this point. I wish I could have controlled myself. This poor woman took the brunt of my frustration.

I sat Michelle in a wheelchair.

When they re-admitted her, her blood pressure was a dismal 60/40 and her hemoglobin was 60g/L, also dangerously low. No wonder she kept fainting. Her brain wasn't getting enough oxygen. The nurse allowed me to come in with her this time. With Covid, this was technically breaking the rules, but they would have had to arrest me at this point if they didn't want me in her room.

I kept asking the nurses and the OB why she had been allowed to leave. They conceded. She shouldn't have been discharged. The fact that they agreed made me more angry. Maybe there was some miscommunication, maybe someone made the wrong call, or maybe they wanted minimal patients in the hospital because of Covid. Either way, I couldn't accept this negligence.

Michelle needed a blood transfusion. She had an IV put in and was scheduled to receive two units of blood.

"How long will she stay here?" I asked.

"We'll need to keep her overnight, and if she looks good, she should most likely come home tomorrow morning." It was now about 5:00 a.m.

"Good," I said. "I don't want her at home." She needed to be monitored.

I walked her to the maternity ward where she would stay the night. "I love you so much, you better be fine now," I jokingly whispered in her ear. Her eyes smiled at me before they started to close, she was exhausted. I wasn't allowed to stay with her, so I gave her a kiss before reluctantly leaving.

"Get some rest and call me later babe, you'll be home tomorrow," I finished whispering. She looked much better after getting some fluids and more blood in her system.

As I left her room and walked down the hallway, I passed the room Claire had nearly died in five years prior. Had I done something wrong in my life? I'd nearly killed two women. Was there something wrong with me, or my sperm? That fucking hospital. I felt like it was haunting me. Why did all this terrible shit keep happening to people I loved?

For the next six months, Michelle would have to get weekly blood tests to measure her HCG (pregnancy hormone) levels. We had to make sure she didn't get pregnant as well. For the first month, her hormones kept coming down nicely, indicating there was nothing left in her uterus. If the HCG level stayed steady or went up, that would be bad news – most likely meaning the growth, or mole, had started to grow again.

For a stretch of three weeks, we never heard back from the OB, so we assumed she was continuing on the right trajectory. To make things even more interesting, she had a hernia that she had dealt with over the years. Since a future pregnancy might make the hernia worse, it seemed like a good time to get it dealt with. The doctors said there was no risk in getting the surgery after what she'd been through. Michelle was on the mend, and we had to wait six months to try to conceive again, anyway. So, she had the procedure done. To say her body had been through a lot was a massive understatement.

We received a call from the OB a week after her hernia surgery. Her hormones had plateaued over the last month. We knew this wasn't good news. She had to go in for more tests.

After another couple of days, we received the call – the final blow in this worst case scenario. We joined the three percent of the one in a thousand partial molar pregnancies. Michelle had cancer.

Chapter 44

Aurora Borealis

—

Gestational Trophoblastic Neoplasia. The cancerous cells were penetrating into her uterus. The mole, which was now classified as a tumor, had grown back. That's why the two D&C's hadn't gotten rid of it. Usually, with a regular mole in this type of pregnancy, the D&C was an effective treatment. Nothing should have been left behind. But a steady or increasing level of HCG for four consecutive weeks was enough to diagnose her with this rare form of cancer.

We were both in complete shock. How the fuck could a pregnancy lead to cancer? We'd never heard of this. Our families had never heard of this. Even our OB had never seen a case of GTN. There was even a possibility that the cancer could metastasize to other parts of her body.

She was scheduled to have her first appointment at the cancer clinic within a few weeks and start chemotherapy. We were both incomprehensibly frustrated and scared. I wanted to drive my fist through a wall to take out my frustration.

I wished I could have taken all of Michelle's pain away. I would fight her cancer for her if I could have. Not long after this diagnosis was laid on us, I was thinking about what we could do to help her fight. We had three weeks to wait until our appointment at the cancer clinic. I remembered what I had told myself after I had gotten my life together three years prior. I would never, ever discount the power of the human mind – specifically Visualization.

I sat Michelle down that night and told her we were making a choice. Our eyes were still bloodshot from the countless hours of crying. We were still attempting to process our new reality.

"Babe, I need you to listen to me. I refuse to just let us sit here and accept this diagnosis. I'm going to marry you and start a family with you one day. You deserve the world and every piece of joy in that fucking world. I need you to get on board with me and say, 'Fuck this cancer.' Are you open to a new regimen of Visualization and a strict diet?"

Her eyes welled with more tears. "Of course. I'm up for anything you want to try."

I continued, "I know my body healed faster in that burn unit because of my mind. People think I'm crazy when I tell them this, but I know it in my heart. I could never have played through the pain that year without Visualization. It gave me a superpower. I would have never made the NHL without it. Maybe you're skeptical too, but I believe we can get rid of this cancer naturally – with your mind and with a strict diet. I've heard of the stories where people's cancer just seemingly disappears out of nowhere. I truly believe in this, and I need you to as well. We're going to do this together, okay? Maybe you will still need some initial chemo treatments, but they can work in tandem."

She cried some more as I tried to keep it together. She not only agreed, but I also knew she was totally onboard and was thankful for this type of support.

We had always eaten pretty clean and mostly organic, but we went super-clean for the foreseeable future. No sugar, dairy, or alcohol. And everything we ate would be organic. We stocked up on antiangiogenic foods and supplements. Angiogenesis is the process in which blood vessels form, delivering nutrients to the body's cells. Cancerous tumor cells also need the formation of new blood vessels to grow. So antiangiogenic agents could help starve the cancer cells from lack of efficient blood flow. I remembered some of these terms from my four years at Brown, in addition to neuroplasticity (more on this later).

We had also lined up some IV treatments at local clinics to give Michelle extremely high doses of certain vitamins.

The most important factor in my mind, however, was the Visualization piece. I got Michelle to visualize three things every day, and I would hold her hand while I visualized with her. For the first few minutes, we visualized her tumor starving for nutrients. All the food and supplements she was putting in her body were contributing to the starvation. I wanted her to imagine that her healthy cells were engulfing this tumor and shrinking it smaller and smaller with every breath she took. As if her body was an army loaded with these powerful cells that overwhelmed the weak tumor. With every new Visualization, the tumor was smaller and weaker than before. The second thing we visualized was a pristine, pink, and healthy uterus. Free and clean of anything abnormal. We imagined a light beaming into her uterus. A healing, nourishing light. Then, for the last few minutes, we both pictured a big, healthy pregnant belly. Then we saw the birth of our child and our baby in our home. There we were – us, Finn, and our baby. I got her to feel the power and joy of breastfeeding this newborn. We wanted to create the experience of this, not just the thought. I liked to end the Visualization with an image of our family picture on the wall, with our new baby.

This was our practice. We felt amazing afterwards. I refused to believe this cancer could beat Michelle. She felt the same, at least most of the time. There were still times when it was difficult to balance all the emotions. We were coping as best as a couple could with a new cancer diagnosis. We continued this regimen for the next few weeks.

Walking into the cancer clinic was one of the most ominous things I have ever experienced. *How did we end up here?* We were handed our information package on what to expect when living with cancer. It felt like some sick initiation packet, welcoming us to Hotel California.

Finally, we were called into the oncologist's office. We sat down while the pit in our stomachs doubled in size. I set the "welcome" package on the bed next to us. Then the doctor spoke.

"So…" There was a pause. She wore a mixed expression of hope and guilt on her face. She took a deep breath. "We don't have conclusive evidence that this case is, in fact, Gestational Trophoblastic Neoplasia. We actually believe it is a hydropic abortion, and was never a partial molar pregnancy."

Our minds raced a mile a minute as we tried to process what the oncologist had just told us.

"So, she doesn't have cancer?" I asked.

"No. We are waiting for one more test, but we are very confident that it is a hydropic abortion. This can present very similarly to partial molar pregnancies and to GTN."

"So, she never even had cancer?"

"That's what it looks like. Initially, all signs pointed to GTN, but there were some inconclusive pathology results. They have been running tests that have taken a few weeks here. After another look, the experts didn't find enough evidence to support that this was, in fact, GTN. Hence the diagnosis of a hydropic abortion. I'm sorry for the immense stress this has caused you, but this is good news."

Aurora Borealis.

Chapter 45

I Do

—

T hroughout all of this, I had been immersed in writing this book. These recent events, some dark and some beautiful, were continuously being added as chapters to my life story.

I also became a director with a charity called Hockey Gives Blood. We have a partnership with Canadian Blood Services. We strive to promote blood donation and stem cell awareness as an integral component of hockey programs' social and community responsibility. I spent most of my time overseeing our player ambassadors in Western Canada and attending different fundraising events. When Stu Middleton, the President of Hockey Gives Blood, called me and asked if I wanted to be part of the initiative, I immediately said yes. I, Michelle, and Claire had all needed blood transfusions at different points in our lives, so this was something that hit very close to home for me. Stu and I played Junior B together in Revelstoke along with some of the other members of the Hockey Gives Blood team.

Michelle had one last hysteroscopy D&C procedure performed to remove the remaining "growth", which turned out to be calcified placental tissue in the end. We could finally repair and move forward.

The woman of my dreams had been in the fight of her life.

The woman I had thought about every day, even before I had met her. Now it was time for us to move forward together.

I had proposed before the cancer diagnosis, when we initially thought the nightmare had ended. The rollercoaster of emotions was real. When Michelle put her hand up to her mouth in shock as I was down on one knee, our world was full of love, truth, and hope. She had made me the happiest man in the world. It felt like I'd been on a journey my whole life to find her, and I knew she felt the same.

We decided to get married that same summer. This didn't leave us a ton of time for planning, but we didn't want to wait to celebrate our love and grow our family. Tomorrow wasn't guaranteed, that was our thought. And she didn't want to be a pregnant bride. We wanted to get back to living our life, experiencing new and exciting things, traveling again, making babies, and fostering our loving relationship. Now we were going to do it as husband and wife.

Our closest friends and family members surrounded us on July 3, 2021. Because of Covid restrictions, we kept the wedding to fifty people. Finn was really excited and even donned the same outfit as me. He was now five and a half years old.

We were on top of a mountain in Salmon Arm, B.C. – her blue eyes penetrated my soul as they always had. On this hot July day, they seemed to speak to me through her energy and spirit. As if to say, *You did it, you found me. I'm right here. Now, and forever.*

We had been through so much, and the love I felt on that day was something that is hard to put into words. It was one of the most powerful moments of my life – almost transcendental. Like time was still, and I was experiencing the moment not as my physical self, but as my spiritual self. I couldn't help but succumb to the fact that I had always been destined to be there at that moment. The mountain top was very fitting for my story, and this new beginning with my wife. Like I had successfully navigated the treacherous terrain on the map of my life. My journey had many paths I could have traveled on, but every turn I made along the way was always meant to lead me here.

I had a moment of gratitude for Michelle and her journey as well. She had traveled the world and could have ended up anywhere, with anyone. If either of us had made one different turn on our respective journeys, we may have never found each other. Or our meeting would have been delayed.

Then, as I was called on to read my vows to Michelle, my physical self returned. That was when the emotion took over. Instead of trying to bury the flashbacks of the trauma we had been through, I welcomed them, albeit briefly. I had once feared there was a chance I wouldn't be able to say "I do" to Michelle because of her diagnosis and all the complications. The tears started flowing as I paused during my vows. I was thankful she was not only there as my wife, but that she was healthy and beaming with her familiar energy. We completed our I do's, kissed the hell out of each other, and included Finn in a tying of the hands ceremony to officially start our blended family together. The officiant bound Finn's hand to Michelle's and mine, and we read our family vows to him. Then we got the party started.

During the speeches later that night, we listened to my dad speak. The ALS had taken away his arms and was now robbing him of his voice. His cadence was much slower, and his speech slurred at times. Not an easy reality to live in when your nickname was "Talkative Tony." He sat in a chair and delivered such a moving speech that had everyone in tears. I couldn't stop thinking about how lucky I was that this man was my father. About all the fun we had together growing up. To have him at the wedding meant the world to me, and I wished more than anything he might still be around for the birth of another grandkid. After his speech, Dad, Mom, Michelle, and I shared another emotional embrace. There was some underlying sadness knowing Dad was progressing much faster now, but he exuded this innate calmness as we hugged.

He pulled me aside later that night, looked me in the eyes and said, "As soon as I met Michelle, I knew she would become your wife. You two have something truly magical, as I know you feel too. Congrats, Hub, you now have what your mom and I have. Now go kiss your wife and never let her go."

I pulled Dad in, and we hugged again. I was full of happiness, but I also felt extremely sad that my mom would be without him in the near future. Thankfully, he had progressed slowly over the years and was there on this special day. He is an extraordinary man, my idol.

It was one thing to get pulled aside by strangers, professing how they loved our love, but when this came from my parents, with the relationship they have, it was the ultimate approbation. I had always wanted the type of love my parents had, and now I did.

Chapter 46

Fighter

—

I don't know how much time Dad has left, but I know it is limited. His ALS seems to be progressing faster now, and I notice changes every time I see him. I still don't know where the positive will lie in his eventual death. He's only sixty years old. What will my mom do when he's gone? She has been battling her own fight, wondering what each passing day will bring. Disease is often hardest on a spouse, and I wish I could ease her pain somehow.

I think about how much of a head start my parents gave me in my life, and I will be forever grateful for that. We will all miss Dad so much when he's gone.

Thankfully, we have been gifted with many years because of the slow onset of his ALS. When Dad was first diagnosed, I tried to get him on board with a new routine. A strict diet, regimented lifestyle, and an intense Visualization practice. I knew there was, and still is, no cure for ALS. But I believed he could, at a very minimum, slow his progression down. While he obliged for the first month, he ultimately decided to live the rest of his life without rules or restraints. I didn't necessarily agree with his decision, but I very much respect it.

Dad has always beat his own drum, and he stays true to himself. I believe that his ability to deal with the stress associated with living alongside ALS for seven years has kept him alive for this long, or at least played a large part. While I initially thought I was unsuccessful in forcing him to visualize his body without ALS, he has chosen to focus on the beautiful things in life every day, not his disease. So, in fact, he *is* living each day as a man undefined by ALS. In his own words, he is living rather than surviving.

He has inspired me to live for each day. He has made me a better man and a better father. He's a guiding star for the man I strive to become. I believe my family and I will look back one day and find some light through this darkness.

As I established myself as a fighter moving up the hockey ranks, I always assumed I had more Papa Jerry in me. I've had some reckless times throughout my life, thrown a lot of punches on and off the ice, and I've embodied that fighter stereotype. This has served me well throughout different points in my life, and also landed me in shit other times.

But I've been wrong. There's been a shift in me as I mature as a man. I still know a small part of Papa Jerry – that paternal Volpatti line – lives in me. I am confident like him, have an innate trust in who I am, and I keep my circle of people small but very close to me. And yes, I also have that short fuse hiding somewhere deep inside me. Dad's disease, however, has made me realize how much of him lives in me. He has faced the biggest fight of his life these last seven years. His perseverance, his defiance of conformity, and his relentless pursuit of happiness and love is what a fighter truly is. Dad, I *am* you. I always have been and will always strive to be.

Spending time with his grandkids has infused energy into his frail body. Finn will always remember Papa, which I will be forever grateful for. We've shared many more "Three Anthony Parties" over the years – usually hockey, fishing, or Rock n Roll themed. Finn has been asking a lot of questions about death and is trying to make sense of it all, as a six-year-old does. He recently asked my dad, "Papa, will you have ALS in Heaven?" Dad smiled, cleared his throat in anticipation of the upcoming effort to speak and replied in a deep, slow cadence, "No Finn. Papa will be strong. Just like your dad. Like I was at his age. I'm going to be running around in the clouds, playing guitar, and singing at the top of my lungs."

Michelle and I hope Dad will get to meet one more grandkid before this final chapter of his life is over, but we have had other miscarriages since the first one. I have faith that if he doesn't get to meet my second child in person, he will look down on us as Finn captains The Buzzard, smiling to see one more addition of the Volpatti clan in the boat.

These miscarriages have been extremely difficult for both Michelle and I. Deep conversations have allowed us to grow stronger as both individuals and as a team. We've allowed trauma to bring us together instead of pulling us apart, which has taken a lot of hard work, vulnerability, and prioritizing. If there's one thing I've learned, it's that you can't over communicate. The energy and love we share grows stronger every day and still gets recognized by the universe. These difficulties are all part of our journey. When our family of three eventually grows to four, it is going to make the destination that much sweeter. That I believe in my heart.

You may be thinking that since we were told Michelle never even had cancer, my potential claim that Visualization healed her is unwarranted. This is a fair point. But regardless of what she had or didn't have, I know one thing. They *diagnosed her* with cancer. She was going to start chemo. That was our reality. Weeks after we started visualizing the reality *we* wanted, she no longer had cancer. Just like that. I fully understand that, medically speaking, this was a coincidence. Or maybe it was a miracle. We will never know with one hundred percent certainty. What I know for certain is that Visualization and the power of the mind proved itself true another time in my life. I'm not saying Visualization alone can cure cancer, but I'm not saying it can't either. I know the mind is the single greatest resource we possess as human beings. Our possibilities are limitless.

My life hasn't been hard by any means. Sure, there have been difficult times, but there are millions of people faced with terminal illness, discrimination, racism, starvation, poverty, abuse, and even war. I've been extremely fortunate in my life. My supportive family and childhood have blessed me with a privilege of predisposed grit and a glass half full attitude. Many others aren't this fortunate. With that said, through my journey and my experiences, I've learned that adversity has been the secret ingredient. Every piece of greatness I've achieved, whether it be in my professional or personal life, has always been preceded by extreme adversity. I know this is no accident. The hard times have always been disguised as a gift, and Visualization has helped me to unwrap that gift. Every event, regardless if it was perceived as positive or negative, has all been part of my journey and set out in my map. I believe we all have a set path in life. Some of us find that path and navigate it. Some of us find it and fall off, or choose not to navigate it. And some of us never find our path. If we never find it, we either never knew about it or refused to believe in its existence. Trust me, it is out there. You are on it right now. It probably won't seem like it at the present time, or when it feels like you are walking through the depths of hell. But I promise you, if you can frame the adversity differently, you will reflect on it one day and be thankful for the journey. Trust in that journey and instill the belief that it can lead somewhere truly amazing, through the perceived good *and* bad times. There will be signs along the way, or forks in the road. Be aware, be open, look and listen for these signs to guide you.

This mindset helps me now and I know it will serve me

well going forward. I still practice Visualization every day. The vision of where I want to go acts as my guiding star, regardless of the surrounding noise. Because of my experiences, I'm now able to appreciate the different roads on life's journey. And while I'm taking in the views, I will always stay true to the fighter inside me.

Fight for the life you want and for what you love. Protect it at all costs. Fight for what you believe in and enjoy the ride. Persevere, for there is a fighter inside all of us.

Afterword

I needed to go on this journey in my post-hockey life in order to write this book; it has led me into this amazing career as a cognitive performance coach, speaker, and author.

After I left my job in wealth management and finished the Ironman, I kicked open other doors. I was very close to buying a local business. Shortly after this fell through at the last minute, the Covid-19 pandemic hit. I was nicely distracted with moving into the new house, but once we settled in, it didn't take long for me to feel lost and antsy about what I was going to do with my life. I needed to be on the move. Doing something. Chasing something. Fulfilling a purpose again.

One day, I went for a walk and meditated on a bench on a pathway by our house.

I let my mind wander. Naturally, I started thinking about Michelle and how much I loved her. This led me to think about my journey to find her. Then I started rewinding through my whole life, when it hit me. My friends had often asked me, "Patti, when are you going to write a book?" It had always been a side project in the back of my mind to tackle one day, but there was always a part of me that wasn't comfortable opening up and telling my story. But on that day, as I sucked in the fresh air on that bench, recapping my life until that point, I knew it was time. I was going to write a book and tell my story of triumph. It would be a project that would take a massive amount of work and diligence, and not only did I want that in my life, I needed it. And that's how *Fighter: Defying The NHL Odds* was born.

After I got about halfway through writing this book, I came to a powerful realization. It was actually more like a proverbial slap in the face, as if to say, "Wake up, how have you not thought of this!" I could help people tap into the powers of Visualization too. I could help change peoples' lives and leave a lasting change in the world. I knew that if I could make the NHL and navigate the other challenges in my life, anyone could achieve their dreams. Anyone could overcome major setbacks in their life and discover true resiliency. Anyone could defy the impossible. I just needed to show them how.

I had taken a deep dive into studying the brain and its plasticity while obtaining my Bachelor of Science in Human Biology at Brown. I've experienced powerful moments in my life thanks to the power of Visualization as you've now read about. I began creating different programs that I could teach other athletes, working in all the techniques that I'd learned through study and through experience. I was slowly cultivating purpose again – a yearning to show other people how powerful their mind really is, and *why* it is so powerful. Visualization re-works the neural circuitry in your brain and changes the energy in your body so you can truly manifest the future you want.

After months of crafting these programs and continuing with this book, I launched my Cognitive Performance Coaching and Motivational Speaking business. I started working with other athletes right away and began speaking to different teams and organizations.

It has been one of the most rewarding endeavors I could have ever asked for. Helping people and opening up their minds to new possibilities is what I was destined to do and has now become my life's mission.

As I mentioned earlier, the odds of making it to the NHL are very low, somewhere around one in four thousand. If you factor in my burn injury and the other events that came after that, I'm sure those odds decrease even more. I often think about how close I was to giving up along the way. How the pain almost broke me and took me down. I almost succumbed to those odds. Thankfully, Visualization helped me be the outlier. I don't know what the combined odds are of everything that has happened in my life post hockey, but I'm sure they are very low as well. But I'm on the other side happier than ever, fulfilled as I've ever been, and extremely appreciative of the journey that has led me here.

Visualization can help you defy the odds in your life, too. We can all tap into the powers of Visualization. This is your life. What do you want the movie of your life to look like? You get to decide! You get to be the director of your movie. No one can predict the future and the curveballs life will throw at you. But you can still *affect* the future. You can rewire your brain for success and create an untouchable sense of belief to achieve anything you want.

Warning: what I'm going to teach you (keep reading) isn't for the faint of heart. True manifestation breeds intense obsession. This isn't a sit back, visualize, and chill – until your dreams come true – type of practice. Quite the opposite. Visualization is powerful, yes. But crafting your movie will push you to explore limits you never knew existed, and that will be very uncomfortable. Pain is a requirement.

Visualization is an integral part of my life to this day, not only as a cognitive performance coach but also as part of my individual practice. When I was younger, I sometimes discounted Visualization and what it had given me. I didn't have the wherewithal to think *what's next?* When the ending of my first movie ended, I thought that was it. But no, there will be several movies in our lives. Once one ends, a new one begins. I'm no longer a hockey player chasing a dream. The movie of my life used to end with a college scholarship. Then the ending changed to the NHL. Now, the movie of my life looks a lot different. But that doesn't mean it can't be equally as beautiful.

I visualize what a successful business means to me – making

an impact, connecting with my clients, giving them a new outlook on life, speaking around the world, and changing peoples' lives by reading this book. I also visualize the life and family I want with Michelle, Finn, and our baby. When I do this, I'm filled with such appreciation and joy. We're writing our own comeback story. This allows me to show up as the person I want to be every day and make appropriate decisions along the way to the ending of this movie. Visualization helped me return to the ice with severe burns, propelled me to the NHL, and it saved my life after hockey. It has been instrumental in helping me deal with the trauma I've faced in my life, and I know I can count on it when adversity comes knocking again. Not only will I never discount it again, but I will also practice it every day for the rest of my life.

I teach several programs and speak to many athletes and organizations. Regardless, there is always overlap in the key message. Visualization can be one of the most powerful practices in your life. Start visualizing what you want in life and where you want to go – for a few minutes a day. No matter what your profession is. The change in your beliefs, thoughts, feelings, and actions will surprise you. The universe can work in unthinkable ways. Start leveraging its power.

Keep reading, as I share my entire twelve week Visualization Mastermind Program. This is really just scratching the surface. It serves as a guideline to help you incorporate Visualization into your life. In my one-on-one and online coaching programs, we delve into these topics much more. If you'd like to learn more, or want to join one of the programs, you can contact me here:

www.aaronvolpatti.com
aaron@aaronvolpatti.com
@aaronvolpatti

Acknowledgements

To Michelle, I'm in awe every day that I found you. That our respective journeys were exactly the paths we were meant to take. I have to pinch myself every day when I wake up next to you. I'm so grateful that we come together as true partners in life – I never knew this kind of love existed. Thank you for supporting and encouraging me through this writing journey. We've had a ton of adversity already, and while it was very difficult at times, it's brought us closer together and made us even stronger. Thank you for being the most amazing bonus mom to Finn. He loves you so much, you'll always be his Miss Mo. I can't wait to grow our family together and make new memories. Let the adventure begin, or should I say continue?

To my parents, Tony and Lana, I love you both so much and look back with such admiration on how you raised Brianne and I. You gave us a surmounting head start for our lives. Every day I strive to cultivate a marriage like you two have. Mom, you are extremely resilient and strong willed like me. You've given me more support than I could possibly imagine, and your loyalty is unwavering. And thankfully, I got your strong legs, not Dad's chicken legs. Dad, you raised me into the man I am today, and I couldn't have accomplished anything in my life without you. Thank you for teaching me the most important things in life – have fun and live for today. I love you.

To Finn, you really are such a special little man. At six years old, you are wise beyond your years, extremely talented, and very caring. You very likely may be a frontman or drummer for the next famous rock band. You heard it here first, world. You really help put things in perspective for me and I'm grateful everyday for you. I know there have been some difficult times over the past few years, but I know you'll be on your way as long as you are surrounded by love and support. With your own love of hockey brewing in your bones, I wish you could have seen me play in the NHL too. But life has a way of working its own wonders dude. Remember the two rules: Always trust Dad and don't have too much fun. ;)

To Claire, I really do cherish the good times we had together. I know there have been difficult times for both of us as well. But like myself, I trust you have found peace in your journey and where it has led you. I hope we can continue to work together as a team for our special little man. I wish you an abundance of joy and happiness.

To my cover design team- Jessica Albert and Michel Vrana, and photographer Heather Pollock, you are all rockstars and made the whole process extremely fun and rewarding.

There are so many more people that deserve thanks here. All my former coaches and teammates, other family members, my close group of friends. I love you all.

Cinematic Mind Mapping

Twelve-Week Visualization Mastermind Program

—

I want to share my twelve-week Visualization Mastermind Program so you can put this practice to work right away. I developed this program for athletes and therefore I speak as if I were working with an athlete. However, it can apply to anyone. The premise of this program is for you, the client, to direct the movie of your life and visualize it every day. The more you do this, the more you will walk around in the present as the person you want to become in the future.

There is a week between lessons because Visualization takes time and practice. Layers should be added to your movie slowly. You will most likely read about the program in this book in less than twelve week's time, so if you'd like to progress faster, go for it. But I'd recommend reading it once through now, then revisiting every lesson on a week-to-week basis. You can start changing your life today. Start shaping the movie of your life. Manifest the ending you want.

Cinematic Mind Mapping

Twelve-Week Visualization Mastermind Program

Week 1

Visualization
Your Undiscovered Superpower

—

The first week of the program serves as an introduction to Visualization, and a deep dive into one of the two types of Visualization – Rehearsal Imagery. When we visualize, neurons (the cells in your brain that transmit information throughout the entire nervous system) that don't normally communicate, start talking to each other. You may have heard of the plasticity of the brain, or neuroplasticity. This refers to the brain's capability of reorganizing, remapping, and rewiring neural connections. We all have the ability to rewire our brains. Remember this as we move throughout the program.

Our thoughts affect our biology, and most of our thoughts are learned, or hardwired in our brain, from past experiences. These make up our subconscious mind. The subconscious mind runs our lives, regardless of our conscious thoughts. Most of us fire these same pathways every day by following the same routines and thinking the same things day in and day out. We essentially live in the past. This further hardwires these familiar pathways, and we continue to feel the same emotions. When we think a thought, a neural circuit fires and the brain releases certain chemical signals, causing us to actually feel the thought.

This is precisely what an emotion is. When we feel an emotion of fear, worry, or pain, we think more about how we're feeling and continue to release more of the same chemicals in our body. It's a vicious positive feedback loop that our brain innately wires and fires, and the reason many of us become stuck in our limiting beliefs. It's why we continue common behaviors our entire lives. This is the exact reason why it's very easy to be common. And why it's difficult to become uncommon and accomplish unthinkable things. We get stuck in our past, and our commonality, because of our limiting subconscious mind. This is the precise reason, for example, why things like diets and New Year's resolutions don't work. They are temporary changes in action, but they don't address the pre-existing pathways in our brain. Therefore, they almost never last.

Think also about someone diagnosed with an illness or disease. Some of these people might exacerbate or speed up the symptoms of that disease. They think about how they're dying, or how their body is falling apart, and their body listens. It sends the appropriate chemical response to these thoughts. Again, I'm not here to claim Visualization or thinking alone can cure disease, but I'm not saying it can't either. There are many stories out there of spontaneous remission from certain cancers and other diseases. This topic is reserved for a completely different book, but the bottom line is, your thoughts matter.

In order to evoke change at a neuronal level, however, we need your thoughts (the movie you're going to direct) to create a powerful experience.

When we are able to create positive experiences and override our pre-existing subconscious pathways, which is possible through consistent practice, we create a unique set of chemical profiles. This will allow us to feel differently. The more we do this, the more we wire new pathways in our brain. These new pathways can take us places we once thought of as impossible.

The other aspect of how Visualization can affect us is from an energetic and spiritual perspective. When we think, feel, and act, we elicit a certain energy – our own electromagnetic signature. We are electric beings because of the synaptic connections in our brain that communicate via electric signaling. This wiring creates neuroelectricity. It's the reason you can feel someone else's energy. When you change your energy and think about where you are in the present moment, what you're grateful for, or where you want to go, you align yourself with that type of energy. I mean this literally. Your own energy waves crave synchronicity with other forms of energy. Meaning they not only seek the same type of energy, but they can also be magnified by these mirrored energy profiles. This is true for both negative and positive emotions, and again why many of us get stuck with our hardwired negative pathways. We become addicted, chemically, and energetically, to that type of thinking. By changing your thoughts, you start vibrating on the same frequency as the person you want to become. This is when "inexplicable" or "coincidental" things happen. The universe truly works in amazing ways. But instead of inexplicable or coincidental, think instead that the energy of the universe is aligning with the energy you are projecting into the world. This is precisely what manifestation is. When you walk around in the present as the person you want to be in the future, your brain, and your body, behave as if that reality is already real. You attract that reality. This was exactly what my body was going through, energetically, and biologically, when I created such a vivid experience in my mind – my movie. If you'd like to learn more about how our energy and biology changes with our thoughts, I'd suggest reading some literature from Dr. Joe Dispenza or Dr. Bruce Lipton. (At the end I suggest two of their books.)

You get to choose what you think and what you believe. We are not victims of our thoughts. Dr. Bruce Lipton is the author of the book, The Biology Of Belief. In his words, "Your belief is greater than your reality. And those beliefs, or perceptions, are translated by the brain into their own chemical profiles that affect our bodies greatly." So, you can effectively distort your current reality, no matter how helpless or grim it may seem, with what you believe. Again, this is accomplished through the rewiring of the subconscious brain. Certain practices, like meditation and Visualization, can help you rewire the subconscious brain. Along my journey, I truly believed in what I was visualizing, which allowed me to perceive a different reality than the one I was physically living in. The perception of my reality trumped the actual reality itself. It did this through the experience I created. This was especially powerful in the burn unit.

Visualization is a form of meditation or guided imagery. In a successful Visualization practice, we are intentionally changing our thoughts through our imagination. We are changing the TV program on our brain's big screen. There are two types of Visualization: Belief (or Manifestation) Imagery and Rehearsal Imagery. The movie you direct from this day on will rewire a new belief system in your brain. But we really dive into Belief Imagery in week three and throughout the rest of the program. The focus during the first two weeks is on Rehearsal Imagery and quick wins. The techniques that can make a difference in your performance right away.

Rehearsal Imagery is what most of us think of when we think of Visualization. It is the execution of a specific act or skill in your mind. I would say "successful" execution, but that is very often not the case. Many of us actually visualize what could go wrong. Even worse, we rarely realize we are executing the potential mistake or a past mistake over and over in our heads. So, we are effectively practicing the mistake! We are sabotaging our performance. This leads to hesitation, lack of confidence, self-doubt, and fear of failure.

But hold up before you start shaming yourself. Our ancestral brains are actually wired to scan for threats and things that could go wrong. Your brain doesn't know the difference between an attack from a saber-tooth tiger or stress resulting from the fear of making a mistake. The brain is wired to protect us, which is where the irony in all this lies. When we sabotage our performance, we are simply firing the pathways in our brain that have been fired so many times before. Remember our innate ability to live in the past and fire those same pathways? Don't beat yourself up, you are hardwired this way. Also, remember the positive feedback loop associated with feelings? The more we feel stress, worry, or fear, the more we think about these feelings, further exacerbating the negative effects. But, since our brain is plastic, we can change these pathways and forge a new level of confidence in ourselves.

Think of a toboggan traveling through the snow down a hill. What happens the more you go down the same pathway? It becomes difficult to go anywhere else, right? And once you're in the track, picking up speed, it's almost impossible to break into the untouched snow. Think of Visualization like a fresh dusting of snow. You can create a new pathway. Of course, it may still feel difficult to get fully out of the old pathway, but you start to touch "new" ground. And eventually, once it snows more, you can break free of this old pathway and forge a new one. The more you travel down this new pathway, the easier it becomes. Then it will become the new default. This is how the rewiring of neural connections happens.

I run into varying levels of Visualization "skill" with all my clients. Some can vividly imagine their movie right from the get-go while others can take several weeks to feel totally comfortable in their practice. It can take some time, so be patient. Dr. Nate Zinsser spoke to a great example of how to practice Visualization: Try this for a few seconds. Close your eyes and imagine holding a lemon in one hand and a sharp knife in the other. Slowly take the knife and cut through the lemon. See the light reflecting off the knife as you place the knife on the lemon and feel it glide through the flesh of the lemon. Then once it's cut in half, take one half and bring it up to your face. Smell the fresh citrus aroma, see the juicy flesh, and feel the lemon in your hand. Feel the bumpy little ridges on the lemon's yellow skin. Then bring it to your mouth and squeeze some lemon juice onto your tongue. The fresh citrus causes your taste buds to jump and ignite with a powerful, fresh citrus explosion.

Okay, what did you feel? There's a good chance you started salivating, right? Your thoughts can drastically affect your biology. This is a very simple example of how powerful the mind-body connection is.

I often get people to do a similar exercise with their favourite food. If you're finding it difficult to visualize, go back to this type of exercise as practice. We want to incorporate every sense we can (which we dive into more in Week Nine).

So how do you visualize successful execution in your sport? I want you to pick three areas in your sport. For example, if you are a golfer, these areas might be tee shots, approach shots from the fairway, and putting. There are obviously many more areas (chipping, bunker play, shot shaping, scrambling, etc) which we will add later. You could start with your driver and start visualizing hitting a perfect drive every time. Think of the pressure points on your feet and the takeaway of the club. Your hand, hip, and head positions play an important role in successful execution too. Imagine, and feel, the ideal positions. Work through your pre-shot routine in your mind, then see and feel the perfect execution of the shot.

You want to pick a few different iterations for each of these three areas. In golf, there are par threes, fours, and fives, so there are three different iterations of tee shots right there. Eventually, you can add different elements like wind, rain, dog legs, different clubs, hitting under immense pressure, and many more. These are added later. Once you've performed a minute or two, move to your approach shots. Again, keep it simple to start. Visualize your one hundred-, one-fifty-, and two-hundred-yard approach shots.

After another minute or two, move to putting. Visualize draining every put from five, ten, and twenty feet. Over and over, keep executing. Then, at the end, I want you to perform a quick highlight reel in your mind of all those shots you just made. Almost like those rapid fire highlights you see on TV. Then briefly just sit with the feelings you have after. You should notice a change in your confidence. It might be small to start, but this will grow.

One important note. If you visualize a missed shot, go back and do it again. Will you make a real mistake in the round? Yes. And we will deal with this more in week two.

As a hockey player, my three main areas were physicality, breakouts, and offence. Physicality was my trademark as a player, so I knew heading into my last year at Brown that I needed to double down on this. I would visualize my skates being one with the ice, almost as if I was cemented into it. Not that I felt slow, I actually visualized feeling quick and fast as well. But I couldn't be knocked over or knocked off the puck. I would visualize making massive hits over and over in my head. If someone even came near me, they would explode off my body. If I had the puck, I would imagine protecting it and executing the perfect pass every time.

A breakout in hockey is when a team is trying to move the puck from their own defensive zone to the neutral zone and then the other team's defensive zone. I was a winger, which meant I was often given a pass by my defenceman. Sometimes this pass was direct, sometimes it was a rim around the boards, or sometimes it just ended up in my vicinity (hockey is a quick game and there are a lot of battles and scrambles). There could be hundreds of different iterations of these breakouts, so I eventually started executing many different plays in my head. I would get the puck and make the best play, depending on the set circumstances. I always took pride in being responsible in my defensive zone, so this was another area I wanted to double down on.

The last area, offence, was where I needed the most improvement. Remember, I wasn't that skilled. I didn't have that element for most of my career. So I would visualize scoring hundreds and hundreds of goals every day. All different types. I knew I would have to put up more points if I wanted an NHL contract. Well, I did. In my last season at Brown, I put up more points than my first three years combined. This was no accident. I owe a lot of this success to rehearsal imagery, and hard fucking work.

My clients often call me in pleasant shock and confusion. The play or plays they had visualized came to fruition in real life, just as they had concocted in their minds. It is truly remarkable. I can't stress enough how much of a superpower rehearsal imagery is. Especially when paired with laser focus and obsession during physical practice. You want to talk about skyrocketing performance, confidence, and swagger? This is how you achieve these things. It's an amazing feeling before a game when you know it's going to go well. Before games, when I had such an extreme sense of confidence, I'd think, *I've already been here. I've played this game in my head hundreds of times already.* This allowed me to play on autopilot, or what you might have heard of as flow state or in the zone. You aren't thinking; you are just playing, and therefore, having a lot of fun doing so. We don't want to be thinking during the game. That's why we do all the thinking leading up to games. When game time comes, you shut everything off and just go out and play. The more you visualize and practice, the more you trust in your preparation.

It is important that the Visualization is as real and as vivid as possible. So put yourself in that upcoming game or match. If I knew I was playing at Harvard in an upcoming game (or say New York in the NHL), I would work through these areas as if I was in Harvard's arena playing against them.

Another question I'm often asked by my clients is whether they should visualize in the first person or the third person. There is no definitive answer to this, but other experiments conclude that the first person is the most effective Visualization technique. So try to immerse yourself in your own body in your Visualization. You're the one performing the skill. With that said, I actually like certain aspects of third person Visualization as well. It can be a good starting point if you're just beginning with Visualization since it can sometimes be easier seeing yourself from afar as opposed to being in the first person. Third person Visualization can also be effective for the highlight reel, which we will talk more about.

To recap, pick three areas in your sport and start visualizing successful execution in the different iterations of those areas. Find a quiet place free of distractions. Put yourself in that upcoming game or match. Do this once a day, at a minimum, for just a few minutes to start. If you can do it longer, then go for it. Ideally, try to practice this twice a day for these first seven days. If it's a game day, do it before the game. I used to do my practice in the morning and again about an hour and a half before the game. There is no right or wrong here. Do what works for you. But I would suggest not doing it minutes before you head out for the game. Remember, by this time, you want to be shutting your brain off and going into autopilot mode. If you don't have any upcoming games or you're in your offseason, it doesn't matter where you are imagining yourself executing in these areas. The important thing is that you are simply working on this practice. The more you do it, the more powerful it will become.

Week 2

Unbreakable

—

Week two is all about mistakes and how to deal with them. We touched on self-sabotage in week one and how we can rewire our brains for success. Mistakes, however, are inevitable. This is just a fact of life. There is no such thing as perfection, especially in sport. This is a hard realization, especially for younger athletes in today's world. With social media, all we see are everyone's highlight reels. Naturally, our brain will expect perfection from the inundation of these highlights. Parental and peer pressure also play a factor in our need for this perfection.

It's how we deal with these mistakes that cause the lasting effects. When we don't know how to cope with them, our minds can become hijacked as we are pulled out of our competition and into the mental weight of our errors. This, in turn, leads to us firing those same negative pathways. We make more mistakes in the next game, feeding this detrimental feedback loop. Give yourself permission to make mistakes. You can't be free and play on autopilot without having this permission from yourself. Recognize that failure and mistakes are enormous opportunities for growth. So go ahead and fuck up, it's alright.

It's important to remember these other two important facts as well. Number one is having fun. We all started playing our respective sport because it was fun. Well, at least we should have. The reason I see a lack of joy in athletes today is because of that pressure to achieve perfection. Once we deliberately work on letting perfection go, we can experience the joy again. In general, focus more on your effort and preparation, and less on the idea of a perfect outcome. This might seem counterintuitive to my message in the first week about successfully executing the skills in your sport perfectly every time. But you can still imagine perfect execution, reap the benefits, and feel ok with mistakes from time to time. It's more of a general perspective shift around an idealistic life.

You may need to remind yourself, especially when things aren't going well, that you are playing a game. Don't let the pressure of competition become greater than the pleasure of competition. And no matter what, your worth as a human being is never on the line. No matter how bad your game is or how many mistakes you make. You are never defined by your performance. You're defined by the resiliency of showing up again, better than the last time. You've learned from your mistakes. All outstanding athletes have short memories. When one game or match ends, no matter how great or poorly it went, they move onto the next game.

Number two. Some anxiety is a good thing. Butterflies or nervousness before competition is our body's way of preparing for the game or match. Think of every game as an opportunity, nothing more. There will always be another opportunity. Remember, short memory. We want the adrenaline in our bodies, as well as some cortisol (the stress hormone). These chemicals allow our reactions to sharpen when game time comes. The problem arises when the stress becomes too high or when we don't get any reprieve from it (when we constantly think about what could go wrong or past mistakes we've made). I've battled this at many points in my life. I know it's easier said than done. Part of this practice is the realization that mistakes are inevitable, and the other part is acknowledging the feelings we're having so we can make adjustments if needed. So, when you feel nervous, acknowledge and welcome the feeling. Know that your body is doing its job. Take a few deep breaths and be content with the nervousness. Give your body permission to feel the excitement and know that feelings of stress are totally fine. They won't harm you or hinder your performance, but you have to believe this first.

As mentioned in week one, we now have the tools and techniques to visualize the outcomes we want. But what do we do when a mistake actually happens? This depends on the person, but I'm going to list the best techniques that I've found to work with my clients.

The technique I find most effective is what I call the consumer. It is the inhalation and exhalation of the mistake and a brief mental execution. Most sports allow for some rest at some point, so here's what you can do when play is stopped. First, remind yourself that you had permission to make the mistake. Then, take a deep breath in, and while you do, I want you to feel like you're breathing the mistake in. Consume the whole thing. Once you have sucked it all the way in, forcefully breathe out as if you are ridding your body and mind of the mistake. When you have finished breathing out, the mistake is gone forever. It is in the past and you won't think about it again. Then I want you to close your eyes and quickly visualize how that exact play will go next time. Execute it successfully in your mind.

Again, I stress quickly because we don't want you thinking during competition. This is just a quick mental adjustment. Once you do this, you've reset everything. Go back to autopilot. You might make more mistakes and that's okay. Do this quickly every time thereafter. If you have time to continue focusing on your breath, that will help too. Inhale and exhale deeply and you will naturally become more relaxed. I like box breathing best and I will introduce it shortly.

Humor is the next best remedy. The psychology behind smiling and laughter is very compelling. Even forcing yourself to do one of these can have profound positive effects, including lowering cortisol levels in the body. It helps to override our natural, negative reactions to our mistakes, which usually spike cortisol levels. You can essentially laugh off a mistake. Maybe the mistake was made because of some rare, possibly funny, set of circumstances. Life isn't perfect, so try to find some humor in it. Even though you may be overwhelmed with anger and frustration because you made the mistake, humor can bring you back to the present.

The last technique is the safe word, or a mistake word. If you find your thoughts being consumed with the mistake and the negative cascade of events that can happen after, this word is your cue to snap out of this trance. It can be anything you want. Maybe it is humorous and you pair this and the former technique together. This can work well with team sports. For example, I could tell my linemate in hockey that my word is pineapple. If they see me make a mistake or see me spiraling mentally after my mistake, they can say the word to me. When I hear the word, I repeat it back and reset. I may even find my teammate and I will naturally share a quick smile after.

In week two, I also introduce a breathing exercise. From now on, every time you practice your Visualization, I want you to do some deep breathing beforehand, preferably the technique below. This will allow you to be more present, calm, and focused. It will also provide you with the best opportunity to change your subconscious mind and your energy. The technique is essentially box breathing with some add-ins. I like five second increments for box breathing, and sometimes I find exhaling for longer helps as well. This is also great practice for breath control, something you can apply to any daily routine.

Box Breathing: 1) Breathe in slowly and deeply for five seconds, or until your lungs are full. When you are performing this inhale, start in the lower diaphragm – your stomach should move first, not your chest. The chest should expand with the last half of the inhale. While inhaling, send that breath and that energy through the top of your head. 2) Hold that for five seconds and continue focusing on the movement of energy towards the top of the head. 3) Then exhale for five seconds (you might find you need to be forceful here or extend past five seconds). I like to exhale for longer, around eight seconds. As you exhale, consciously send any bad energy or toxins out of your body with that breath, while imagining that new energy you just consumed is still present. 4) Hold again for five seconds and get present with feelings in your body. You will notice your heart rate change, some tightness in your chest, and potentially some flashes on your mind's big screen TV. Sit with this and really feel the effects of the exercise. Then repeat until you do a minimum of five rounds. If you'd like to do more, great! You might find that four second increments or even six is optimal for you. Give yourself flexibility to find what works best. You should find that your heart rate has dropped, and you feel calm, focused, and ready to visualize.

What I want you to do next is imagine that your mind is a blank slate, with endless possibilities. Or even as a mountain with fresh snow and unlimited pathways to be forged. You're at the top with your toboggan or skies, ready to make your own path. You get the drift, be creative here. Spend a minute or two and just imagine the endless possibilities. Then go into your Visualization.

The Visualization practice for week two is the same as week one except we've added the breathing exercise and the brief Visualization of your mind as a blank canvas. After this, go into your rehearsal imagery areas at least once a day. Really focus on your Visualization. Put yourself in the game or match. The first two weeks are repetitive on purpose. This may have felt unnatural during the first week. Just like meditation, Visualization takes practice. Towards the end of week two, you should notice a change in how you think about your performance and your mistakes.

Week 3

Start With The End In Mind

—

Stephen R. Covey said it best regarding defining your destination. "To begin with the end in mind means to start with a clear understanding of your destination. It means to know where you're going so that you better understand where you are now and so that the steps you take are always in the right direction." This week is focused on writing the ending to your movie. Where do you want to go?

Before you define this, let's talk more about the second type of Visualization – Belief (Manifestation) Imagery. Sometimes my clients balk when I tell them that simply thinking about something can make it happen. Hopefully now you realize how the impossible can become the possible. Every one of my clients feels differently by the end of these twelve weeks. I've lived it, my clients have lived it, and so have many other athletes. The reason Belief Imagery and visualizing your movie is so powerful is because you are creating an experience for your brain, and therefore, an emotion for your body. In order to evoke lasting change, we need to create emotion. Experience equals emotion. So, if our thoughts don't evoke emotion, we haven't yet created an experience. Again, this takes some practice. Have faith, it will come. When the brain believes that the experience you are creating in your mind is real, you become that person and attract that reality. Your energy changes. This is when the rewiring of the subconscious mind starts to take place. When obsession and trust in your journey become fortified in your soul.

"There is no doubt that human beings have a great capacity for sticking to false beliefs with great passion and tenacity"- Dr.

Bruce Lipton. Many of us have limiting beliefs about what we're truly capable of in life. Think of an iceberg. Above the water's surface is only about five percent of the total iceberg. Ninety-five percent of the iceberg exists below the water's surface. The conscious mind is akin to the ice above the surface and the subconscious is everything below – Ninety-five percent of our beliefs, emotions, thoughts, values, habits, memories, and actions are determined by our subconscious mind. This is where the hardwired, limiting pathways exist – often unbeknownst to us.

Okay, so that's the potential bad news. Many of us are not hardwired for success. But the good news is that we can change this. Similar to rehearsal imagery, we can rewire our brain through repetitive, emotion-evoking Visualization. Some other methods of rewiring the subconscious include hypnosis and PSYCH-K Therapy, which are out of the realm of my current practice.

I should stress repetitiveness. This will take some time. There is no definitive answer on how long, but you should notice more and more change as time goes on. But you have to be diligent. Remember the toboggan analogy? Belief Imagery and the subconscious mind are no different. The more you visualize your movie and the destination you want, the more you travel outside of that negative path in the snow. Eventually, you will create new pathways of great belief, determination, resilience, and grit. You will believe that you can achieve your dreams and you will relentlessly pursue that dream, no matter what. This belief will manifest since your energy changes, attracting the mirror image of that same energy in the universe.

I can't guarantee that if you go through this program, you will win an Olympic gold medal. But I can guarantee that you will notice monumental changes in your beliefs, thoughts, feelings, and actions if you are diligent with your Visualization practice. And I know in my heart that you will surprise the shit out of yourself if you travel down the paths of your life's journey.

Roger Bannister was a track athlete in the 1950s. He was the first person to run a sub four-minute mile. His story is now referred to as the Bannister Effect. Running a sub four-minute mile was only deemed possible if attempted under a set of perfect parameters. As other athletes continued to fail in their attempts to break the four minute mark, the psychological barrier seemed to become insurmountable. Roger Bannister set out to defy the seemingly impossible, in conditions that were different than those suggested by experts. Every day, he visualized success. He visualized every step of the race, including the time on the clock reading 3:59 when he ran across the finish line. He evoked the feelings and emotions associated with defying the impossible. Of course, you probably know where I'm going with this. He broke the record. He manifested this reality.

My point in sharing this story with you is twofold. First, it is another example of the power of Visualization and manifestation. But it is also a testament to the effects of the human belief system. What do you think started happening after Roger Bannister broke the four-minute mile record? Other athletes around the world started breaking that mark as well. Why? Because they believed it was possible. Any limiting belief they had hard-wired in their subconscious had changed. People thought, *Hey, if he can do it, so can I.*

I want to help you knock down these walls in your mind with my story. If I can make it to the NHL, trust me, you can become anyone you want. Things seem impossible... until they're not.

So let's circle back. Where do you want to go? What are your dreams? What's going to be the ending to your movie?

I want you to think big here. This dream is going to be your guiding star. Our imagination is something we need to use more. It is a magnificent gift. Kobe Bryant said it best regarding our dreams. He said we need to hold onto our dreams and keep them close to our hearts. As we age, we rob ourselves of these dreams and the belief that we can achieve them. We put more and more governors on our dreams the older we get.

You might think of this like goal setting. But I want you to reframe the idea of goals. I don't believe in goals. Goals are hopes and wishes. How many people in the world write down their goals and do nothing to truly pursue them? A lot! They end up in the massive goal dumpster with everyone else's hopes and wishes. Again, I can't guarantee that you will achieve this dream. But reframing it in your mind will allow you to relentlessly pursue this dream with extreme tenacity.

So for week three, I want you to get a whiteboard or a large piece of paper and title it something that has meaning to you. Something that will reframe the notion of goals. Call it a To-Do List, or My Future, or Johnny's List of Awesomeness. Whatever you like, just don't have the word goals on it. Then put it somewhere you will see every day. In your bedroom, bathroom, kitchen, wherever. You could even put several boards in different areas of your house. My board is called Aaron's To-Fucking-Do List. So go ahead and swear if it moves you.

No one thought I would play in the NHL, let alone come back from my burn injury. The fuck you mentality was part of my "prove people wrong mentality". If someone asks you what your goals are, tell them you don't have any. You now have items or things you are simply going to do, no questions asked. This will send a message of belief to your subconscious every time you talk about it or simply look at this whiteboard.

After you've come up with your title, I want you to write three items on the list. A short-term, a medium-term, and the long-term one. The long-term is your dream – the guiding star and ending to your movie. To give you context, here were my three during my senior year at Brown. Short-term: 30 points, Medium: Sign NHL contract, Long-term: Play in the NHL.

Now it's time to visualize. We're simply adding another layer, or chapter, to your movie. Just like week two, start with your box breathing exercise and a few minutes of rehearsal imagery. Then go into the belief imagery and your ending. Work through these three items on your list. See yourself achieving them. What does it look like? What do you feel? It should feel great. Perform another few minutes here.

The total Visualization practice should be a minimum of five to six minutes, not including the breathing. Again, the minimum for this practice is once daily. If you can sneak in another session, even better. If you're having a hard time visualizing your dreams or you're distracted, that's okay. Give yourself permission to explore your imagination. If you're distracted, consciously bring yourself back to the task at hand.

Think about what makes a good movie. Especially the ending of a good movie. These endings evoke an emotional response in you, right? That's what you want to accomplish with your own movie. The ending of my movie was me walking onto the ice for my first NHL game. Then I briefly reflected on my journey to get there. I looked up to my parents in the stands and knew they were looking back. It evoked an intense emotional response of pride, joy, and confirmation that I was unstoppable.

When I was in the burn unit, my Visualization practice hadn't evolved to the directing of my movie yet. I simply visualized where I wanted to go. I saw myself playing for the Vipers and receiving the scholarship to Brown. Every little detail associated with these dreams was included in my Visualization. It wasn't until Brown that I had developed this idea of creating my movie in my mind. I made it so real my brain believed it had already happened. I walked around everyday living in that new reality.

Here are a couple of other great examples of movie endings from some of my clients. One of them played college hockey like me. His dream was to play in the NHL as well. His beginning (which we write in next week's lesson) involved himself as a child. A child that was full of uncertainty and adversity. For his ending, he walked down the tunnel from the dressing room to the ice for his first NHL game. As he walked out, he saw his younger self as one of the kids giving the athletes high fives from above the tunnel. He then locked eyes with his younger self. They shared a moment before he gave him a high five. Then he said to his younger self, "You're going to be okay, look at us now. Look what we did." He continues walking to the ice and everything fades to black. Now that's an ending.

Another client was a professional golfer. Her ending was her walking up to the eighteenth green for her first LPGA tour win. The crowd was cheering and as she looked back behind her, she saw that her best friend was following her. This friend committed suicide just years prior. It was a devastating event that filled her with struggles for many years. But this friend was now the inspiration for her to relentlessly pursue her dream. She wanted to leave a legacy bigger than herself. This included raising money and awareness for mental health and suicide prevention. She lifted the trophy and shared an emotional embrace with her friend as her movie ended.

These are the endings you want to write for your own movie. When you visualize this ending every day and create an experience, you change the energy you are sending out into the world, slowly manifesting that ending.

"Everything you can imagine is real."- Pablo Picasso.

Week 4

The Beginning, The Now

—

We all come from somewhere, right? I'm not one to dwell on the past, nor do I think you should. The past can't be changed, and we don't want to focus on our limiting pathways that force us to relive anything negative. But thinking about positive or powerful moments in your past can create nostalgia and ignite your imagination, something we obviously want for the rest of your movie. It's time to set the stage for the opening of your movie. We also want to determine where you're at now.

What are your first childhood memories that pertain to your sport? There's a good chance you fell in love with your sport at a young age. Think back to some of these memories. The beginning of my movie was at four years old. I was skating on our makeshift rink in the backyard, constantly asking my dad where the ball was. He wouldn't give it to me until he finished shoveling the snow because I would shoot it into the snow and lose it. When the ice was clear, we would pretend like we were playing for the Vancouver Canucks in the Stanley Cup Final. I set the stage for my movie with a true love for the game of hockey.

Then I would cut scene and fast forward through the rest of my childhood. I would think about how I was really such a long shot to ever make it to the NHL. This led me to my burn accident. I briefly acknowledged the fact that if I could overcome my injuries to come back to play hockey and achieve my scholarship to Brown, I could do anything I wanted. This comeback was my superpower. I would visualize myself becoming stronger and stronger with each breath as I reflected on this injury.

Maybe you have had no bouts of adversity yet. That's okay.

Simply set the stage with those first memories. But if you had any bouts of adversity growing up, use them in a positive way. One important note on this: we don't want to focus on the negative piece of this adversity, as you've probably realized by now. So, if you're unable to remove the negative emotion, or if there is any type of trauma associated with these memories, we need to rework this. I'm not a designated professional in dealing with trauma, so I would also suggest getting professional help to unpack this. We don't want you to keep firing these same pathways. But think about what makes a great movie. A comeback story, or an underdog story. Adversity will strengthen you – with the caveat that any trauma is dealt with properly. Use it as fuel in life and in your movie. And don't worry, if you haven't experienced any real adversity yet, you will at some point. It's also important to remember that adversity and trauma is relative and specific to each person, so don't compare yourself to other types of adversity that exist in the world.

The recovery from my burn injury is a great example here. There has definitely been trauma associated with this at different points in my life. However, it made the early chapters of my movie powerful because I was able to channel this adversity in the right way. It made my movie the ultimate comeback story, therefore evoking intense emotion.

Let's now identify where you are currently. Where is this in relation to your dream? If it is far away, then perfect, your story and movie will be that much better. I want you to think that today is the start of a massive change. A fork in the road or a pivotal moment where you make the choice to relentlessly pursue your dream. For this part of your movie, we are also going to incorporate a few affirmations. For example, I want you to consciously think how you are right where you're supposed to be. You're ready for the journey ahead (this is next week's lesson). Then think about how strong, fast, energetic, and focused you are. Again, these are some examples, but you get my drift. What are your affirmations?

Self-image is an integral part of Visualization. Confidence, swagger, cockiness (not too much, but a little can be good), whatever you want to call it – it all stems from self-image. How do you view yourself? How do you feel about your identity and your capabilities? Remember, your brain has recorded everything you've said to yourself and every thought or image you've conjured up in your head. From now on, we want you to create an empowering self-image. Think and act like the athlete and person you want to be. When things don't go your way, override those negative thoughts that creep in. And if you don't feel like you are embodying this self-image, that's okay, just keep overriding it. That's right, you can fake it til' you make it. Because one day you will become it.

The beginning and the now of your movie will be much shorter in relation to the rest of the movie. We are simply setting the stage here and we don't want to focus too much on the past. But it is still an important part of any movie. Try to keep this part of the movie to one minute – two max. For week four, your Visualization practice should go as follows. Breathing exercise, beginning, current (start of a big change, self-image, attributes), rehearsal imagery areas, then your To-Do List and ending of your movie. You should try to visualize for around six to eight minutes now. Again, this is not including the breathing exercise and the quick recognition of your mind as a blank canvas. If you want to go longer, great! If distractions become overwhelming, go back to cutting the lemon or enjoying your favourite food.

You've now written the early scenes of your movie, congrats!

Week 5

The Journey

—

"The fight is won or lost far away from the witnesses, behind the lines, in the gym, and out there on the road, long before I dance under those lights"- Muhammad Ali. It's time to write some of the most important scenes in your movie and take ownership of your journey. It will be a long road. This is by design. As Ali has famously said, people only see the finished product. They don't see the blood, sweat, and tears that went into the masterpiece. The journey of your movie, and therefore your life, will be a lonely one at times. Many people in your circle won't understand the sacrifices you will have to make. The best are obsessed. You have written these three items down on your personal To-Do List. We reframed the notion of goal setting. In this program, we identify, attack, and conquer your dreams. But you need to become obsessed. Visualization will guide you through this newfound obsession.

I'm not Muhammad Ali by any stretch, but I became obsessed with achieving my dreams. It led me to some dark and lonely places along the way, but my movie guided me to the top.

Here's what I want you to insert for the journey scenes of your movie. There are three parts to this. First, I want you to go through a highlight reel of your past performances. Pull thirty seconds of memories where you played the game or match of your life. What specific plays or moments made it really special? Go back to those and visualize them. Become *that* person. This acts as a segue from the beginning and now of your movie to your journey. A simple highlight reel will greatly increase your confidence and reinforce the natural abilities you possess. The energy you will feel from personifying yourself in the highlight reel will transfer to the rehearsal areas.

Now I want you to insert those rehearsal imagery areas you've been working on since the first week. Again, see yourself in that upcoming game or match, if you have one. Feel that confidence growing inside you.

For the last part of your journey, I want you to think of the Rocky movies. If you haven't seen them, that's okay, just keep reading. Of course, we can't predict the future. But we can influence it. I want you to see yourself as this obsessed, unstoppable, and unbreakable athlete as you are putting in the sacrifices, in the future. Rocky Balboa was constantly putting in the miles on the road when no one else was watching. He was throwing logs over his head, getting punished in the gym, and working on his boxing skills religiously. You can even visualize yourself visualizing in the future. Feel the power it gives you.

Then I'd like you to insert the first two items on your To-Do List along your journey. Sit with each of them briefly, thinking about the triumph and how they are just a stop on the way to your dream or ending. Since these first two are short and medium-term targets, you will need to come up with new ones once you conquer them. If you fail, simply pick a new one and re-work the journey of your movie. And remember, you haven't failed. You simply have to take a different turn on your map.

Remember self-image? See this new you in the future too. Natalie Cook's story is an impressive one of self-image. She won gold in beach volleyball for Australia in the 2000 Olympics. But again, this was the finished product. It was a long journey to the top for Natalie. It all started with a dream. When she was seven years old, she decided this was her calling in life. She became obsessed with everything gold. Gold clothing, sunglasses, bedding, and eventually a gold car. Everything became gold.

She came across naysayers and people who thought she was crazy. But she stood by her dream with conviction. What do you think this was doing to her subconscious brain? It was wiring it for success. She was able to live a gold medal life every day. It allowed her to push through the darkest times because she refused to give up her dream of gold. Become the person you want to be today, and also visualize that person along the journey and at the top.

By week five, the rough outline of your movie is complete. It may be a little foggy still, but as we go along, it will become clearer every day. Try to creep up to eight minutes total for your Visualization practice this week.

There is also some flexibility if it is a game day for you. You absolutely want to visualize before your game. If I had a game, I would visualize my movie just as I had every time before that. I would spend a little extra time on my rehearsal imagery areas for that game, but I still went through my movie. Remember, the beginning and current shouldn't be too long compared to the rest. Some people I work with would rather just go through their rehearsal imagery areas on game days. That's fine too. If this is you, I would recommend visualizing your movie once in the morning and only perform the rehearsal imagery areas an hour or more before game time.

Visualize the full movie on all non-game days. Experiment with this. In a perfect world, this is the ratio I'd get you to aim for: Beginning/Current: one minute, Journey/Rehearsal Imagery: five minutes, Ending: four or five minutes. This doesn't need to be exact. There can be flexibility, within reason. If your beginning was creeping towards two minutes, for example, we would look to shorten this and focus more on the journey and the ending.

Week 6

Think, Rewire, Write

—

In week six, we add another layer of manifestation. We're trying to control your thoughts as much as we can each day. Journaling can help us channel our thoughts and create intention. It provides another opportunity to create your ideal self-image. It can help you walk around in the present as if you're the person you want to become in the future.

When you write your thoughts down, they become real. For me, and for the sake of this program, we write affirmations. If you would like to journal and write more in depth about these affirmations, that would be great. But just the act of writing affirmations can help rewire your brain for success.

So, go buy yourself a meaningful book, not your high school Hilroy notebook. Find something that speaks to you. You can even add your To-Do-List title on the front or a saying that resonates with you. Every day, you're going to write these affirmations in this book. Once a day is the minimum, but the more the better. When you put pen to paper, your brain will naturally think about what you're writing. By changing your thoughts again, you are helping rewire your brain for success. When do you write these affirmations down? I find writing right after my morning Visualization the most impactful. My mind is the clearest in the morning and my focus is the highest. It also sets the day with intention. But if you find a different time of day that works better, then that's fine.

You're probably wondering what you should write down. Again, there can be flexibility here. The only mandatory items are the items on your To-Do List. End with those three things. I want you to come up with a minimum of three other affirmations. They can be feelings, traits, stats, et cetera. You can also add any affirmations as you continue through the program, especially if a weakness creeps into your game that you want to address. Here were my affirmations leading up to, and during, my last year at Brown:

I am strong and powerful

I am unstoppable

Burn survivor

30 points

Sign an NHL contract

I will play in the NHL

I wrote these affirmations down every day. Now, my affirmations look very different. I visualize and write what I want in my personal life, and in my coaching and speaking business. And of course, I think and write about impacting peoples' lives with this book you're reading.

Week 7

Soundtrack

—

Adding a soundtrack to your movie can make a world of difference. When people ask me about "Hero of the Day" by Metallica, and whether I get sick and tired of hearing it, I reply with, "You don't understand." Just by hearing the song, I'm transported back to the movie I created for my life as a hockey player. And it was a damn good movie. So no, I absolutely do not get tired of hearing it. I must have listened to that song thousands and thousands of times by now.

Music has been known to activate the same areas of the brain that respond to other euphoric stimuli like food, sex, and drugs. Our brains find music very rewarding. The soundtrack to your movie can make a massive difference in its realism and vividness. Many things we see, or think we see, are largely determined by what we hear.

If you've seen the Rocky movies, you would most likely recognize the iconic theme song. It transports me right into a Rocky movie. Just like "Hero of the Day" transports me into my movie. Have you ever listened to a song after a breakup or on a road trip – blasting it with the windows rolled down? The right song can have profound emotional effects. This is because there is an alignment of energy between you and the song. Think about some of the best movies you've seen. What if you removed the soundtrack? It wouldn't have nearly the same effect, would it? Or what about a memorable concert you've been to? Have you ever gotten goosebumps from the emotion evoked at a live concert? I know I have. This is the type of emotion we're trying to evoke in your movie.

What will the soundtrack to your movie be? Have some fun with selecting your song. Some people have a good idea right away and others have a longer selection phase. Get out your Spotify, Apple music, record player, or however you listen to your music. See what fits your movie the best. Eventually, you will notice ideal transition points to cue you to move to different parts in your movie. I like songs that start slower for the beginning and current, and then ramp up a bit for my journey and ending. One important note: it is helpful if the lyrics have meaning to you and your journey. Can you resonate with them? Once in a while, the odd client I work with will find lyrics distracting, so if you fall into this category, try to find a song with minimal or no lyrics at all. Maybe your soundtrack is just instrumental or even classical music. This can be just as powerful.

Again, there can be some flexibility with this. I enjoyed listening to "Hero of the Day" twice, back-to-back. Some of my clients pick two songs, or even three. Some start with an instrumental only and follow that up with a song or two. Just try to land somewhere near ten minutes total for your whole movie. Some of my clients even like to have a specific song for the writing of their affirmations.

One note on the rhythm of your soundtrack, specifically as it pertains to the rehearsal imagery part of your movie. Ideally, you want a song with rhythm that aligns with the movement or "feeling" of your sport. If you're a hockey player, you might remember Don Cherry's Rock 'em Sock 'em videos. The soundtrack to the highlight reels worked very well together. The ebbs and flows of a song should work well with your own highlight reel. They will also cue you to move onto the next successful execution or next chapter of your movie. To reiterate, with regards to rehearsal imagery, each specific execution might only last a few seconds. The rhythm of your soundtrack can help you navigate your way through each rehearsal.

Of all the clients I've worked with, there have been songs repeated. The most popular song has probably been Dream On by Aerosmith. I mean, it's literally called Dream On, so I think it's great. Here is a simple exercise for you as you're reading this, especially if you haven't started writing your movie yet. Play Dream On right now. Not too loud, keep it low to medium. Then close your eyes and think about your dream. Usually, athletes know what their dream or ending is. If you aren't an athlete, you must still have dreams. Maybe a dream job, dream family, dream lifestyle. Think of achieving that dream.

Become that person and try to *experience* the feelings associated with being that person. Again, what does this look like? What does it feel like? Immerse yourself in the feeling of conquering that dream.

I bet that felt pretty good, right? When music is paired with Visualization, it can be extremely powerful.

Week 8

Why?

—

This is one of the most important weeks of the entire course. The secret ingredient. Your purpose. Working hard to simply work hard isn't sustainable and won't get you to where you want to go. Your why is your purpose. Intention is the vehicle you travel in to fulfill your purpose. Incorporating Visualization is like traveling in a locomotive. You make the right choices every day and bring energy and intention to every task. No matter how difficult the terrain, you're able to push through because you have a deep purpose. You will come across days where you don't feel like putting in the extra work. When you visualize your movie and circle back to your why, you make the hard choice to get up and put in the work.

To be clear, here is what a clearly defined purpose does not do: it doesn't imply you will enjoy training at all times, and it doesn't mean that learning will be easy. The road to success hurts and it can be lonely. But I enjoyed that part. I took pride in doing shit other people wouldn't do. I had many days where I wanted to give up or take it easy, but my purpose made that hard choice an easier one.

Here's what a clearly defined purpose *will* do: it will provide intrinsic motivation to push through the difficult times, give you an appreciation for the process and the journey, help hardwire resilience and effort levels, and it will trump talent. I've played with hundreds and hundreds of players way more talented than I was. I passed them all because they fell off the wagon. As they climbed the ranks in hockey, things got harder, and they didn't have the mindset to push through. When you identify your why, the choices you make every day become clearly defined. You bring that energy and intention to every movement and every thought.

You want to incorporate this purpose throughout your movie, especially for the journey and the ending. As you visualize your movie, remind yourself why you are chasing your dreams. When I walked through the tunnel onto the ice for my NHL game, I circled back to a quick thought of my purpose. *Look at me now. I proved everyone wrong and myself right. I did it. I've arrived.*

Here was my why: to honor my true potential, protect what I loved (my dream of an NCAA scholarship and later the NHL), and become someone nobody thought I could be. Everyone from doctors, family, and teammates told me I should give up my hockey dreams. Or that I wouldn't be able to play hockey. I set out to prove them all wrong. I was never supposed to make the NHL. I took pride in defying the odds. This was a big part of my why. But I set out to honor my true potential and what I knew I was capable of deep within myself.

Remember the endings to the movies I mentioned in week three? Walking out of the tunnel for that first NHL game and locking eyes with his younger self? Well, his why was to make his younger self proud. Remember the ending of the golfer who walks up to the eighteenth green for her first LPGA victory, with her deceased best friend walking right behind her? Well, her why was to leave a legacy bigger than herself and create awareness for mental health and suicide prevention.

At the ending of your movie, it's important to always circle back to your why. When I visualized myself in the NHL, I always circled back quickly to the image of myself bed ridden in the burn unit. A quick recognition of what I was capable of. A brief revisit to the thought of proving everyone wrong and myself right.

Other powerful whys could be: honoring a family member,

providing for your family, or honoring something within yourself, like a core value. So, what is your why? Why did you write these items on your To-Do List? When I work with my clients, I usually turn into that annoying little kid who keeps asking why to every response. We need to peel back the layers of the onion. When I ask someone why they would like to play in the NHL, for example, I often get a response like, "It would be really fun." "Why?" "Because I would get paid to play the game I love." "Why is that important?" "Because I want to play the game I love for as long as possible." "Why?" You get my drift.

This can sometimes go in circles and become uncomfortable for some people. But it's supposed to get uncomfortable. It's important to have a clearly defined why. Eventually, people will usually discover their why after this exercise. But sometimes there is more work to be done. It's okay if you're not sure what your why is yet. But it is important to remember that it is out there. Here are some things you can do to help discover your true purpose: read, daydream (continue visualizing your movie), journal about what brings you happiness, listen to what others appreciate about you, venture out into the world, kick new doors open, build community, and express gratitude.

If anything, make decisions. Right or wrong, it's very empowering to simply make a choice and act on that choice. This is how we learn, grow, and discover ourselves. Many of us think we need experience before we venture out and do something scary, or something new, or interview for that job. But that's backwards. You need to get uncomfortable and try new things *in order* to get that valuable experience. You don't just wake up and all of a sudden feel more comfortable and armed with experience. This mindset is a choice. The road of life is paved with flat squirrels that couldn't make a choice.

So, what is your why? Start incorporating it into your movie.

Week 9

Senses

—

Remember when I said that we want your Visualizations to be as vivid as possible. You want to feel like you're really living in your movie. So how do we accomplish this? By utilizing all our senses. Remember the cutting of the lemon? The watering of your mouth was because of the vividness of the Visualization. We incorporated all the senses.

If you think of the word Visualization, you most likely think of the sense of sight. And yes, I would agree that sight is the most important part of Visualization. But sight is only one of the five senses. We haven't fully incorporated touch, sound, smell, and taste. If I said your movie could be eighty percent more vivid by incorporating the other senses, I would probably be stretching it since sight is the most important. It is the first layer of a Visualization, the foundational piece. But I would say we are leaving at least fifty percent on the table without incorporating the other senses.

I've had people ask me, "How am I supposed to taste or smell my dreams?" Well, you can, you just have to get creative. I do, however, have a list of importance for these senses when it comes to Visualization. The order is: sight, touch, sound, smell, and taste.

In week nine, we go through your whole movie and see where we can pull in these other senses. I'll give you some examples of how I pulled the other senses into my movie.

For my beginning, I would revisit my first memories of hockey. I could smell my equipment and the pungent, yet pleasant, scent of old, small-town arenas (all the hockey players will know what I'm talking about). I remember eating popsicles and oranges during tournaments, so I would imagine eating these. They were great memories.

When I went back to the burn unit and my recovery, it was easy to pull in other senses. The smell of my charred flesh, the feel of bandages on my skin, and, of course, the pain. The taste of those Krispy Kreme donuts and my delightful cream of wheat. I recalled the conversations I had with doctors and my parents. And especially those phone calls that changed my life. I replayed the sounds in my mind.

Touch is a massive component of rehearsal imagery. I would feel the puck on my stick with every play I made in my head. I could feel my skates cut through the ice and feel opponents bounce off my rock-solid body. I loved feeling the embrace of my teammates as I scored that big goal over and over.

Sound is also important here. Hockey is a loud game. I heard the roar of the crowd and my teammates during all the goals I scored. If I was battling with an opponent in the corner, I would feel my strength overpower him and then hear my teammate yell for a pass. I'd turn my head, see him, and then feel the puck leave my stick. I would see and hear it hit his stick and watch the puck go into the back of the net.

For my ending, I tried to incorporate all the senses. The touch and smell of my first NHL jersey was something I imagined. I could feel the excitement in my bones leading up to that first game. I imagined what gourmet food would smell and taste like while in an NHL dressing room. What my new equipment would smell like. I visualized myself talking to scouts. Hearing them and shaking their hands. I even visualized the feeling of the pen in my hand as I signed my first NHL contract. I could see the blue pen and hear my parents' voices as I told them about the news over the phone.

These are just some examples of how to incorporate all the

senses into your movie. As you work through it, try to find out where you can add different senses in. It helps to write your movie script down to gain clarity of where each sense can be included.

So go ahead, see, touch, hear, smell, and taste your dreams.

When reporters asked Michael Phelps how it felt after he won all his medals, he replied with, "It felt like I imagined it would." He had already been there. He'd been living that dream his entire life.

Week 10

The Premiere

—

By week ten, your movie should be pretty clear. It might not be perfect yet, and you may still find yourself distracted, but you've come a long way. Your beliefs, thoughts, feelings, actions, and results have all seen vast improvements.

There isn't a new topic for week ten. It is called the premiere because we go through every little detail of your movie. I want to know what you're visualizing at every moment of your soundtrack. We find out exactly where your transition points are and identify any areas we can improve on.

Since you are reading this book and we're not going through your movie together, it's helpful to write out all the details of every scene in your movie. Think of it like a script. In my one-on-one and online programs, we work through a script together so everything and every idea is written down and organized. Write the times in your song, or songs, of when you are visualizing these scenes. You want your movie to be very predictable and repetitive. Of course, it will take slightly different forms over the long term. And for rehearsal imagery areas, put yourself in that upcoming game or match if you have one.

If there is an area you are struggling with, you could tweak some of these rehearsal imagery areas to address these struggles. This is where we also try to expand on the rehearsal imagery areas. Is there another, totally separate area we can incorporate? Going back to the golf example, maybe this is where we add bunker shots in. If I'm a centreman in hockey, it could mean adding in faceoffs. And we can add more iterations to the existing rehearsal imagery areas. This may mean extending this part of your movie slightly, but we are also looking to optimize the time spent on these scenes of the movie.

Week 11

Grit and Habits

—

When most of us hear the word grit, we think of physical grit, right? But grit lives in the mind first. The physical grit is simply a byproduct. My acronym for Grit is: Growth, Resilience, Intention, Tenacity.

Many of you have probably heard of growth versus fixed mindset. I've already talked about the fixed mindset throughout this program – the hardwired pathways in our brains that limit us and cap our true potential. We often unintentionally sabotage our performance by firing those pathways of fear, doubt, and worry. Visualization helps break down the walls of a fixed mindset to one of growth. Someone with a growth mindset embraces adversity and frames failure differently. Thomas Edison once said, "I haven't failed. I've just found ten thousand ways that won't work." That's a growth mindset. When we break down these walls, the mistakes that once crippled us no longer seem to affect us because we've adopted a growth mindset.

Josh Waitzkin, chess champion and martial artist, has a great quote on the fixed mindset: "The moment we believe that success is determined by an ingrained level of ability, we will be brittle in the face of adversity." Remember, our perception is our reality, and our belief is our perception. If you truly believe you can accomplish something, then you can. But if you don't, you will absolutely fall short and be brittle in the face of adversity.

Resilience is a byproduct of a growth mindset. It is something that is learned and gained through your experiences. One doesn't just obtain resilience. You have to go out and find it. How? By making choices – right or wrong. Failing, learning, and getting up. Then either trying again or trying something different. That's all part of your map and your journey. It takes resilience and experience to navigate it. The average person can only get knocked down a certain number of times before giving up. For a truly resilient person, this number is infinite.

Intention. Remember, intention is the vehicle you travel in to fulfill your purpose. Energy plus intention equals a fulfilled purpose. We've talked about how you can change your electromagnetic profile by changing your thoughts. What intention are you bringing to each day? Throughout the first ten weeks of this course, you have worked on aligning your dreams with your intentions. Keep visualizing and make those hard choices every day.

Tenacity. Like resilience, this isn't something you just get one day out of nowhere. You have to obtain the right mindset in order to attack every day with tenacity. Visualization and mental grit will equip you with the tenacity to train like an animal and put in that extra work. Tenacity is doing shit other people don't want to do. When you're truly tenacious, other people might think you're crazy. If you ever get told you're crazy, you know you are on the right track. In order to achieve your dreams, you have to get better every day and be tenacious. And remember, getting better doesn't mean never failing. You will and you must fail.

Visualizing your movie every day will equip you with a Grit Mindset. Now it's time to bring your body along for the ride and look at your actions and habits. You've worked on your mindset, and it will continue to guide you. Now it's time to walk the walk.

There is an unparalleled level of confidence when you look across from a teammate during tryouts, or an opposing player, or even a coworker, and know there is no way they have put in the work that you have. Their preparation must pale in comparison to yours. If you've been through extreme adversity and come out the other side, use this to your advantage. Let it fuel you. This level of confidence is obtained through extreme obsession, sacrifice, and hard fucking work. Period. It's something that you can carry in your back pocket. This was an important factor in my success during my senior year at Brown.

In week eleven, I introduce the idea of an alter ego or animal totem. This has been really helpful for some of my clients. Everyone has a dark side they can tap into. This dark side embodies grit. It craves the uncomfortable, doesn't care what anyone thinks, and has a killer instinct. Try adopting this alter ego in your Visualizations, in your training, and in your games. When you're not putting in the work, turn this switch off and go back to yourself. But when it's time to mentally prepare, practice, or play, adopt your alter ego. Imagine it growing stronger and more powerful each day. You feed it every time you visualize or put in the physical work. The same can be said for adopting a spirit or predatory animal. Feed that wolf, or lion, or whatever animal you resonate most with. This isn't mandatory, but it can be powerful for some people.

As an athlete, you have a finite window to achieve your dreams. In some sports, this age can be different. But there are rarely forty-year-old Olympians. I always tell my clients that they have the rest of their life to "chill". If you really want to chase that dream, there has to be sacrifice and hard work. You only have so long to put in the sacrifice now. Don't wake up one day ten years from now and regret that you didn't give it everything you had. And as I've said many times already, Visualization will push you to put in that extra work because of the belief it has instilled in your subconscious. There is no option of giving up. I can't put in the work for you. That is up to you.

I'm not saying you can't have fun. I was obsessed and relentless. But I also needed to let loose once in a while to reset and escape. This allowed me to come back to my movie and obsession with more and more tenacity. It's important to have different hobbies or even a vice or two to reset yourself. Think of your life as a pie. There needs to be some of that pie reserved for rest and recovery. And some reserved for other hobbies or activities that make you happy. There can even be a sliver in there for going out with your friends and having some drinks. I knew I could go out on the town and still be in the best shape on the entire team. I'd earned my rest time and my time to let loose and have fun. It's all about the energy you bring to your Visualization, training, practice, and games. You can't bring the required energy for all twenty-four hours in a day. But you could definitely bring it for half of that. It's all about the collective habits that make up the pie. You are the sum of your habits.

So, let's look at these habits. I'm not talking about the hours you need to put in the gym or in your training. This is the bare minimum. I'm talking about the little things that will make a big difference in the long run. Your actions now have to align with your new mindset.

Habits can also be another layer in manifestation. Changing your habits can also be thought of as biohacking. Biohacking is incorporating small changes to your everyday life to change your health and wellbeing, as well as obtaining a peak state of mind. Here are some examples: optimizing sleep, cold water exposure, optimizing diet/hydration (this actually has many subcategories like mindful eating, optimizing ph, et cetera), morning routine, and time in nature. You have already changed your habits for the better by incorporating Visualization, journaling, box breathing, and harnessing the power of music. So great job!

What else can you do? A good morning routine can include many of the items listed above. If I could suggest a simple and very effective morning routine, it would look like this: wake up (no snooze), make your bed, slam a glass of room temperature lemon water (kickstarts your system by providing hydration after a night's sleep and brings ph into balance), a round of the box breathing exercise, ten-minute Visualization, and cold shower for a couple minutes. This would take you all of twenty minutes. You've set your day with intention by visualizing your movie and accomplished things that were hard and uncomfortable.

Cold water exposure is probably my favourite. Aside from the health benefits such as improved sleep, decreased stress, muscle recovery, immune system boost, and several others, it is more important to do little things that suck early in the day. This will give you a confidence boost and further set that intention for the day. Let me ask you this: if you can't make your bed and battle a cold shower for a few minutes, how the hell do you expect to achieve the things you wrote on that personal To-Do List? Your journey is going to force you to endure a lot more than a little cold shower. The pain and sacrifice you will have to endure in your training will dwarf this brief bout of discomfort. I still have cold showers to this day. After a while, they stop feeling cold because, like many things, that degree of being uncomfortable you once had only existed in your mind.

What else can you do? You can always do more. You have your whole life to chill. The time is now to chase your dreams. Start aligning your habits with this new mindset you've adopted through Visualization.

Week 12

The Journey Continues

—

This week serves as a wrap up and a fine tuning of your movie. Let it guide you throughout your journey. Congratulations on becoming a director. Remember, neurons that fire together wire together. Think of the toboggan analogy. You can wire your brain for success. Your mind is the greatest tool and resource you possess. Visualization applies to everyone, not only athletes.

Twelve weeks is a brief time in relation to your journey. Stick with this practice. Let it grow and become more and more powerful each day. Be consistent. You get to take this movie with you and live in that reality every day. Remember, you get choices every day. What choices are you making?

Fight for your dreams. Manifest the future you want.

Testimonials

"Aaron's program has given me a newfound belief in my journey as a hockey player. I feel more confident and prepared going into every game. I never imagined these techniques would have such a huge impact on my game!"
Nick Lappin – Professional hockey player (NHL, AHL)

"I have tried to practice different methods of Visualization and manifestation throughout my college and pro career and know that it works, but Aaron's program helped me enhance the effects tenfold. I noticed results right away and I've never looked forward to a season as much as my upcoming one, thanks to Aaron."
Anthony Greco – Professional hockey player (NHL, AHL, Swedish Hockey League)

"After just a few weeks of working with Aaron, I have such a clear understanding of my journey as an athlete. I am now able to attack every day with more focus and clarity. I've noticed a huge change in my feelings and my performance has reaped the benefits!"
Kate Griffiths – Professional Golfer

"I've become obsessed with progress and growth. I feel like the skill of Visualization has brought such a tremendous level of commitment and calmness to my whole process. I used to put so much emphasis on every event, every shot. But now I feel like I'm able to accept things as they happen because I'm so laser focused on the big picture. I'm forever appreciative of this gift you've given me. Thank you."
Chris Poli – Amateur Golfer

"I first looked into Aaron's program as a course for my clients. I ended up participating myself and am grateful I did. I have always had dreams but not the courage or plan to put them into action. Aaron helped me change hope into belief. His Visualization Masterclass helped me lift restrictions on what I thought was possible and gave me the courage to act. I now have tools that I'll use forever in all areas of my life."
Katinka Devrainne – Equestrian athlete. ELITE Sport Horses Ltd.

"Prior to working with Aaron I really struggled with being too critical of myself and focusing on things that were out of my control. Now, after incorporating the Visualization techniques Aaron taught me, my confidence in myself as a person and a player are at an all time high. I feel great about where I'm at in my journey."
Ben Tupker – Cornell Big Red

"Wow! Our fifteen-year-old-daughter Danica completed Aaron's Twelve-Week Visualization Masterclass and we noticed results instantly! She was captivated by Aaron's powerful, relatable and inspiring sessions. Danica instantly became engaged in writing her own movie and on her very next elite hockey showcase she put her new Visualization skills to work, walking away with the award for Top Defenceman of the showcase. Danica has learned that training her mind is just as important as training her body on and off the ice. She will forever remember to always believe! We highly recommend Aaron's program! We can't thank you enough!"
Dean & Thasha Maynard – parents to Danica

"Aaron's Mastermind Course instilled a new belief in myself and has given me the confidence I need to attack each and every day. Visualization is now a huge part of my daily and game day routine."
Devin Pimm – Carleton Place Canadians, CCHL

"Our daughter struggled with low self-confidence and anxiety, especially before games! We saw immediate results in her anxiety after working with Aaron. Thanks for giving our girl one of the best gifts she will ever receive- To believe in herself!"

Kristin Buckler – Mom to Phoenix

References

Covey, Stephen. (2020). *The 7 Habits Of Highly Effective People* / Stephen R. Covey– 30th anniversary edition. Simon & Schuster.

Dispenza, Joe. (2017). *Becoming Supernatural: How Common People Are Doing the Uncommon* / Dr. Joe Dispenza. Hay House.

Lipton, Bruce H. (2015). *The Biology Of Belief: Unleashing the power of consciousness, matter & miracles* / Bruce H. Lipton, Ph. D. –10th anniversary edition. Hay House.

Revelstoke Mountain Resort. https://bit.ly/3QsBKEB

Taylor, Bill. (2018). *What Breaking the 4-Minute Mile Taught Us About the Limits of Conventional Thinking.* Harvard Business Review. https://hbr.org/2018/03/what-breaking-the-4-minute-mile-taught-us-about-the-limits-of-conventional-thinking

Waitzkin, Josh. https://www.brainyquote.com/quotes/joshua_waitzkin_536461

Zinsser, Nate. (2022). *The Confident Mind: A battle-tested guide to unshakable performance* / Dr. Nate Zinsser. Harper Collins.

About the Author

Aaron Volpatti is an Author, Cognitive Performance and Injury Coach, Speaker, retired NHL player, burn survivor, and a graduate from Brown University – B.Sc Human Biology.

A pioneer in Cinematic Visualization and athletic performance, Aaron's unique practice has helped athletes all over the world.

Born and raised in Revelstoke, British Columbia, he is a guitar aficionado and wannabe rockstar. He's a professional dabbler – spending his free time fishing, hunting, camping, golfing, playing squash, or learning a new musical instrument or language.

Aaron resides in the beautiful Okanagan in British Columbia with his wife Michelle, and his son Finn. You can visit him online at www.aaronvolpatti.com or on Twitter and Instagram (@aaronvolpatti)